FIVE YEARS AFTER

FIVE YEARS AFTER
The Long-Term Effects
of Welfare-to-Work Programs

≈≈≈≈≈≈≈≈≈≈≈≈≈≈≈≈

DANIEL FRIEDLANDER
GARY BURTLESS

*A Manpower Demonstration
Research Corporation Study*

RUSSELL SAGE FOUNDATION / NEW YORK

The Russell Sage Foundation

The Russell Sage Foundation, one of the oldest of America's general purpose foundations, was established in 1907 by Mrs. Margaret Olivia Sage for "the improvement of social and living conditions in the United States." The Foundation seeks to fulfill this mandate by fostering the development and dissemination of knowledge about the country's political, social, and economic problems. While the Foundation endeavors to assure the accuracy and objectivity of each book it publishes, the conclusions and interpretations in Russell Sage Foundation publications are those of the authors and not of the Foundation, its Trustees, or its staff. Publication by Russell Sage, therefore, does not imply Foundation endorsement.

Library of Congress Cataloging-in-Publication Data

Friedlander, Daniel.
    Five years after : the long-term effects of welfare-to-work
programs / Daniel Friedlander and Gary Burtless.
      p. cm.
    Includes bibliographical references and index.
    ISBN 0-87154-266-8
    1. Welfare recipients—Employment—United States. 2. Public
welfare—United States. 3. Public welfare—Evaluation.
I. Burtless, Gary T., 1950-   . II. Title.
HV95.F68   1994
362.5'8'0973—dc20   94-20932
                                                                         CIP

The Manpower Demonstration Research Corporation's preparation of this volume was supported by the Russell Sage Foundation, the Ford Foundation, and the U.S. Department of Health and Human Services (HHS). The JOBS evaluation, of which this is a part, is funded by HHS under a competitive award, Contract No. HHS-100-89-0030. The findings and conclusions presented herein do not necessarily represent the official positions or policies of the funders.

The paper used in this publication meets the minimum requirements of American National Standard for Information Sciences—Permanence of Paper for Printed Library Materials. ANSI Z39.48-1992.

Text design by John Johnston.

RUSSELL SAGE FOUNDATION
112 East 64th Street, New York, New York 10021

10 9 8 7 6 5 4 3 2 1

Contents

Preface and Acknowledgments

A central goal of efforts to change the current welfare system in the United States has been to move recipients from public assistance to stable employment. During the 1980s, a number of states tried to expand and intensify their welfare-to-work programs. But their efforts were hampered because public officials lacked the information necessary to guide them in designing and running programs that would best achieve their objectives. They encountered considerable difficulty in trying to estimate, with a high degree of reliability, just how much work and earnings could be increased and welfare receipt reduced.

At the same time, however, some social scientists were borrowing classical experimental methods from the natural sciences and adapting them for use in large-scale field studies of the effectiveness of welfare-to-work programs. Working closely with federal, state, and local program administrators, the Manpower Demonstration Research Corporation (MDRC) designed and implemented a set of eight social experiments in various localities under the collective title, The Demonstration of State Work/Welfare Initiatives. MDRC also conducted one subsequent experiment to evaluate the Saturation Work Initiative Model (SWIM) in San Diego, a demonstration program sponsored by the U.S. Department of Health and Human Services (HHS). The MDRC field trials were orginally planned as studies of short-term behavior, with data tracking the work and welfare activity of employment program enrollees for about two years in most sites. The initial findings from the experiments were helpful to policymaking, but those results also made it clear that the full effects of the programs could not be measured with only two or even three years of follow-up data. A number of important questions about long-term program effects remained unanswered.

In embarking on the research that led to this book, we were motivated by a desire to address some of these important open questions. Given the intense national interest in welfare reform, we felt that the answers would be useful not only to scholars but also to the broader community of policymakers and public opinion leaders. At the time we began this inquiry, the existing evidence showed that welfare-to-work programs did, to some extent, increase employment and earnings and decrease welfare receipt and welfare expenditures in the short run. But we did not know whether individuals were *permanently* affected by their program experiences. Were their gains in employment and earnings temporary, or did they persist for many years? Were program graduates able to retain employment, or did most of them soon lose their new jobs? Did individuals *without* the program eventually come to earn as much as those *with* the program? Like many of the readers of the MDRC studies, we also wanted to know about program participants' subsequent welfare experiences. Did the programs affect long-term welfare receipt? Did the programs increase or reduce the likelihood that recipients would return to the welfare rolls after their initial exits? More fundamentally, did more costly investment in remedial education and occupational training produce more lasting effects? And would some of the programs eventually produce financial benefits for *both* welfare recipients *and* government budgets?

This book attempts to answer these questions and, in doing so, to highlight some of the critical problems that must be solved if employment and training programs are to succeed in moving large numbers of families from welfare to unsubsidized employment. What made the research possible was the acquisition of new, longer-term data for four of the MDRC experiments. These data allowed us to examine the behavior of sample members over a period of at least five years, an unusually long follow-up for this kind of research and considerably more than was available for the original evaluation studies. The first contribution we hoped to make to the knowledge base was to provide estimates of the longer-term effects of these four programs on employment, earnings, welfare receipt, and welfare payments.

As our second contribution, we wished to develop new measures of work and welfare behavior, measures that would reflect the often sporadic nature of employment, interspersed with episodes of joblessness and welfare receipt, that is characteristic of this population. The lengthier follow-up, we believed, would enable us to go beyond the usual "average" measures of employment and welfare receipt of the initial evaluation studies to explore the underlying patterns of behavior that make program effects appear to rise and fall over time. In designing our new measures, we avoided certain procedures (such as event history analysis) that require moving away from the individual sample member as the focus of analysis or which necessitate making strong assumptions about future behavior to predict what will happen after the end of the observation period. We worked with measures that dealt only with individuals and only with behavior actually observed. The challenge, as we saw it, was to create measures that would mesh naturally with the experimental designs yet provide information about patterns of behavior not investigated in the original analyses.

We hope that the results of this study will be useful to those who wish to know the full effects of the relatively low- to moderate-cost interventions tried in the last decade. We hope that the results will also help people understand the roles of job loss and welfare recidivism in producing those effects. At the same time, we must caution the reader to bear in mind some limitations and uncertainties inherent in the findings. The programs we were able to study illustrate some of the key choices that must be made in designing welfare-to-work programs. In some important ways, however, they differ from the succeeding generation of programs and from reform strategies that have been proposed for the future. They lack the emphasis on basic education embodied in subsequent federal legislation. In addition, only one of the programs had authority to require participation by the large group of welfare mothers with a child under school age, authority that has since been granted all states under law. None of the programs operated under a two- or three-year time limit on AFDC receipt. Lastly, although our ability to look at programs with comparable research designs is an asset not usually available to the researcher, our total of four program evaluations is not a large enough number from which to make sweeping generalizations with certainty. Our results should be viewed in the context of other completed and ongoing field research. An overview of that research has been provided in an earlier Russell Sage volume, *From Welfare to Work*, by Judith Gueron and Edward Pauly.

The detailed and often technical nature of our material created problems in presenting our results in a way that would be accessible, especially to non-statisticians. To solve this problem, we collected the main empirical themes and findings into a single summary chapter at the beginning and stated most of our broader interpretative conclusions in a chapter at the end. Those who wish to examine the underpinnings will find them in the intervening chapters, which develop the empirical points summarized in the first chapter. The middle chapters lay out in detail the goals of the study, key features of the programs, methodological issues, the nature of the data and the characteristics of the samples, the estimated five-year program effects, and the estimated effects on underlying patterns of employment and welfare behavior.

Four organizations and a number of individuals made possible the analysis of longer-term data or contributed to its fruitfulness. We owe a great debt of gratitude to the Russell Sage Foundation for supplying the initial impetus and principal funding for the project, for providing continuing encouragement and support, and for publishing our findings. We are especially grateful to the Foundation's President, Eric Wanner, who recognized the untapped value of the welfare-to-work data sets and the unusual opportunity to extend past analyses with additional follow-up data. We also thank Lisa Nachtigall, Director of Publications, and Charlotte Shelby, Managing Editor, for their care in handling our manuscript.

At a critical point in the project, help from HHS made possible the realization of the full scope of research. The study would be far less complete without the financial assistance of HHS in collecting and analyzing portions of the extended follow-up data. We particularly wish to thank Howard Rolston, currently of the Administration for Children and Families, who, over a number of years, has persistently challenged researchers to produce more pertinent and higher quality information to aid the making of policy.

No list of thanks would be complete without acknowledging the crucial part played by the Ford Foundation. From the beginning of the welfare-to-work experiments, their support and guidance has been unfailing. Their financial contribution to the analysis of longer-term data was essential in seeing the project through to completion and is greatly appreciated.

Finally, we find it difficult to express adequately how much we owe to Daniel Friedlander's colleagues at MDRC. The set of field experiments of which the four in this book are a part depended on a long and very close collaboration among diverse and devoted staff working in field operations, data processing, and analysis. Daniel Friedlander was privileged to participate directly in that process as an MDRC staffer. Gary Burtless, serving as an external advisor to MDRC, has been involved in the welfare-to-work studies for a number of years. Both authors' approach to the data and interpretation of the results have benefited from more than a decade of internal discussion and debate among researchers at MDRC. The actual empirical analysis was made possible by the outstanding research assistance provided by Dan Edelstein and Scott Susin.

Our most persistent source of encouragement, and also our most probing reviewer, was Judith Gueron, MDRC's President. Many of the ideas in the present study derive specifically from a prior paper written jointly by Dr. Gueron and Daniel Friedlander. Gordon Berlin and Barbara Goldman read a number of drafts of this book, and their comments and criticism helped shape it into its present form. Our thanks also go to MDRC's Board Committee on Welfare Studies for the benefit we gained from their collective knowledge and insight in reviewing this study. Outside MDRC, David Greenberg of the University of Maryland deserves special mention for having provided us with detailed notes from his close reading of the manuscript. If our study fails to make good use of the wise guidance offered by these reviewers, the responsibility is ours.

DANIEL FRIEDLANDER, *MDRC*
GARY BURTLESS, *The Brookings Institution*

1

Findings of This Study

OVERVIEW AND SUMMARY

Strong interest by the public and the states and by Congress and the Clinton administration has placed welfare reform high on the national agenda. At the same time, the implementation of the Family Support Act (FSA) of 1988, including the Job Opportunities and Basic Skills Training (JOBS) Program, has raised pointed questions about ways to improve the effectiveness of employment and training programs for recipients of Aid to Families with Dependent Children (AFDC), the nation's largest cash welfare program. This study addresses some of these questions using data from four social experiments designed to test the effectiveness of alternative welfare-to-work strategies. Three of the experiments evaluated state-initiated programs, created under the Work Incentive (WIN) Program system.[1] They tested special services and procedures to encourage welfare recipients to find work and leave the welfare rolls. The programs were evaluated between 1982 and 1987 by the Manpower Demonstration Research Corporation (MDRC) as part of a series of experiments known collectively as the Demonstration of State Work/Welfare Initiatives (Work/Welfare). The fourth experiment was the Saturation Work Initiative Model (SWIM) in San Diego (1985–1988), a specially funded federal demonstration program, also evaluated by MDRC.

---

[1] WIN was the national employment and training system for AFDC recipients that preceded JOBS. Under provisions of a 1981 law, states could elect to reorganize their WIN programs as WIN Demonstration programs, which could be operated with greater flexibility. The three programs mentioned in the text were operated under WIN Demonstration authority.

1

The present study expands on previous work in two ways. We use information covering a much longer follow-up period, and we examine new measures of employment and welfare behavior. The analysis is based on five years of follow-up data, two to three years more than was available previously, providing valuable information about the longer-term impacts of welfare-to-work programs. Long-term impact estimates are critical in understanding the full effect of a program. They tell us whether permanent changes were made in the lives of program enrollees. Even rather modest continuing impacts can dramatically improve the overall assessment of program results.

In addition to analyzing longer-term follow-up, we analyze new measures that describe patterns of work and welfare behavior over time. For example, we examine *employment stability* to see how long program enrollees hold on to jobs once they have found them. We also analyze *AFDC recidivism*, the tendency of some individuals who exit AFDC to return after a time.

The study yields a number of conclusions. The four programs appear to have used their modest resources in a cost-effective way. They encouraged more enrollees to enter employment or to start working sooner than they would have without the programs. More enrollees working and faster job finding led to increased total employment, and increased employment led to increases in total earnings. For all four programs, the gains in enrollees' earnings were several times larger than program net cost. Increased employment also meant that program enrollees left AFDC sooner. The resulting reductions in AFDC payments were usually smaller than earnings gains, but were still large enough to more than offset program costs in two programs. When impacts on transfers other than AFDC are factored in, the savings were about equal to program costs in a third program. We also find that program enrollees who left AFDC were no more likely to return to the welfare rolls than people who were not enrolled in a program. These findings suggest that the tested programs achieved solid, though not spectacular, results.

But we also find some shortcomings. The programs, with one exception, were not successful in helping their graduates find better-paying jobs. Nor did they help enrollees find jobs offering noticeably better job security. In two of the four programs, earnings gains achieved by the programs produced little or no improvement in the financial position of enrollees: those earnings gains were largely offset by AFDC benefit reductions. The one program where employed program graduates did obtain better-paying jobs produced the longest-lasting impact on total earnings. It clearly improved the financial position of enrollees. This program offered more generous education and training than would be typical of many programs, but it did not produce significant reductions in AFDC payments and therefore produced no savings for government budgets. In addition, most of the earnings gains appear to have accrued to a small number of program enrollees. Finally, the four programs had limited success in reducing the number of enrollees who face long future spells of joblessness and AFDC receipt. Modest reductions in long AFDC spells were obtained in two of the programs, but future programs will need to achieve greater impact on long spells if they are to have a larger total impact on AFDC.

These shortcomings may be addressed by a new generation of welfare-to-work programs. JOBS has moved beyond previous policy, especially in permitting a more enriched mix of services and supports to a larger population and in promoting attention to the more disadvantaged groups within that population. Learning how to make more expensive services most effectively increase earnings for individuals with moderate to severe skill deficits is one of the great challenges facing policymakers. Through creative combinations of past practice and careful innovation, JOBS may be able to achieve better results with the long-term AFDC caseload. This is necessary if the program is to have a larger and more sustained impact on enrollees' self-sufficiency and income.

PROGRAMS AND METHODOLOGY

Programs

AFDC provides cash payments for needy children who have lost the support of a parent who is absent, incapacitated, deceased, or unemployed. The great majority of AFDC children reside in single-parent families. The monthly AFDC benefit includes an amount for the support of the children's caretaker, but AFDC payments end when the children become ineligible (generally on their 18th birthday). States administer AFDC and set their own monthly benefit levels, which differ widely. Federal funds cover from 50 to 80 percent of AFDC payments in a state, depending on the state's per capita income. In 1992, some 4.8 million families and 13.6 million individuals received $22.2 billion in AFDC. Families receiving AFDC are automatically eligible for Medicaid and may receive food stamps and other assistance. Earnings are counted against the AFDC grant and may reduce it, but some work expenses and other allowances may be deducted from earnings first. Most families receiving AFDC do not have reported earnings. It is possible, however, for a family with a part-time or low-pay worker to receive some AFDC, and, in states with higher AFDC benefit levels, greater earnings would ordinarily be possible before the monthly AFDC amount goes to zero.

The four welfare-to-work programs under study operated in the states of Virginia and Arkansas and in the cities of Baltimore, Maryland, and San Diego, California.[2] All four programs aimed at increasing employment and earnings and reducing AFDC receipt. The target populations consisted mainly of single-parent family heads receiving AFDC. Most were women. Baltimore and San Diego also worked in smaller numbers with two-parent families with an unemployed head (AFDC-U cases, mostly males), but we do not examine their experiences in this study.

The most common program activity was some form of structured job search, which provided guidance in job-hunting techniques and assigned job search tasks, either individually or in a group setting. In three of the four programs, job search was normally required as the first program activity. Enrollees who failed to find a job could be assigned to three-month unpaid work positions in public or nonprofit institutions. Education and training, which are more expensive to provide, were a significant part of program services in Baltimore and San Diego SWIM. But neither of these programs emphasized immediate assignment to basic education to the degree of some subsequent JOBS programs.

The programs were similar in some respects. All were relatively large scale. All four were *broad-coverage* programs, designed to reach or "cover" all eligible individuals in a particular target population, without selectively screening out potential enrollees on the basis of lack of "job readiness," "poor motivation," or other subjective criteria. Participation in a program was mandatory in the sense that AFDC recipients who did not com-

---

[2] Details of the format, services, participation, and short-term impact and benefit-cost results for the four programs examined in this study may be found for Virginia in Friedlander (1988a), Riccio, Cave, Freedman, and Price (1986), and Price (1985); for Arkansas in Friedlander (1988b); Friedlander, Hoerz, Quint, and Riccio (1985), and Quint (1984a); for Baltimore in Friedlander (1987), Friedlander, Hoerz, Long, and Quint (1985), and Quint (1984b); and for San Diego SWIM in Friedlander and Hamilton (1993), Hamilton and Friedlander (1989), and Hamilton (1988). More general reviews, including results for other programs and cross-program comparisons, may be found in Friedlander and Gueron (1992), Greenberg and Wiseman (1992), and Gueron and Pauly (1991).

ply with an activity assignment risked a financial *sanction*, a temporary loss of a portion of their monthly AFDC grant. Single parents with any children under six years of age were exempted from the enrollment requirement, as prescribed by federal statute. Thus, roughly two-thirds of the total population receiving AFDC did not have to participate. In Arkansas, by special federal waiver, this exemption was available only to single parents with a child under the age of three. In all four sites, program staff granted many *deferrals* from immediate participation to enrollees for "good cause" excuses (such as illness of self or a child).

Given the emphasis on broad coverage and mandatory participation, the programs comprised more than just a set of activities. They also incorporated procedures for client outreach, enrollment, and orientation; provisions for support services such as transportation and child care; staff and procedures for assessing enrollee capabilities and needs, for assigning them to activities, and for monitoring and enforcing compliance; and a set of regulations detailing enrollee obligations and penalties for noncompliance. Typically, about half of program enrollees actually participated in a formal program activity. Among the remaining enrollees, many left AFDC before their participation could begin, some were sanctioned for noncompliance, some were excused from participating, and some were not reached by the program.

In several respects, the four programs differed in philosophy, goals, resources, and operating environment. As a result of these differences, the programs differed in the mix of services they offered, in program structure, and in their level of enforcement and overall "mandatoriness." The programs can conveniently be divided into two contrasting pairs: Virginia and Arkansas on the one hand and Baltimore and San Diego SWIM on the other. Virginia and Arkansas were both low-cost, job-search-first programs, without major investments in education or training. Both were implemented in a large number of urban and rural counties. In some ways, Virginia is the most representative program of the four. AFDC grants in that state were near the national median, and program net costs, at $430 per sample member, were near the middle of the cost range for the four programs. The great bulk of program activity was low-cost job search (assigned first), but three-month unpaid work assignments were commonly used as well.[3] Arkansas was the lowest-cost program, at $118 per sam-

---

[3] Some Virginia enrollees were referred to education and job skills training opportunities in their communities, but they participated in such activities only slightly more than the control group.

ple member. Almost all formal activity was in group job search, although a small number of enrollees were assigned to three-month unpaid work positions. Arkansas has comparatively low AFDC grant levels, and the population enrolled in the Arkansas program was consequently very disadvantaged.

Baltimore and San Diego SWIM programs cost more than those in Virginia and Arkansas. Net costs per sample member were moderate: $953 in Baltimore and $920 in San Diego SWIM. Both programs were run in major metropolitan areas, and both offered some moderately expensive education and training services in addition to low-cost job search and unpaid work assignments. The two programs differed in important ways, however. Baltimore was oriented towards the goal of increasing enrollee employment in better-paying jobs. Instead of mandating a particular sequence of activities, the program made an effort to assess enrollees' capabilities and needs and to match individuals with the most suitable kinds of activities. Job search and three-month unpaid work assignments were heavily utilized, but Baltimore was the only one of the four programs in which job search was not automatically assigned as the first activity. It was also the only one to encourage enrollee choice of activity, when openings to particular activities permitted. Sanctioning was rare, and staff tended to secure enrollee compliance through persuasion. Notwithstanding the limited use of sanctions, participation was treated as mandatory, and staff efforts to obtain cooperation yielded participation rates that were no lower than the other programs.

Philosophically and practically, San Diego SWIM was very different. The objective of the program, which was a specially funded demonstration rather than an ongoing local program, was to have as many enrollees as possible participate in activities for as long as possible while they remained on AFDC. This strategy is sometimes referred to as "caseload saturation." Initial activities were assigned in a fixed sequence: job search, then three-month unpaid work experience, followed by education and training. SWIM offered much less scope for client choice than was the case in Baltimore.[4] Financial penalties were applied at

---

[4]Enrollee choice was possible at several points under the SWIM program design. For example, assignment to activities could be put off for enrollees who were already employed part-time or already engaged, on their own initiative, in qualifying education or training. In addition, there was room for enrollee choice after completion of the basic job search and unpaid work sequence, at which point various education or training activities, or additional job search, could be assigned.

a relatively high rate. More than 10 percent of all SWIM enrollees were sanctioned. Unlike Baltimore, the goals of increased employment and reduced AFDC receipt were emphasized over improved job quality. AFDC benefits in California are among the highest in the nation, whereas those in Maryland are in the middle range. Finally, SWIM was unique in that the obligation to participate in the program while on AFDC could, in theory, extend for a very long time, perhaps even years. In the other programs, if an enrollee did not find a job, participation would usually end when the original course of assigned activities was completed. In Virginia and Arkansas, this usually occurred after fewer than six months of program involvement.

Analysis Issues

Our fundamental unit of analysis is the individual program enrollee. Data are organized to show the experiences of a representative group of enrollees forward in time from the date they entered a program through a follow-up period of about five years. Persons who enrolled in each program were randomly assigned to either an experimental or control group. Members of the *experimental group* were eligible for special program services and were subject to program participation requirements; members of the *control group* were not eligible for program services and were not subject to program participation requirements, although they could find and participate in services available elsewhere in the community, outside the program. Average outcomes for experimentals minus average outcomes for controls provide unbiased estimates of program impacts. Because randomization makes the two groups similar at the start, they differ only in their exposure to the program. Any subsequent difference in behavior between the two groups can therefore be safely attributed to the program.

Experimentals who do not participate in the program are nevertheless retained in the research analysis as part of the experimental group. Employment, earnings, AFDC receipt, and AFDC payments are thus averaged over nonparticipants as well as participants. Sample members who do not become employed are still included (as zeroes) in the averages when we calculate average earnings. Sample members who leave AFDC are counted (as zeroes) in our averages for AFDC payments. The reported group differences thus represent the desired result: "average program impact per experimental sample member." Similarly, *net cost* is the difference between average cost per experimental and average cost per control (for any similar services received by controls in the community).

The evaluations utilized three kinds of data: background demographic information obtained from a one-page questionnaire given to the sample members just before random assignment; earnings obtained from the computerized tapes of state Unemployment Insurance (UI) systems; and AFDC payments obtained from automated payment ledgers maintained by the state or local welfare agencies. The use of administrative records data offers important advantages in cost, but imposes some limitations as well. We do not observe some outcomes, such as hourly wage rates, which would be helpful in assessing the tested programs. In addition, some earnings are not covered by or not reported to the UI system, which tends to bias measured earnings impacts somewhat towards zero.

The Duration Issue

The availability of five-year follow-up data offers opportunities to explore important questions about long-term program impacts. But the lengthy follow-up period also gives rise to certain problems of interpretation. One important issue concerns the duration of each experiment. Ideally, estimates of the five-year impacts of a program would be based on five years of continuing program treatment for experimental sample members and a corresponding five-year prohibition or *embargo* against program services and participation requirements for control sample members. The original evaluations, however, were not designed to examine long-term impacts. The original evaluation designs planned only a short-term follow-up. After about two years of follow-up, each experiment formally ended, and so did the embargo on providing services to the control group. Thus, after about two years, some controls may have become subject to the same program mandate and may have participated in the same or very similar services as did experimentals. Any activity by controls could influence experimental-control behavioral differences observed in the later part of follow-up.

In three of the programs, we do not know how many controls participated in program services late in the follow-up period; the possible effect of such participation is also unknown. For SWIM, researchers returned to San Diego after five years and obtained participation data from SWIM's successor program, California's Greater Avenues for Independence (GAIN) Program. About one-fifth of SWIM experimentals *and* controls participated in GAIN; and we also know that GAIN was effective in raising earnings and decreasing AFDC payments.[5] It is therefore likely that the estimates of SWIM's impacts for the end of the follow-up period are less than what they would have been had SWIM been a permanent program, instead of a two-year demonstration, and had the research embargo on control services lasted a full five years. If controls had not received services through GAIN, it is likely that their employment and AFDC receipt would have "caught up" to experimentals more slowly, resulting in larger and longer-lasting experimental-control differences in those outcomes in the latter half of the SWIM follow-up period.

Post-experiment participation among controls may have been lower in the other programs, which were not superseded (as was SWIM) by new programs making special outreach efforts to engage controls. Notwithstanding, impact estimates for years three, four, and five in the extended follow-up for all four evaluation samples ought to be treated conservatively as lower-bound estimates of the long-term effects of a permanent program. Had the embargo on working with controls continued indefinitely in each of the programs, the estimates of impacts on employment, earnings, AFDC receipt, and AFDC payments would probably have been larger in the last years of follow-up and might have persisted longer.

EMPIRICAL FINDINGS

Five-Year Program Impacts

Figure 1-1 shows the net costs for the four programs and the dollar impacts on earnings and AFDC payments during the five-year follow-up period.[6] AFDC impacts are shown as negative because they represent reductions in payments. It should be noted that length of follow-up differed across programs, running through quarter 20 in Virginia, 22 in Arkansas, and 21 in San Diego SWIM. In Baltimore, follow-up data for earnings ended in quarter 21, but quarters 13 through 18 were not available; AFDC payments were available only through year three (month 36).

---

[5] For details of the SWIM/GAIN participation study, see Friedlander and Hamilton (1993). For short-term GAIN impacts, see Friedlander, Riccio, and Freedman (1993).

[6] Throughout this study, differences, sums, and percentages shown in figures, tables, or text are computed on unrounded estimates and may differ slightly from those obtained with a hand calculator on the rounded estimates.

> • *In all four programs, the five-year earnings of experimentals exceeded those of controls by amounts that were at least double the net costs of program operations; earnings impacts sometimes exceeded net costs by much more. The five-year earnings impacts were two to four times those observable over the originally planned two-year evaluation periods, showing the importance of the longer-term perspective in assessing total program impact.*

For Virginia, the data reveal that experimentals obtained, on average, $13,098 in earnings over five years (including zeroes for non-earners). Controls obtained an average of $11,919 in earnings. The difference of $1,179 per experimental sample member is the five-year impact of the Virginia program shown in Figure 1-1. The estimate represents a 9.9 percent gain over the control mean earnings level. The observed dollar impact is nearly triple the net cost of the program.

Dollar earnings impacts were lowest in Arkansas, which had the lowest net costs, although the $1,079 total earnings gain was close to the gain in Virginia. The earnings impact in Arkansas was 16 percent of the control mean. The earnings gain was nine times the net cost of the Arkansas program, the highest impact/net cost ratio among the four programs. The high impact/net cost ratios for Virginia and Arkansas show that job search and unpaid work activities can be implemented quite cost-effectively.

The observed earnings impact for Baltimore was only $1,380, but this effect occurred in a follow-up period with a gap of six missing quarters. It is almost certain that the missing data would show that the total five-year earnings impact in Baltimore was somewhat larger. If we credit the missing interval with an impact that is the average of the earnings impacts in the year prior to the gap and the three quarters available after the gap, we obtain a five-year total earnings impact estimate of $2,119 per experimental sample member for Baltimore (shown in Figure 1-1 with the interpolated amount more lightly shaded). The five-year earnings gain in Baltimore was then about the same as the gain in San Diego, which was $2,076 per experimental sample member. In percentage terms, five-year earnings impacts in Baltimore and SWIM were also similar: 14 and 15 percent of average control-group earnings, respectively.

Across the four programs, earnings impacts appear to have increased with net cost. Net costs in Baltimore and San Diego SWIM were about twice the net cost in Virginia and an even greater multiple of net cost in Arkansas. But both of the more

FIGURE 1-1

Observed Program Impacts on Earnings and AFDC Payments

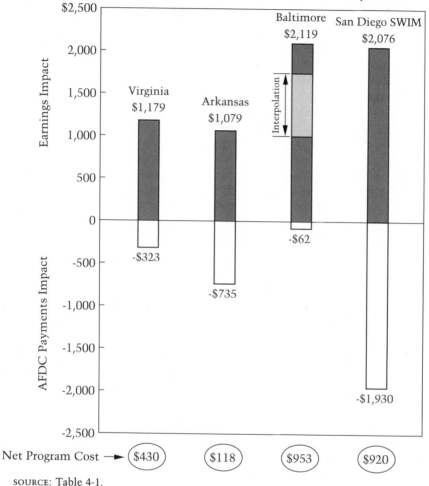

SOURCE: Table 4-1.

costly programs produced five-year earnings gains that were larger than those of the two lower-cost programs and also exceeded twice their own net costs. This raises the question of whether greater effort might bring still larger impacts. At the same time, the somewhat lower impact/net cost ratio in Baltimore and San Diego SWIM compared with Virginia and Arkansas suggests that returns to more expensive education and training are decreasing. That is, adding more expensive education and training to a mix of program services may eventually cease producing additional impacts.

As noted earlier, the formal experiments came to an end after the first two years. Had the reporting of impacts ceased with follow-up year two, observed total earnings impacts would have been considerably lower. In Virginia, earnings gains for years one and two totalled $352; the five-year estimate was more than three times this amount.[7] In Arkansas, the five-year earnings gain was nearly triple the gain in the first two years. Similar results were obtained for the two moderate-cost programs. In San Diego SWIM, the five-year gain was more than double the two-year estimate, and so was the five-year gain in Baltimore, even with the missing earnings quarters. These results show why it is useful to collect and analyze longer-term follow-up data. Long-term impacts are often important in determining the full impact of even quite low-cost programs. As discussed earlier, impact estimates for the later years of these four evaluations should be considered lower-bound estimates of the impacts of ongoing, permanent programs.

- *AFDC savings over five years were large enough to pay government budgets back for the cost of two of the four programs. AFDC savings were more than twice program cost in San Diego SWIM and more than six times cost in Arkansas. AFDC savings plus other impacts on transfers paid back program costs in Virginia. Little if any welfare savings were obtained in Baltimore.*

Reductions in AFDC payments were usually smaller than earnings gains and were not found for every program. The relationship between earnings gains and AFDC reductions is not straightforward. In Virginia, observed total AFDC payments to controls over the five-year period were $6,641 (including zeroes for periods off AFDC); average payments to experimentals were $6,318. The $323 difference (Figure 1-1) amounted to 4.9 percent of average payments received by controls. When lower Medicaid payments, higher tax collections, and reduced administrative costs for transfer programs are factored in, the Virginia program almost certainly broke even.

The Arkansas program produced larger five-year AFDC reductions, $735 per experimental sample member, or 14.3 percent of five-year AFDC payments to controls. These savings were double

---

[7] Estimates for years one and two are taken from Table 4-2.

those in Virginia. They were more than six times net program cost in Arkansas, indicating that, even ignoring effects on other transfers, the program more than paid back its costs to government budgets. San Diego SWIM produced a still larger dollar amount of AFDC savings: $1,930 per experimental, or 10.3 percent of average payments to controls.[8] In fact, the AFDC dollar impact for SWIM is the largest found for an experimentally evaluated broad-coverage program of the 1980s.[9] The impact was more than twice net costs, again indicating that the program more than paid for itself from the perspective of government budgets. As with earnings, five-year impacts on AFDC payments for Virginia, Arkansas, and San Diego SWIM were more than double the impacts that would have been observed at the end of the two-year experiments.[10]

Despite the absence of welfare information from the fourth and fifth years, it is clear that the AFDC impacts in Baltimore were the smallest of the four programs. The dollar impact amount was close to zero and equaled only 1 percent of control-group payments. AFDC savings alone were clearly insufficient to pay the net costs of the Baltimore program. Enrollees, on the other hand, obtained the benefit of increased earnings without much of an offset from reduced AFDC income. This combination of relatively large earnings impacts without corresponding AFDC impacts can occur if earnings effects accrue mainly to program enrollees who are not likely to remain on AFDC for long. In such a case, the increased earnings may not speed case closure any more than would have occurred in the absence of the program.

- *As a result of the programs, enrollees depended more on their own earnings and less on AFDC for income over the five-year follow-up. This increase in "self-sufficiency" may have yielded benefits—or costs—to enrollees that cannot be measured in purely financial terms.*

- *Subtracting AFDC reductions from earnings gains, however,*

---

[8]In order to conform with data in Virginia, Arkansas, and Baltimore, data for San Diego SWIM in this study are organized differently from other SWIM studies. These differences result in slight discrepancies between impact estimates for SWIM in this study and the others.

[9]More recently, two-year impacts for several counties in the California GAIN evaluation showed AFDC savings of $1,397 per experimental sample member in Riverside County, an impact larger than dollar savings for the first two years in SWIM. See Friedlander, Riccio, and Freedman (1993), Table 2.1.

[10]Estimates for years one and two are taken from Table 4-2.

indicates that the overall financial position of enrollees improved in only two of the four programs.

• *Enrollees gained most where government budgets gained least, suggesting a possible trade-off of income gains for budgetary savings.*

By at least one measure, the programs increased self-sufficiency: experimental sample members obtained a larger share of income through their own efforts in unsubsidized employment and a smaller share through AFDC. Increased productive work, in and of itself, is seen by some as a high-priority goal for welfare employment programs.

In the four evaluations, directly measurable financial benefits to enrollees consist of gains in earnings minus reductions in AFDC payments. In theory, it is possible for both enrollees and government budgets to gain, which would be the case if AFDC reductions plus related transfer effects were large enough to cover program costs but earnings gains were even larger. Virginia came closest to this result: government budgets made back approximately what they spent on the program, but, from the enrollee perspective, the modest AFDC reductions offset less than a third of the earnings gain. Among the four programs as a group, however, net financial benefits received by enrollees were obtained at the expense of financial benefits for government budgets. Financial benefits to enrollees were largest in Baltimore, where there was almost no offset to earnings gains from reduced AFDC. Government budgets paid out more to operate the program than they got back in welfare savings and other transfer reductions. Arkansas and San Diego SWIM were the two programs that yielded the most benefit to government budgets. Reduced AFDC payments offset more than two-thirds of earnings gains in Arkansas and nearly all the earnings gains in SWIM.

The trade-off between financial gains for enrollees and for government budgets may be greatly influenced by the format of a welfare-to-work program. A comparison of Baltimore and San Diego SWIM illustrates this point. These two programs differed in the goals they stressed. Baltimore gave a high priority to helping enrollees obtain better jobs, even if that meant staying longer on AFDC to complete a course of education or training. SWIM emphasized maximum participation, rapid employment, and AFDC case closings. These differences were reflected in the program formats. The Baltimore program was designed to encourage participation in activities that would most increase earnings for an individual. Enrollees were given some latitude to pursue activities with the biggest payoff to themselves. As a by-product, the program may have encouraged participation most among individuals who expected to leave AFDC in the short run and who therefore saw clear benefits from increasing their earning power. In addition, the program may have lowered potential AFDC savings by encouraging some participants in education or training to remain on AFDC longer than they otherwise would have.

In contrast, San Diego SWIM enrollees were given less leeway. To achieve maximum monthly participation at large scale, activities were assigned in a fixed sequence and few exceptions from that sequence were allowed. Sanctioning rates were relatively high. This approach may have affected enrollees with longer expected future AFDC stays and therefore with more AFDC income to lose if they became employed.

Impacts Over Time

- *Control-group earnings approximately tripled from year one to year five in all samples. Over the same period, AFDC payments to controls dropped by one-third to two-thirds.*

An oft-expressed concern over low- to moderate-cost welfare-to-work programs is that program effects will "wear off," that many program graduates will lose or leave their newly found jobs and return to AFDC. Wearing-off may, however, play less of a role than control-group catch-up. For earnings, the tendency to catch up occurs because many controls find jobs on their own and because earnings on the job increase with pay raises or promotions or movement to better jobs. This upward drift in control earnings can narrow the initial difference created by the program between experimentals and controls. At the same time, the receipt of AFDC declines gradually, partly because of the growth in earnings. Marriage or reconciliation also contributes to the decline in AFDC receipt. And AFDC benefits for both experimentals and controls must sooner or later fall all the way to zero simply because their children grow up and become too old to qualify for AFDC. Impacts on AFDC must therefore be driven to zero eventually for any group of program enrollees. In these four studies, AFDC receipt among controls declined steadily from year to year until, by year five, only about 25 to 35 percent were receiving AFDC. This pronounced decline in AFDC receipt may be expected to shrink the experimental-control AFDC differential by the end of follow-up.

Control catch-up is inevitable for AFDC impacts, but it need not always occur for employment and earnings impacts. There is no ceiling on enrollees' earnings. Earnings for experimentals could climb indefinitely. The programs could have created a permanent differential in earnings between experimentals and controls. Control catch-up might not completely eliminate the differential. In the fifth follow-up year, less than half of controls at any site were employed in any given quarter. If some of the long-term joblessness and intermittent employment could be converted into stable, ongoing employment, a program could continue to generate earnings-gains in the late follow-up period and beyond.

- *Experimental-control differences in earnings and AFDC payments remained strong for three to four years, but both effects declined thereafter. Additional impacts occurring after follow-up year five were probably much smaller than in earlier years except in Baltimore.*

Figure 1-2 displays impacts on earnings and AFDC payments for each program and for each year of follow-up with time increasing toward the right. As before, AFDC impacts are negative amounts, and larger savings are plotted farther below the zero line.

Earnings impacts remained statistically significant for at least three or four years in all programs. By year five, however, a pattern of peak-then-decline is clear in three of the four programs, though not in Baltimore. Year-five earnings impacts fell by a third from the peak earnings gain in Virginia and fell by two-thirds from the peak gain in Arkansas and San Diego SWIM. For AFDC payments, the pattern is similar. The modest AFDC impacts in Virginia almost completely disappeared by year five. In Arkansas, dollar savings continued and remained statistically significant through year four and, in San Diego SWIM, through year five.[11] The peak for these two programs occurred in year two, however, and dollar impacts had declined by more than half by year five. The limited sixth-year information that is available for Arkansas and SWIM indicates that the downward trend in AFDC effect was continuing. Baltimore achieved virtually no AFDC impacts in any year.

It seems likely that additions to total impacts after the fifth

---

[11] In Friedlander and Hamilton (1993), AFDC payments impacts for San Diego SWIM were statistically significant only through year four owing to a slightly different organization of data over time periods.

FIGURE 1-2(*a*)
Year-by-Year Impacts on Earnings

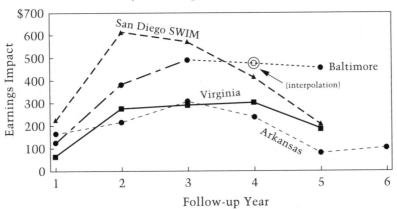

SOURCE: Table 4-2.

FIGURE 1-2(*b*)
Year-by-Year Impacts on AFDC Payments

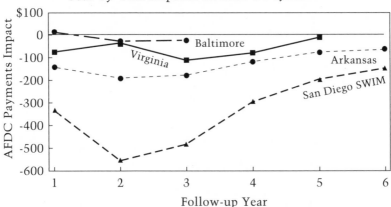

SOURCE: Table 4-2.

year will be much smaller than in preceding years and may eventually approach zero for earnings as well as AFDC payments. Longer follow-up would be useful in confirming this inference. The general pattern of growth and then decline of impacts is traditionally referred to as impact "decay," which connotes a wearing-off of program effect, a failure of the program treatment to "take hold" or "stick" for any length of time. Given the probable importance of control-group catch-up, however, we prefer to describe the narrowing of the experimental-control difference with the more neutral term "convergence." Catch-up and convergence may also have been assisted by possible receipt of program services by controls after the end of the formal experiments, as discussed earlier.

The one exception to the usual time pattern of effects is the earnings impacts in Baltimore. The relatively large $475 fifth-year earnings impact in Baltimore was only slightly below the peak earnings impact of $506 observed in year three, and it was more than twice the fifth-year earnings impact of any of the other programs. The continuing differential constitutes a major program achievement. It boosts the observed impact on earnings and raises our assessment of the program's financial value for enrollees.

Patterns of Employment

The results presented in the preceding section were based on a comparison of the full experimental group with the full control group in each site. This is the pure experimental method. In going beyond the traditional analysis, we must often make use of methods that are *non*experimental in nature. That is, we must make comparisons between subsamples of experimental and control groups that are selected on the basis of outcomes which occur after random assignment. Nonexperimental estimates pose problems for making valid inferences. The behavioral differences between selected subsamples may reflect differences in unobservable characteristics between subsamples rather than real effects of the program. Therefore, some care must be taken in interpreting the various nonexperimental estimates, and the conclusions must be viewed as less certain than those based on pure experimental comparisons.

Table 1-1 summarizes the principal relationships revealed by the analysis of earnings. As shown at the top of the table, the total earnings impact of a program is produced by at least two kinds of effects: an initial program impact, represented in the table by impacts in year two, and a longer-term program impact, represented by impacts in the final follow-up year. These effects are illustrated in graphic format. Each full block represents $100 of earnings. The effects that are critical to our overall understanding of these results appear in boldface. Critical impacts include the large initial earnings impacts and small late-period earnings impacts in San Diego SWIM and the large late-period earnings impacts in Baltimore. The lower part of the table shows

TABLE 1-1

Summary: Components of Program Impact on Earnings

	Results by Program			
Impact and Component	Virginia	Arkansas	Baltimore	San Diego SWIM
Earnings Impacts				
S = Initial impact (year two)				
L = Longer-term impact (final year)				
	S L	S L	S L	S L
Component Effects				
Shorter initial joblessness				
Faster job finding	x	x	x	x
New employment for long-term jobless	x			*MAX*
Higher earnings while employed			*MAX*	
Longer employment spells		x		

SOURCES: Tables 5-1, 5-2, 5-3.

NOTE: Each vertical block represents $100 in earnings impact.

the component effects that we found produced the earnings impacts for each program. We mark with an "x" where effects were found but were of average or unexceptional magnitude. We indicate the largest effects—those associated with the critical impacts—with "*MAX*" in boldface.

To summarize, we find that programs produced their *initial* impacts on earnings by shortening enrollees' initial episodes of joblessness, not by raising their earnings on the job or lengthening their employment spells. All programs got people to work sooner, in large part through faster job finding among enrollees who would eventually have found work anyway. One program produced major earnings gains through an additional mechanism: San Diego SWIM achieved a large "new employment" effect. That is, the program brought about employment among many enrollees who would not have worked at all during the five-year follow-up period. Its success on this score was more than twice as great as any of the other programs. This success did not appear to produce longer-term earnings impacts, however. In contrast, Baltimore produced the most persistent, longer-term earnings impact while inducing only a small new employment effect. The large longer-term impact came mainly through increased earnings on the job, possibly the result of Baltimore's human capital development activities.

Table 1-2 shows details of our analysis of the components of

TABLE 1-2

Details: Components of Program Impact on Earnings

Impact and Component	Summary of Findings	Empirical Measure	Results by Program			
			Virginia	Arkansas	Baltimore	San Diego SWIM
Total Impact on Earnings	Observed impacts on earnings were similar in Arkansas and Virginia, larger and similar in Baltimore and San Diego SWIM, but impacts in Baltimore after five years could increase total impact substantially.	Impact on earnings over the follow-up period	+$1,179*	+$1,079	+$2,119[a]	+$2,076**
		plus	+	+	+	+
		Final-year earnings impact projected into future years	modest future addition	small future addition	**large future addition**	modest future addition
Components of Earnings Impact						
Initial impact on earnings	The largest short-term earnings impacts were found in San Diego SWIM, followed by Baltimore.	Impact on earnings in year two	+$282**	+$224	+$395***	+$626***
Shorter initial joblessness	Virtually all short-term earnings impacts were achieved by shortening the time until experimentals found employment.	Program impact on number of quarters of initial joblessness	−0.72***	−0.87**	−0.98***	−1.89***
Faster job finding	Much of this reduction in initial joblessness came from faster job finding by experimentals who would have found work eventually, even without program assistance . . .	Experimental-control difference in number of quarters until first employed among persons ever employed [z]	−0.26	−0.86	−0.84	−1.04
New employment	. . . but one-third to three-quarters was accounted for by job finding among experimentals who would not have worked during the five-year follow-up. The smallest effect was in Baltimore, and the largest effect was in San Diego SWIM	Impact on percent ever employed during the follow-up period	+3.5**	+2.8	+2.1	+7.1***

		Virginia	Arkansas	Baltimore	San Diego SWIM
Earnings on the job	Experimental-control difference in earnings per quarter of employment in year two (z)	+$25	−$28	+$76	+$19
Duration of employment	Experimental-control difference in length of first employment spell (z)	No effect	Small increase	No effect	No effect
Longer-term earnings impact	Impact on earnings in final year Dollar impact Percent of peak-year earnings impact	+$201 (63%)	+$84 (26%)	+$475* (94%)	+$148 (24%)
Control catch-up	Impact on percent ever employed in year Year two Final year	+5.2*** +1.6	+4.9** +4.9*	+4.6*** +0.4	+10.4*** +1.6
Job loss	Experimental-control difference in joblessness after starting first job (z)	No effect	Decreased	No effect	No effect
Earnings on the job	Experimental-control difference in earnings per quarter of employment in final year (z)	+$64	−$182	+$167	−$9

SOURCES: Tables 5-1, 5-2, 5-3.

NOTES: The follow-up period was defined as quarters two through the last quarter available for each program: Virginia, quarter twenty; Arkansas, quarter twenty-two; Baltimore, quarter twenty-one (quarters thirteen through eighteen missing); San Diego SWIM, quarter twenty-one. The "final year" was defined as the last four quarters available (in Baltimore, the last three available).

A two-tailed t-test was applied to experimental differences. Statistical significance levels are indicated as: * = 10 percent; ** = 5 percent; *** = 1 percent. (z) indicates that the comparison is nonexperimental: no test of statistical significance was performed.

[a]The estimate for Baltimore imputes the missing six quarters from year three and year five earnings impacts estimates. The estimate for the actual follow-up, excluding the missing quarters, is +$1,380***.

earnings impacts. The table links each behavioral component of earnings impacts with relevant empirical results and their interpretation. The left column of the table lists the effects examined: first the total earnings impact and below that the component effects contributing to total earnings impact. A brief interpretive statement of findings pertaining to each component is given in the next column to the right. The third column names one or two empirical measures we defined to investigate the component effect. The last set of columns then describes the estimates for those measures for each program, which constitute the evidence supporting our interpretive statement of findings. Nonexperimental measures are marked with a "z" footnote reference. Estimates of particular interest are shown in boldface.

The labels on the left of Table 1-2 follow the same scheme as in Table 1-1, but with a more detailed catalogue of component effects. As before, the total earnings impact of a program is divided into two major categories of effects: initial program effects occurring during the first few years of follow-up and longer-term program effects. The initial impact on earnings is determined by reductions in the initial period of joblessness and by increases in initial earnings on the job and duration of initial employment. Reduced initial joblessness, in turn, comes from faster job finding and new employment. Given the initial impact on earnings, the longer-term earnings impact is determined by control-group catch-up, the eventual rate of job loss among experimentals, and long-term increases in earnings on the job.

- *In accord with program efforts to get enrollees into jobs quickly, the main initial impact in all four sites was shorter initial spells of joblessness. Experimentals found employment that was similar in earnings levels and duration to employment found by controls, but experimentals found employment sooner than controls.*

During the first two to three years after random assignment, nearly all the impacts on earnings were attributable to increases in the average number of quarters of employment. Very little of the total earnings impacts occurred because employed experimentals earned more during quarters in which they were employed than controls. Of the increase in quarters of employment, nearly all occurred because the initial spells of joblessness of experimentals were shorter than those of controls, not because experimentals remained employed longer. Once employed, experimentals tended to remain employed about as long as controls who found jobs. In large part, the programs speeded up job finding among enrollees who would have worked within a few years anyway. But from one-third (Baltimore) to three-quarters (Virginia) of the decrease in quarters of initial joblessness came from job finding by enrollees who would not have worked at all during the five-year follow-up period.

As shown in Table 1-2, initial earnings impacts were largest in San Diego SWIM, followed by Baltimore and then Virginia and Arkansas. San Diego SWIM had the largest initial earnings impact because it had the greatest success in putting enrollees to work quickly. That is, SWIM had the greatest success in shortening the initial period of joblessness. To examine effects on initial joblessness, we counted the number of quarters for each sample member until the first employment spell started or until the end of follow-up, whichever came first. We then compared experimentals and controls on this measure. As shown in Table 1-2, the reduction in the number of quarters of initial joblessness was similar in Virginia, Arkansas, and Baltimore, ranging from 0.7 to 1.0 quarter. But San Diego SWIM achieved an average reduction of nearly half a year (1.89 quarters), about twice that in the other programs.

The decrease in duration of initial joblessness was partly due to faster job finding among enrollees who would have worked anyway, but this effect did not appear to be the main factor in cross-program differences. For example, as shown in Table 1-2, the speedup of about one quarter in SWIM was not much better than in Arkansas and Baltimore. But San Diego SWIM also had success in encouraging employment among enrollees who would not have worked at all during the follow-up, and this seems to have given it an advantage in producing large initial impacts. About a third of San Diego controls (32.5 percent) reported no earnings at any time during the follow-up, a typical rate for the four programs. SWIM decreased this long-term jobless rate to 25.4 percent for experimentals, for an impact of 7.1 percentage points. In other words, about one in five SWIM enrollees who would not have worked in the absence of the program did work at some point with it. As shown in Table 1-2, this new employment effect was twice that of the nearest program, Virginia, and more than three times that of Baltimore, where the effect was smallest. Our calculations indicate that the new employment effect accounted for about two-thirds of the overall decrease in initial joblessness in San Diego SWIM.

The initial effects of the four programs did not include significant improvements in initial job quality. We examined two dimensions of job quality: earnings per quarter employed and length of first employment spell. Average earnings per quarter employed for controls in year two ranged from $1,300 in Arkansas to $1,900 in San Diego. These averages reflect both the low hourly wage rates of this population and the fact that many sample members who worked in a quarter did not work the full quarter, either because they worked part-time or because they started or ended a job during the quarter. Table 1-2 shows that differences between experimentals and controls on this measure were small. The other dimension of job quality, duration of first employment spell, was not much affected by the four programs either. Experimentals who got jobs during the initial part of follow-up were tracked for two years after they started work. Over those two years, the average duration of the first employment spell was only a little more than one year for all four programs. Differences in spell length between experimentals and controls were minor: the largest difference (in Arkansas) gave experimentals only one-third of a quarter longer first employment spell.

· *Effects on long-term employment patterns differed across programs. The most persistent earnings impact (in Baltimore) was associated not with more job finding but with improved on-the-job earnings, possibly the result of skill enhancement.*

Rates of employment among controls increased over time in all four sites. By the last four quarters of follow-up—the "final year" in Table 1-2—impacts on employment had declined substantially in every program except Arkansas. Control catch-up, however, is not the only possible explanation for the decline in employment impacts over time. Job loss among experimentals, which was high, could also be a contributing factor. Across programs, 50 to 70 percent of sample members (both experimentals and controls) who found work during the follow-up no longer held full-year employment by the final follow-up year. Although they were high, rates of job loss were generally no higher among experimentals than among controls. But the similarity in job loss rates for experimentals and controls meant that job loss played a role along with control catch-up in explaining the observed convergence of employment rates over time.

Job loss had its largest effect in San Diego SWIM, which was the only program to show a decline in employment rates among experimentals following a peak in the middle of follow-up. Some 50.6 percent of experimentals worked in year two, but only 43.4

percent worked in the final year. This employment decline implies that some SWIM enrollees obtained fairly short-lived employment around the time of their initial involvement with the program but subsequently lost their initial jobs and did not resume working quickly.

Keeping enrollees employed longer might be one way to increase impacts on the total amount of time employed and on total earnings, but this does not necessarily have to be so. The overall effect on earnings may depend on how the continuing employment is achieved. A case in point is Arkansas, which was the only program to increase the probability of remaining employed after first finding work. The greater tendency of experimentals to continue working kept their employment rate above that of controls through the end of the follow-up period. Table 1-2 shows that the impact on the probability of being employed at any time during the year was the same in the final follow-up year as in the second year (4.9 percentage points and statistically significant). The table also shows, however, that earnings per quarter of employment in the final year were $182 *lower* for experimentals than for controls, a difference of nearly 10 percent. In part, then, the program experience led some intermittently employed, part-time, or poorly paid workers to stay in the labor market when they might otherwise have left it. We hypothesize that this came about because the experience of some enrollees, either in the program or on the job later, shifted their attitudes more in favor of work over welfare. This change in attitude kept them from giving up on employment and returning to AFDC. But because earnings on the job did not rise, the additional employment did little to increase the program's impact on total earnings. In fact, the impact on total earnings for the final year in Arkansas was well below its peak level, even though there was the continuing impact on employment.

The most persistent earnings impact, that for Baltimore, was associated with a long-term increase in earnings on the job. The final-year earnings impact in Baltimore was large relative to the other programs both in dollar amount and as a percentage of the peak-year earnings impact. Employment impacts in Baltimore, as elsewhere, declined over time. But the Baltimore program boosted long-term earnings among working experimentals. Higher earnings per quarter employed accounted for two-thirds of the $475 final-year earnings impact. This suggests that a staff assessment/enrollee choice approach, going beyond job search and unpaid work assignments to include some education and training, may pay off in longer-term improvements in earning power. These improvements do not necessarily show up quickly in the form of higher-paying initial jobs. After some time, though, this strategy may lead to higher levels of earnings on the job. These improvements in earning power, rather than faster initial employment, can produce permanent increases in earnings for the program-eligible population. In these four programs, it was higher earnings per quarter employed, not increased employment, that produced the largest longer-term earnings impacts.

Patterns of AFDC Receipt

Table 1-3 summarizes findings about the patterns of AFDC receipt. Entries in boldface, as before, indicate critical impacts and major component effects. We find that impacts on AFDC occurred as a result of faster case closure, rather than reduced monthly payments. Large total AFDC reductions in Arkansas and San Diego SWIM were associated with at least modest reductions in long-term AFDC receipt. Return to AFDC after the initial case closure, the behavior known as "recidivism," was common among sample members, but no more common among experimentals than among controls. Catch-up by controls and not recidivism among experimentals was the main factor explaining the decline of AFDC impacts over time.

Table 1-4 presents detailed results for patterns of AFDC receipt. The table is organized in analogous fashion to the detailed table for employment patterns: from left to right, the columns

TABLE 1-3

Summary: Components of Program Impact on AFDC Payments

	Results by Program			
Impact and Component	Virginia	Arkansas	Baltimore	San Diego SWIM
AFDC Payments Impacts				
Total	Some	**LARGE**	None	**LARGE**
Component Effects				
Faster case closure	x	*MAX*		*MAX*
Reduced monthly grants	x			
Reduced recidivism		x		
Reduced long-term AFDC receipt		**Some**		**Some**

SOURCES: Tables 6-1, 6-2, 6-3.

list the total AFDC impact and contributory component effects; the capsule findings for each; the empirical measures utilized to estimate each component effect; and the estimates for those measures for each program. As before, nonexperimental measures are marked with the *"z"* footnote reference, and estimates of particular interest are shown in boldface.

- *AFDC impacts, where they were obtained, came mainly through speedier termination of AFDC receipt.*

- *AFDC recidivism, common among experimentals and controls, was not markedly affected by the programs. Recidivism played only a minor role in offsetting the faster case closures that produced the AFDC reductions. Most of the convergence of experimental and control AFDC outcomes over time is attributable to "catch-up" of case closures among controls, not to recidivism.*

Initial program impacts on AFDC may come either from more rapid case termination or reduced monthly grant amounts. For all four programs, initial AFDC impacts occurred overwhelmingly as a result of more rapid AFDC case closure. More rapid case closure, in turn, reduced the total number of months that experimentals spent on AFDC. If the initial effects of a program on case closure were small, total AFDC impacts were also small. If initial case closure effects were large, then total AFDC impacts were large. Thus, initial AFDC spells were reduced only slightly (by half a month) in Baltimore and by about a month in Virginia but were reduced by an average three months in Arkansas and by nearly four months in San Diego SWIM. Reduced total months on AFDC accounted for more than 80 percent of the large savings in Arkansas and San Diego SWIM.

Reduced monthly grant amounts for experimentals who remained on AFDC played, at most, a minor role in overall AFDC impacts. For none of the four programs were average monthly grant payments to experimentals more than 2 percent below those of controls (not shown). Grant adjustments in response to earnings for recipients working while on welfare were therefore not a major source of AFDC savings. Sanctioning, which partially and temporarily reduces the monthly grant, also appears to have had a very small *direct* effect in producing AFDC reductions, even in San Diego SWIM, where sanctions were most common. The indirect effect of the threat of a sanction in promoting cooperation by program enrollees could not be measured, however, and it might have been important.

TABLE 1-4

Details: Components of Program Impact on AFDC Payments

Impact and Component	Summary of Findings	Empirical Measure	Results by Program			
			Virginia	Arkansas	Baltimore	San Diego SWIM
Total Impact on AFDC Payments	AFDC impacts were largest in San Diego SWIM and were also large in Arkansas, were modest in Virginia, and were not found in Baltimore.	Total impact on AFDC payments over the follow-up period	−$323	−$735***	−$62[a]	−$1,930***
Components of AFDC Impact Faster case closure	More rapid AFDC case closure resulted in fewer total months on AFDC, which, in turn, accounted for the bulk of AFDC impacts.	Impact on months observed in initial AFDC spell	−0.98	−3.03***	−0.50	−3.89***
Reduced monthly grant amounts	Reductions in monthly grants from sanctioning or part-time employment played a minor role.	Percent of impact on AFDC payments accounted for by lower monthly grant amounts.	37%	11%	No effect	18%

Return to AFDC (recidivism)				
Although common, return to AFDC after initial case closure did not explain the decline in AFDC impact over time. "Catch-up" of case closures among controls was the main factor.	Experimental-control difference in months back on AFDC after first exit [z]	No effect	Reduced recidivism	No effect	No effect
Reduced long-term AFDC receipt				
Modest reductions in future long-term AFDC receipt were found in Arkansas and San Diego SWIM, but these made greater than proportionate contributions to total AFDC impacts.	Impacts on AFDC payments to potential five-year recipients				
	Percent reduction	No effect	−8.3%	No effect[b]	−6.7%
	Share of total AFDC impact	No effect	up to 1/3	No effect[b]	1/3

SOURCES: Tables 6-1, 6-2, 6-3.

NOTES: The follow-up period was defined as months one through the last month available for each program: Virginia, month sixty; Arkansas, month sixty-six; Baltimore, month thirty-six; San Diego SWIM, month sixty-three.

A two-tailed t-test was applied to experimental differences. Statistical significance levels are indicated as : * = 10 percent; ** = 5 percent; *** = 1 percent. [z] indicates that the comparison is nonexperimental: no test of statistical significance was performed.

[a] Estimate for Baltimore includes only years one, two, and three. Later years are not available.
[b] No computation was performed for Baltimore because AFDC data were not available for follow-up years four and five, but, given the results for the first three years, no longer-term impact is expected.

29

After the initial speedup in case closure, there was a gradual long-term decline in AFDC impacts that continued through the end of follow-up. This decline may stem either from experimentals returning to the rolls—AFDC recidivism—or from the rate of case closure among controls catching up to that for experimentals. AFDC recidivism was common in all four sites. If we define an individual's first month with a zero AFDC payment as an "exit from welfare," about 40 percent of sample members who exited AFDC returned within a year. If episodes of one or two months off AFDC are not counted as true exits, the rates of return to welfare range from 20 to 30 percent. By and large, however, the programs had little effect on recidivism. Among experimentals and controls who left AFDC, there was little difference in the probability of being back on the rolls in any subsequent observed month. In Arkansas, there was actually a small reduction in recidivism among experimentals. The absence of an AFDC impact in Baltimore stemmed from the absence of any significant case closure effect there, not from recidivism.

  · *Impacts on long-term AFDC receipt—benefit receipt lasting ten years or more—are difficult to project beyond the end of the available data. In Arkansas and San Diego SWIM, however, AFDC reductions were achieved for a modest number of sample members who would still have been on AFDC in the last year of follow-up. Despite the small numbers affected, impacts on these five- and six-year recipients appear to have made a disproportionately large contribution to total AFDC impacts in these two programs, helping to boost the overall impacts of these programs on AFDC.*

One determinant of the magnitude and duration of AFDC impacts is a program's effect on potential long-term AFDC recipients. For any sample member, "future" AFDC receipt is defined relative to the point of enrollment into the welfare-to-work program. From that point forward, some individuals will experience only a short period of future AFDC receipt and others will spend many years on the rolls. Speeding case closures for experimental sample members who would otherwise have been short-term recipients cannot produce long-lasting AFDC impacts because, by definition, similar short-term controls will soon be off AFDC, too. In theory, the greatest *potential* for lasting reductions in AFDC is among individuals who would become future long-term recipients. Impacts obtained for these potential long-term recipients will not be subject to control-group catch-up for many years.

It is therefore of considerable interest to determine whether any of the four programs were able to produce impacts on potential long-term AFDC recipients.[12] To investigate this issue, we may look for program effects on sample members who, in the absence of intervention, would still be on AFDC at the end of follow-up, five or six years after random assignment. We include individuals who remain on continuously and those who leave and then return. Any sustained impact on potential long-termers must show up as experimental-control differences in AFDC during the final follow-up year.

In Virginia and Baltimore, such effects (as seen in Figure 1-2) were close to zero. The interpretation of results for Arkansas and San Diego SWIM is more challenging. For those programs, the AFDC reductions in years five and six (Figure 1-2) appear modest relative to the earlier years and are not statistically significant, except for year five in SWIM. It is difficult to project these estimates beyond the end of the follow-up period; effects on AFDC receipt at eight or ten years may well be quite small. Nonetheless, in the last twelve months of follow-up, the Arkansas and SWIM programs produced average AFDC payment reductions of 8.3 percent and 6.7 percent, respectively, of the control mean AFDC payments during that year. Estimates of the percentage impacts on the number of months of receipt of AFDC in the final year are almost as large. It is worth noting that these two programs, which had the largest total AFDC impacts, were also the only programs to show even modest effects on enrollees who would have still been on AFDC five or six years after random assignment. In SWIM, impacts on those potential long-term AFDC recipients may account for as much as one-third of the total AFDC impact over the full follow-up period, although the exact share cannot be determined with certainty. In Arkansas, the contribution of impacts on potential long-termers was probably smaller but still significant. Thus, effects on five- and six-year AFDC recipients, even though modest, appear to have helped these two programs achieve relatively large overall AFDC reductions.

---

[12] In thinking about program impact on "long-term AFDC receipt," we must distinguish individuals with long future spells of receipt from those who have already been on the rolls for several years. Previously published research (Friedlander 1988c) has found that, among adults, AFDC recipients with two or more years of *prior* AFDC receipt have contributed a substantial share of total program AFDC impacts.

CONCLUSIONS

A number of analysts have pointed out the somewhat surprising finding that almost all (eleven of thirteen) the welfare-to-work programs for adult single women evaluated with experimental impact designs have shown positive impacts on earnings, beginning with the National Supported Work Demonstration in the late 1970s. Our analysis of the new, extended follow-up data from four of the experiments also yields an optimistic picture. The programs used their limited resources in a cost-effective way to achieve several, though not all, of the goals of welfare-to-work programs. Commensurate with their modest cost, the programs increased employment among AFDC recipients; reduced AFDC receipt; increased the share of sample members' income coming from earnings; and, in two of the four programs, saved money for government budgets (a third program probably broke even). In achieving other goals, these four programs were much less successful. In two of the programs, we find evidence for little or no improvement in the financial position of program enrollees. Only in Baltimore was there clear evidence of higher pay on the job. Impacts on potential long-term AFDC receipt were not achieved by two of the programs and appear to be modest at best in the other two.

In pursuit of the general policy goals just mentioned, employment and training programs have three immediate operational objectives: speeding up job finding and AFDC case closure; increasing earnings on the job; and decreasing long-term joblessness and AFDC receipt. The four programs we studied were most successful in achieving the first objective. Faster job finding meant more employment and higher total earnings, which, for two programs, led to more rapid case closure and saved taxpayers money. These achievements constitute a solid foundation upon which to build more sophisticated and comprehensive programs in the future.

The programs had less success in achieving the second operational objective. Most of the programs did not increase the quality of jobs held by enrollees once they began to work. The employment found by experimentals was usually similar to that of controls, both in duration and on-the-job earnings. Only in Baltimore did employed experimentals make more money than employed controls. The quarterly earnings increase was not large, but it produced the only sustained impact on total earnings. The fact that Baltimore allowed more staff discretion and enrollee choice than the other programs and provided some education and training suggests that matching enrollees individually to appropriate human capital development activities may be important in achieving long-term earnings impacts. It should be noted, however, that Baltimore did not achieve AFDC savings. In addition, we cannot say at this point whether the earnings result was caused by the assessment/choice format, by the education and training activities, by the nationally recognized management abilities of the Baltimore program agency, or by some interaction of these factors. Moreover, Baltimore is only one evaluation, and the findings from that site should not be accepted as definitive without further tests of similar programs elsewhere.

The contrast between AFDC impacts for Baltimore and San Diego SWIM offers lessons about the nature and consequences of "mandatoriness" in welfare-to-work programs. Sanctioning was used much more frequently in SWIM, but sanctioning by itself does not explain AFDC impacts that are mostly the result of reductions in months on welfare rather than reductions in monthly payments. One alternative explanation is that the strong effort in SWIM to attain maximum participation, with a fixed sequence of activities that limited staff and enrollee discretion, enabled the program to exert its influence on a higher proportion of the enrollee population. In Baltimore, the program acted primarily on enrollees who could obtain financial gains from participating in the services offered. In SWIM, the program format engaged many more enrollees who did not perceive that participation would lead to financial benefits for themselves. In extending the program reach in this fashion, sanctioning may have played an important role in supporting staff authority without necessarily creating direct AFDC impacts by itself.

The programs were least successful in achieving the third operational objective, that is, in converting long future spells of joblessness and AFDC receipt into steady employment and sustained self-sufficiency. Substantial numbers of program enrollees remained without work and on AFDC five or six years after their initial program experiences. Of the four programs, only Arkansas and San Diego SWIM made even modest inroads into long-term AFDC receipt. Those modest reductions in long-term AFDC receipt appear, however, to have been helpful in achieving the relatively large overall AFDC reductions observed for those two programs. Further reductions in long-term receipt may be necessary if greater overall AFDC impacts are to be achieved in the future.

Limited program effect on potential long-termers meant that wearing-off of initial program impacts through job loss and return to AFDC among program graduates would not be the sole factor shaping experimental-control differences over time. Rather, the gradual narrowing of the experimental-control differences in the later follow-up years came both from catch-up by controls and from wearing-off of the treatment effect. As more controls got jobs and moved up pay ladders, either on their own or possibly through program experiences they might have had after the formal end of the experiments, their levels of employment and earnings rose to converge with those of experimentals. Although there was substantial job loss and intermittent employment among experimentals, there was no more than among controls, and job loss does not appear to have been the main reason for convergence. Likewise, the eventual narrowing of the experimental-control differential in AFDC appears not to have been the result of recidivism related to wearing-off of program effects. Most program graduates who left AFDC did not come back to the rolls quickly. Many did come back, but the level of such recidivism was similar in the experimental and control groups. Convergence over time in AFDC receipt and AFDC payments seems to be the result of normal welfare turnover among controls resulting in catch-up: with each passing year, more and more controls left welfare, and case closings for controls gradually approached those achieved for experimentals in earlier years.

The secondary role played by job loss and return to AFDC in generating the observed pattern of impacts for the four programs studied does not mean that job loss and recidivism should not be important concerns. If the four programs had achieved larger initial impacts on potential long-termers, job loss and recidivism might well have become more severe offsets to impact in the later follow-up years. In this connection, it is significant that San Diego SWIM, which showed the greatest initial effect on long-term joblessness and a modest effect on long-term AFDC receipt as well, did show evidence of some partial erosion of impacts through job loss and recidivism. Program approaches specifically intended to achieve larger impacts with potential long-termers may be hampered more by job loss and recidivism than was the case in these four programs.

Finding ways to address more effectively the needs of potential long-term AFDC recipients is a critical problem for welfare-to-work policy in the years ahead. But substantial risk is entailed in moving programs to focus more on the more disadvantaged, potential long-term recipient. Intensive and expensive services may be needed to raise severely deficient skills to marketable levels. A complex mix of job search, unpaid work assignments, and various kinds of basic and remedial education and occupational training may be necessary for achieving a larger impact within a given program budget. The effectiveness of such services may hinge on the proper combination of program structure, rewards and sanctions, and support services and work incentives. Targeting the more expensive activities to individuals that can be most helped by them and establishing program performance standards that will ensure high-quality and effective services remain difficult unsolved problems. Given the cost of large-scale implementation, there is a risk that significant sums might be spent ineffectively, before adequate development and testing. There is the additional risk that energy might be diverted from operating proven approaches for speeding job finding and from improving approaches for increasing on-the-job earnings for other groups in the caseload. Results from the next round of field experiments, now in progress, should reduce these risks and provide guidance for systematic improvement of JOBS over time.

2

Goals of This Study

Since the late 1960s, a central goal of U.S. welfare policy has been to increase employment among working-age welfare recipients. As discussed in Chapter 1, the Family Support Act (FSA) of 1988, for example, created the JOBS program to provide education and training, work experience, and assistance in finding unsubsidized work in the regular labor market to persons applying to or receiving help in the AFDC program. Like the welfare-to-work programs that preceded it, JOBS provides authority for states to require participation among eligible, able-bodied members of the AFDC caseload. The law permits states to reduce AFDC payments to JOBS program enrollees who do not participate in their assigned employment and training activities.

The popularity of welfare-to-work programs raises important questions about their impact. How effective are these programs in increasing employment and decreasing AFDC receipt? What are the prospects for improving their effectiveness? It is too early to attempt a full assessment of the state level of programs launched under JOBS over the last few years. A rigorous evaluation of program effectiveness will not be completed for a few more years. In the interim, we are fortunate to have information from several experimental evaluations of welfare-to-work programs established in the early and mid-1980s prior to JOBS. These social experiments were designed originally to test the feasibility and effectiveness of large-scale or potential large-scale interventions that could be operated for low to moderate cost per enrollee. This study analyzes four of these social experiments, as described in Chapter 1.

Short-term findings from these evaluations have already been published and have contributed to the national debate over welfare reform.[1] Several crucial issues could not be investigated in those earlier studies, however. This study expands on previous work in two ways. First, we analyze a substantially longer follow-up period than was covered by the data available at the time of the original evaluations. Second, we create a variety of new measures of employment and welfare behavior that were not examined in the original project reports.

The analysis of a longer span of follow-up data is made possible by the accumulation of additional follow-up information. Five years of follow-up data on earnings and AFDC payments are now available for the four evaluation samples. These new data extend the length of time we can observe sample members' behavior by two to three years beyond the earlier evaluation studies. Follow-up data of this duration for four comparable programs with similar evaluation designs are unique.

Longer-term data also permit us to develop and analyze new measures of individual behavior and program impact. In this study, we reorganize the longer-term earnings and AFDC data into new variables that describe quarterly patterns of employment and monthly patterns of AFDC receipt. In analyzing these novel measures, we provide new insight into the nature of long-term program effects, particularly the processes by which impacts can grow or fade over time. Unlike the authors of the original evaluation studies, we have enough follow-up data to go beyond simple averages when measuring employment and welfare receipt.

KEY FEATURES OF THE EVALUATIONS

A complete description of the programs may be found in the next chapter, but some key features should be noted at the outset. The intent of all four programs was to increase employment and earnings and decrease AFDC receipt and AFDC payments. All four were relatively large-scale programs or were prototypes for large-scale programs.[2] People enrolled in the experiments were adult heads of AFDC families. The ones we will analyze

[1] See, for example, "A symposium on the Family Support Act of 1988," published in the *Journal of Policy Analysis and Management* (1991), on research and the passage of the Family Support Act.

[2] The Baltimore program was originally limited to one thousand slots, but was expanded to a claimed six thousand slots during the five-year follow-up period.

here were single parents; nearly all of them were women.[3] The programs were not selective in enrollment; on the contrary, they were *broad-coverage* programs, designed to reach or "cover" all eligible individuals in a particular target population. Enrollment and participation in a program were mandatory in the sense that AFDC recipients who did not participate in an assigned activity risked a temporary reduction of their monthly AFDC grant. This penalty is known as a *sanction*. Single parents with any children under six years of age were exempted from the enrollment requirement in three states, as prescribed by federal statute. This is roughly two-thirds of the total AFDC population.[4] The remaining group, targeted by the programs, is known as the traditional *WIN-mandatory* population. In Arkansas, by special federal waiver, the child age exemption was granted only if the youngest child was under three. Aside from the enrollment exemption for single parents of preschoolers, *deferrals* from immediate participation were granted to many enrollees for "good cause" excuses (such as illness of self or a child).[5]

Activities (known as program *components*) in all four programs included job search assistance, either one-on-one with enrollee and staff or in a group format, and three-month assignments to work without pay at a public or nonprofit agency. Some education and training was part of three programs, though not of the program tested in Arkansas. While there was a rough similarity in the basic list of employment and training activities, the programs differed from one another in philosophies and goals, in format and duration, in degree of "mandatoriness," and in cost per enrollee. The average program net cost ranged from a low of about $100 per enrollee up to a high of about $1,000. In three of the programs, job search was usually assigned before any other activity. In this regard, the Baltimore program differed from the

---

[3] The basic AFDC support is for children in single-parent families and the single parent. The AFDC Unemployed Parent (AFDC-U) program provides support for children and their parents in two-parent families with an unemployed head. Most AFDC-U case heads are male. The rules for AFDC-U eligibility and requirements for employment program participation are different from those for the AFDC basic program. Two of the four social experiments we examine incorporated samples of AFDC-Us but, owing to the differences between them and the regular AFDCs, the AFDC-Us are not included in the present study.

[4] Also exempt were household heads who were under sixteen years of age or sixty-five or older, under twenty-one and enrolled full-time in school, sick or incapacitated, living in a remote area, or caretakers of a sick person.

[5] Deferral of participation could be granted to enrollees with child care problems, housing problems, and the like. Deferral of immediate participation for a program enrollee is not the same as exemption from the enrollment requirement.

other three and was similar to many JOBS programs today. Participation in Baltimore began with an initial assessment of enrollee needs and capabilities, and some latitude was afforded to staff and enrollee in deciding whether education or training should be the first assigned activity.

The San Diego program was also distinctive but for other reasons. Unlike the other programs, it was not an ongoing local program but, rather, was a special demonstration undertaken at federal initiative. Its purpose was to test the feasibility of requiring sustained participation in an employment-directed activity by a high percentage of the target caseload. This "caseload saturation" strategy reflects one view of what welfare reform should aim for. The other programs were not organized to require sustained participation after enrollees completed their first set of assigned activities. In Virginia and Arkansas, participation in employment-directed activities was often relatively brief. The full sequence of activities could be completed within a matter of months. These and other differences across the four programs invite comparisons of results to help us judge which approach might be superior in achieving a given policy goal. These comparisons are not straightforward, however. The economic and policy environments differed in the four sites. For example, local unemployment rates and AFDC grant levels varied widely.

All four sites tested welfare-to-work strategies in the context of a classical experiment with randomized assignment of program enrollees to program and comparison groups. The program group, also known as the experimental group or "experimentals," was assigned to the tested program services and was subject to the regular participation requirements and sanctions. The comparison group, called the control group or "controls," could not participate in these program services and was not subject to program requirements or sanctions. The differences in earnings and AFDC benefits between the two groups represent our best estimates of the programs' impacts. Because randomization makes the experimental and control groups similar except in their program experiences, the impact estimates are internally valid and unbiased. It should be noted that some controls, on their own initiative, sought out and participated in employment and training opportunities available outside the experiments. The experimental-control difference therefore measures the impact of the participation mandate plus the additional services offered by the program above and beyond the services that AFDC recipients would voluntarily obtain on their own.

The rigor of the experimental evaluation design is a great asset in analyzing the behavioral response to the tested treatments. To answer some research questions, however, we occasionally rely on *non*experimental methods in this study. The interpretation of the nonexperimental empirical estimates entails less certainty than in a pure experimental analysis. In addition, it should be noted that the long period of follow-up data, although it is invaluable in addressing particular questions, also presents some difficulties in interpretation. In particular, there is an important issue regarding the duration of the experiments. In all four programs, the formal experiments ended, as originally planned, after about two years. In extending the follow-up to five years, we are analyzing responses that occurred long after the formal experiments ended. For reasons discussed in the next chapter, this means that our estimates of program impact in the last years of follow-up are likely to underestimate the size and durability of impacts that would be obtained from a permanent program evaluated with a formal experiment period of five years instead of two. Another issue concerns a gap in the data that occurred during part of the extended follow-up period in Baltimore. As we indicate later, this gap reduces somewhat our certainty about the pattern of effects in that site.

GOALS OF THIS STUDY AND ANALYSIS STRATEGY

The original evaluations of these four programs and other studies have shown that welfare-to-work programs can increase employment and earnings and, to a lesser extent, reduce AFDC receipt and AFDC payments. On average, these impacts were comparatively modest, although estimates of total earnings gains have generally equaled or exceeded program costs. In addition, total AFDC benefit reductions were often large enough to pay back all program costs to government budgets. In some of the experiments, program effects began to appear almost immediately (i.e., within a few months of enrollment in the program). In other experiments, program effects took as long as a year and a half to show up. How long the effects of the program persisted—whether two years, three years, or permanently—was not ascertainable from the short-term follow-up data available in previous studies. The dearth of longer follow-up has also made it uncertain whether the programs affected long *future* AFDC spells, even though the results indicated that a major share of total AFDC impacts accrued to people with lengthy *prior* AFDC receipt. In addition, little has been done to investigate possible program effects on stability of employment among program graduates and on the length of time graduates remained off AFDC. The basic evaluation studies have therefore left major gaps in our understanding of the total impact of these programs and how those impacts were achieved.

Our first research goal, as stated earlier, is to use the new five-year follow-up data to estimate longer-term program impacts on the earnings and AFDC payments of enrollees. We want to measure the total impact during the five years, and we also want to see whether the programs produced lasting effects that might extend into later years. As part of this analysis, we will use our longer-term estimates to determine whether revisions must be made to previously published conclusions about total benefits and costs to program enrollees and government budgets. Our second research goal is to look more closely at program effects on the underlying time patterns of employment and welfare receipt that make up the total or average impact of a program. In doing so, we must develop new measures of outcomes and new ways of analyzing them. We must look at the speed with which jobs are found, the levels of earnings once employed, and the stability of employment after starting to work. On the welfare side, we must look at the speed of AFDC case closure and the frequency and timing of return to public assistance. Understanding these detailed patterns yields additional insights into how these programs worked, what behaviors they affected, and where they succeeded and failed. From this investigation, we hope to draw conclusions about the potential for improving future welfare-to-work programs, particularly with regard to more intensive and expensive treatments than were tested in these four program evaluations.

Our fundamental unit of observation is the individual program enrollee. Our data are organized in such a way as to show the experience of a representative group of enrollees from the point at which they entered the program, tracing their employment, earnings, and AFDC receipt year-by-year, quarter-by-quarter, for about five years. Within this framework, "year one" for the representative group begins with program entry, which coincides with their random assignment. Subsequent years are designated "year two," "year three," and so on. When we speak, for example, of "impacts in year three" we mean the third year of follow-up for the representative group, not the third year of program operations. Thus, the phrase "short-term impacts" means impacts that occur for the representative group near the time they enroll in the program and first participate in it, or shortly thereafter; "longer-term impacts" are impacts that occur for the group several years after their initial program experiences. In this context, "short" and "long" are terms relative to individual enrollment, not to the date of establishment of the program. The terms do not refer to the program start-up and steady-state phases of operation. Groups that enroll in a program after the experiment has finished might still be expected to obtain a pattern of short- and longer-term impacts similar to the one estimated for the original experimental sample.

In analyzing these data, we make an important distinction between "outcomes" and "impacts." Behavioral *outcomes* are simply the observed levels of the variables of interest at any point during the follow-up period. For example, one outcome of interest is the average quarterly employment rate among program enrollees in year three of follow-up. An *impact* is the difference between an outcome that is observed for a group of enrollees and the level of the outcome that would have occurred in the absence of the special program. Thus, if a group of enrollees is observed to have a 35 percent employment rate in year three and is estimated to have had a 30 percent employment rate without the program, then the program impact is the difference of 5 percentage points. Typical outcomes for a group of enrollees include percent employed, average earnings, percent receiving AFDC, and average dollar amount of AFDC payments received. Experimental-control differences in these outcomes represent the employment and earnings "gains" and the AFDC "reductions" achieved by the program.

We look at the data in a variety of ways. We compute total earnings and AFDC payments over the observation period, earnings and payments for each year, speed of initial job finding and AFDC case closure, duration of employment and AFDC spells, earnings on the job, prevalence and speed of return to AFDC for those who leave it, comparisons of early and late follow-up periods, and other measures. Using multiple indicators allows us to describe the many facets of work and welfare behavior and allows us to confirm conclusions we reach from one analysis against the results of another analysis.

Our presentation is structured as follows: The next chapter describes the programs and data and discusses important analysis issues. Chapter 4 presents the basic five-year impact estimates for the full follow-up as a whole and for each follow-up year. Chapter 5 then analyzes the patterns of employment that shape the basic program impacts. In Chapter 6, we look at the program effects on detailed patterns of AFDC receipt. Finally, in Chapter 7, we interpret the array of empirical findings and formulate general conclusions about the nature of program effects; and we close by discussing the implications for welfare employment policy.

3

Analysis Issues, Programs, Data

In this chapter, we provide the basics for understanding the research projects analyzed in this study. We begin by explaining the social experiment research methodology that was used to estimate program impacts. We then discuss the nature of broad coverage, which was a central feature of all of the programs that were evaluated. We proceed with a detailed description of the programs under study. Next, we devote some attention to the duration issue, which stems from the availability of program services for control sample members after the end of the formal experiment in each site. We follow up with a summary description of the data and conclude with a presentation of the characteristics of the four research samples.

EXPERIMENTAL DESIGN

As mentioned in Chapter 2, the concept of program impact is based on a comparison of the outcomes observed for a group of program enrollees with the outcomes that would have occurred for the same group in the absence of the program. It is the difference between these two levels, the observed outcome level for program enrollees and some measure of the unobserved outcome level they would have obtained, that constitutes program impact. Outcomes for program enrollees are relatively easy to observe. Estimating what those outcomes would have been without the program is the principal challenge for impact research. One method of estimating unobserved outcomes is to collect information from some comparison sample of individuals who are not enrolled in the program. But if the comparison group differs in background characteristics from the program group, then differences in average outcomes may result from this basic lack of group similarity and not from any effect of the program. Impact estimates will, in this case, be biased.

In a classical experimental design, randomized assignment is intended to create two groups that are similar in all measurable and unmeasurable characteristics, so that they differ only in their exposure to the program. Because the two groups are similar at the start and their subsequent differences in treatment derive only from the program under study, any subsequent difference between them can be safely attributed to the program.[1] The resulting estimate is generally stated as impact "per experimental sample member" or impact "per enrollee" rather than impact "per participant," since experimentals do not generally all participate in formal program activities.

An analogous approach is used to estimate program costs. Net cost is estimated as the average level of program costs for experimentals minus the average cost of whatever community services are utilized by controls. As with impacts, net program cost is stated "per experimental sample member" rather than "per participant." The fact that the same sample is used to calculate impacts and costs means that impact and cost estimates are directly comparable. It is thus straightforward to determine a program's *cost-effectiveness*, which may be defined as the amount of impact per dollar of net program cost. It is also possible to add up all impacts and subtract out all net costs pertaining to government budgets to estimate the bottom-line financial effect in a *benefit-cost* analysis. Similar benefit-cost analyses may be performed to tally up all measured financial effects accruing to sample members and to other members of society.

To preserve the similarity between experimental and control groups upon which all else rests, no changes may be made in research group membership after random assignment has occurred. Experimentals always remain experimentals; controls always remain controls. Experimentals who do not participate in the program are still retained as part of the experimental group. Employment, earnings, AFDC receipt, and AFDC payments are averaged over nonparticipants as well as participants. In addi-

---

[1] In practice, it is usually the case that extensive on-site monitoring must occur during the experiment to ensure that true randomization and separate treatment are maintained for experimentals and controls and that no extraneous elements influence behavior or the quality of data differently for the two research groups.

tion, sample members who do not become employed are still included (as zeroes) in the averages for earnings. Sample members who leave AFDC are counted (as zeroes) in the averages for AFDC payments. The reported group differences thus reflect the average program impact per experimental sample member.[2]

To increase the accuracy of the basic impact estimates, experimental and control average outcomes may be statistically adjusted by regression techniques. Regression adjustment corrects for any small differences between experimentals and controls in background characteristics that are still present after randomization. Under some circumstances, it also increases the statistical precision of the impact estimates by removing some of the statistical noise. Both these benefits of regression are usually quite small under experimental impact designs and lead to only minor differences between the regression-adjusted and "raw" (unadjusted) impact estimates.

The accuracy of impact estimates is affected by a number of factors, one of which is the size of the research sample. For any individual, employment and AFDC outcomes are partly shaped by chance events: a "lucky break" in job search, an unexpected layoff, a serious illness of the case head or a family member, and the like. In large samples, chance events tend to cancel out; in small samples, the role of chance may be more pronounced. Thus, the accuracy of impact estimates generally increases as sample size increases. In this study, all four samples are of adequate size to yield reasonably precise impact estimates. It may be noted, however, that the Arkansas sample is the smallest and is less than half the size of any of the other samples. Estimates for Arkansas are therefore less precise than those for the other programs.

Statistical tests are applied to impact estimates to help in interpreting the results. These tests are intended to rule out the role of chance where that is possible. Greater certainty attaches to impact estimates that are statistically significant than to those that are not. However, statistical significance should not be equated with policy significance. When samples are large

---

[2] Some exceptions to the rule forbidding the dropping of sample members usually occur in practice. For example, the handful of sample members who do not have Social Security numbers at the time of random assignment are often dropped because earnings from the UI earnings data (and sometimes AFDC payments data) cannot be obtained for them. On the other hand, sample members who lack less important baseline information (e.g., ethnicity or length of prior AFDC history) are generally retained in the impact and benefit-cost analyses.

enough, even quite small impact estimates will be statistically significant. Conversely, programs that have large impacts may not show statistically significant results in small samples. Finally, some results may be important precisely because they are small and not statistically significant. In formulating conclusions from the empirical findings, we therefore draw confidence not only from statistical significance but also from consistent patterns in the estimates.

In succeeding chapters, we will often have recourse to *non*experimental estimates. Nonexperimental estimates are distinguished from pure experimental estimates in that they utilize portions of the experimental and control samples that are selected on the basis of individual behaviors that occur *after* random assignment has occurred. For example, we may wish to compare earnings per person employed during the follow-up period for experimentals and controls. To calculate this statistic, we omit people in the experimental and control groups who are not employed. Because we are dropping sample members without earnings from this estimate it is not a pure experimental estimate. The difference we observe in average earnings may be the result of the program or it may simply occur because there are background (i.e., pre-random assignment) differences between the experimentals and controls who are employed and, hence, are selected for this nonexperimental estimate. Great care must therefore be used in interpreting the nonexperimental estimates we report. The conclusions that depend on nonexperimental comparisons must be viewed as less certain than those based on pure experimental comparisons. In this study, we have elected not to apply statistical tests to nonexperimental estimates of differences between research groups.[3]

BROAD COVERAGE

As broad-coverage programs, all four of the programs were designed to reach or cover every eligible person in a target group defined by objective characteristics. No subjective screening cri-

---

[3] The issue of statistical tests for nonexperimental estimates that are derived from experimental estimates is a complicated one. It may be argued that a statistical test of a derived estimate would be inappropriate, given that the source estimates have already been subject to a test. On the other hand, it would often be useful to know which of several derived estimates are the most reliable components of the overall effect from which all are derived.

teria were imposed for program enrollment. "Job readiness" or "motivation" were not considered in enrolling individuals in the programs. The broad coverage of these four programs sets them apart from another class of programs that have been evaluated experimentally. Programs in this other class are known as *selective-voluntary* because screening criteria, often subjective ones, may be utilized by program staff to select who is suitable to enroll and because participation is voluntary on the part of the enrollee.[4]

The broad-coverage programs in this study have two distinctive features. The first is implementation on a large scale or the potential for implementation on a large scale. For example, SWIM, even though it operated in only a portion of San Diego, enrolled more than ten thousand AFDC applicants and recipients during the two years of intake. By way of contrast, the selective-voluntary National Supported Work Demonstration, the first major welfare-to-work experiment, covered a total of seven sites, including such large cities as New York, Chicago, and Newark, but worked with a total of only about eight hundred AFDC recipients.[5]

Second, broad-coverage programs must be thought of as complete *service delivery systems* rather than individual activities. Part of the intent of these systems is to coordinate job search, unpaid work assignments, and other activities for the enrollee population. Moreover, in addition to offering specific activities, these systems include procedures for client outreach, enrollment, and orientation; provisions for support services such as transportation and child care; staff and procedures for assessing enrollee capabilities and needs, for assigning enrollees to specific activities, and for monitoring and enforcing compliance; and a set of regulations detailing enrollee obligations and penalties for noncompliance.

Broad-coverage programs that are mandatory may have effects on enrollees who do not actually participate in formal program activities. After enrolling in the program, many people find jobs or otherwise leave AFDC before they can begin a program activity. Some of these individuals may leave AFDC in order to avoid having to participate. This behavior may be thought of as a *deter-*

---

[4]For further discussion of the important distinction between broad-coverage and selective-voluntary programs, see Friedlander and Gueron (1992).

[5]The AFDC sample for Supported Work was about 1,620, but half of these were control sample members.

rence effect. In addition, some individuals refuse to participate and are sanctioned. Finding a job, leaving welfare, or incurring a sanction may all be impacts of the program that occur even if an individual does not participate in a formal program activity.

In order to measure program effects on nonparticipants, evaluation samples for broad-coverage programs are typically drawn before individuals actually begin to participate, early in the sequence of steps leading up to participation, often at the time an AFDC recipient is first enrolled in or informed about the program. In addition, studies of broad-coverage programs, including the four experiments studied here, usually calculate program impacts for samples that include all enrollees, "participants" and "nonparticipants" alike. As indicated in the preceding section, the correct and generally accepted practice is to report "impact per enrollee" or "impact per experimental sample member" rather than "impact per participant." Actual rates of participation in formal activities within these samples have tended to be around 50 percent. As shown below, the participation rates for the four programs in this study fall in the typical range.

THE PROGRAMS

Table 3-1 presents information about the format, activities, participation, and cost of each of the four programs examined in this study. Except for SWIM, all the programs were implemented beginning in the period 1982–1983, under WIN, following federal legislation of 1981 that enhanced the ability of states to run mandatory welfare-to-work programs.[6] All except SWIM were put in place as permanent, ongoing programs for their jurisdictions, rather than as special demonstrations that ended with the research evaluation. All except SWIM had only the funding sources normally available to programs in the WIN system, although the Baltimore program was funded at a higher level than other WIN programs in Maryland. Unlike the other programs,

---

[6]The Omnibus Budget Reconciliation Act (OBRA) of 1981 and legislation that followed shortly thereafter (a) permitted states to transfer to their AFDC agencies the authority for operating employment programs that served the AFDC population; (b) established the Community Work Experience Program (CWEP), which allowed states to require program enrollees, for as long as they remained on AFDC, to work at public or private nonprofit jobs in return for their AFDC check (with monthly hours not to exceed the monthly AFDC payment amount divided by the minimum wage); and (c) increased program authority to require applicants to and recipients of AFDC to participate in job search.

TABLE 3-1

Descriptions of Experiments

	Virginia ESP	Arkansas WORK Program	Baltimore Options Program	San Diego SWIM
Evaluation Began	1983	1983	1982	1985
Mandatory or Voluntary	Mandatory	Mandatory	Mandatory	Mandatory
Study Group	AFDC single parents with no children under 6	AFDC single parents with no children under 3	AFDC single parents with no children under 6	AFDC single parents with no children under 6
Format and Major Program Activities	Fixed sequence: mainly job search and three-month unpaid work assignments	Fixed sequence: job search with some three-month unpaid work assignments	Initial assessment and some choice among job search, unpaid work assignments, or education/training	Ongoing participation requirement, fixed sequence: job search, three-month unpaid work assignments, then some education/training
Activity Rates[a]				
Any activity	58.3%	38.0%	45.0%	64.4%
Job search	51.0%	27.3%[b]	24.7%	50.6%
Unpaid work	9.5%	2.9%	17.5%	19.5%
Education, training, other	11.6%	—	17.3%	24.3%
Sanction[c]	3.8%	[d]	Rare	10.6%
Program Net Cost Per Experimental Sample Member	$430	$118	$953	$920
AFDC Benefit[e]	$255	$140	$295	$526
Unemployment[f]	6.6%	11.0%	7.0%	9.0%
Study Scale	11 of 124 county welfare agencies	2 of 75 counties	10 of 18 city welfare offices	2 of 7 city welfare offices
Sample Size	3,150	1,127	2,757	3,211

SOURCES: Friedlander and Robins 1992, Gueron and Pauly 1991.

[a] Rates are for the experimental sample.
[b] Excludes participation by 23.3 percent in individual job search.
[c] Request for sanction.
[d] In Arkansas, administrative records indicate that 3 to 5 percent of all persons who participated in a program assessment (not just sample members) were sanctioned or dropped from the program (i.e., were deregistered) for noncompliance.
[e] Guarantee for family of three, as of October 1, 1982.
[f] Average female unemployment rate in state during 1983.

SWIM was a specially funded federal demonstration project, set up to enroll and work with clients for three years only (1985–1988).

The programs were similar in several respects other than broad coverage. To summarize what has already been stated: All four programs were mandatory (as is typical of broad-coverage programs), and all were designed under the same federal rules governing mandatory participation. In accordance with the mandatory format of the programs, enrollees were told they were required to participate in certain activities; those who failed to participate and could not provide a "good cause" excuse could have their welfare payments reduced for several months through sanctioning.[7] The target populations were, in all cases, applicants to and recipients of AFDC. All of the programs made extensive use of some kind of supervised job search. All included some form of unpaid work assignments, and all except Arkansas assigned or referred some enrollees to education or training. In important respects, however, the four programs differed in philosophy and goals, resources, and operating environment. And from these basic differences came differences in the mix of services offered, in program structure, and in the level of enforcement and overall "mandatoriness."

In many ways, Virginia's was the most representative program. AFDC grants in that state were near the national median, and program net costs, at $430 per sample member, were near the middle of the cost range for the four programs. Typical of this kind of program, the Virginia program was intended to reach as many people as possible. It was a multicounty program, covering rural as well as urban areas, and it enrolled all AFDC applicants and recipients who met the existing legal definition of mandatory. The effort to cover this large population with a limited budget determined the structure of the program and intensity of services. It led to the predominance of job search activities, which are much less expensive than other employment-directed services. Job search took precedence over other activities. It was to be assigned first, without assessment of individual enrollees' skills or abilities. In this respect, the sequence of activities was fixed, at least in part, rather than individualized. In addition, most of the job search in Virginia consisted of assigning enrollees to look for work—commonly known as "indi-

---

[7]For the first sanction, the parent's portion of the AFDC grant was eliminated for three months. For the second and subsequent sanctions, the grant reduction remained in effect for six months.

vidual job search"—which is less intensive and less expensive than staff-led classes in job search techniques and in-group supervised search. Finally, job search was short, four weeks or less, although enrollees could be reassigned to job search after completing other program activities. As shown in Table 3-1, the bulk of program activity was in job search, with slightly more than half of the experimental sample participating.

Unpaid work assignments, which lasted thirteen weeks and were restricted to no more than eighty hours per month, were much less common, with less than 10 percent of experimentals participating. About 12 percent of experimentals participated in some form of education or training. Owing to budgetary constraints, education and training were not provided directly by program staff but, instead, by referring enrollees to other training institutions in the local community. Control sample members had access to the same local institutions, and they enrolled in training programs about as often as members of the experimental group. Consequently, researchers in the original evaluation deemed it likely that most of the program impact occurred as a result of job search and unpaid work activities.

In all, 58.3 percent of experimental sample members in Virginia participated in some program activity. Most of the others left AFDC or became ineligible for program services before participating in any program activity. Sanctioning was infrequent. Only 3.8 percent of experimentals were sanctioned during their enrollment. Fewer than 10 percent of experimentals remained in the program without being covered by the obligation to participate, work, leave AFDC, or be sanctioned. It should be noted, however, that the program was not designed to impose an obligation for continuous, long-term participation on enrollees. Most of the services actually provided were of fairly short duration.

The Arkansas program was also designed to reach large numbers. The impact evaluation was carried out only in Little Rock and Pine Bluff, but the program itself was a multicounty program. Coverage under the tested program was further extended by obtaining a federal waiver to include in the mandatory target group all single parents whose youngest child was at least three years old. Arkansas's was the lowest-cost program, with net costs of $118 per sample member. Arkansas was distinguished by the state's comparatively low AFDC grant levels, and the program population was relatively disadvantaged.

As in Virginia, activities in Arkansas were assigned in a fixed sequence: two weeks of group job search training and supervision, followed by up to sixty days of individual job search, although the latter was often assigned as a first activity for individuals regarded as more employable. Enrollees who were still not employed after these activities were completed were to be assigned to an unpaid work position for up to twelve weeks. After completing this sequence, enrollees could be reassigned to any activity or occasionally to a new one. As shown in Table 3-1, job search turned out to be the main activity, with very few experimental sample members participating in work experience. In all, 27.3 percent of experimentals participated in group job search and 23.3 percent participated in individual job search. As in Virginia, participation in Arkansas was usually short in duration.

A high proportion of program enrollees in Arkansas were AFDC applicants who did not complete the application process for AFDC. More than a quarter of the experimental sample received no AFDC payments within nine months after their enrollment. Their quick exit from the system reduced program participation rates within the experimental group. The overall participation rate among experimentals was only 38.0 percent, lower than in Virginia and the lowest of the four programs. Nevertheless, short-term follow-up indicated that only about a quarter of experimental sample members remained on AFDC and still formally enrolled in the program without participating in a program activity. The other three quarters were covered by the program mandate to participate, work, leave AFDC, or be sanctioned. This rate of coverage occurred, in part, as a result of the many rapid exits from AFDC among applicants. Sanctioning, as in Virginia, appeared to be relatively infrequent.

Baltimore differed from the other programs in philosophy and goals, administrative structure, and format of activities. It was implemented as one of nine special initiatives in Maryland. Funds were concentrated in the special initiatives rather than spread thinly over all WIN programs in the state. Management of the Baltimore program was entrusted to a nationally recognized employment and training agency rather than to the existing WIN agency.[8] The special funding and management arrangements

---

[8] Technically, Maryland operated a WIN Demonstration program rather than regular WIN, as permitted under federal legislation of 1981. Under WIN Demo, as it was called, authority for employment activities and AFDC administration were combined in a single agency and not split between the welfare agency and the employment service. This arrangement existed in Maryland prior to WIN Demo. Notwithstanding, responsibility for operation of the new program in Baltimore was delegated to the local Job Training Partnership Act (JTPA) agency, which was perceived as more innovative than the WIN agency.

were intended to allow the Baltimore program to provide high-quality services and enough program openings to accommodate all suitable enrollees. In harmony with this objective, the Baltimore program did not attempt to enroll all eligible individuals in its target area. Instead, it took only individuals newly entering the mandatory category, either as applicants to AFDC or as longer-term recipients whose youngest child had just turned six. Enrollments were limited in order to maintain a slot level of one thousand initially. It may be noted that, unlike the other programs, controls in Baltimore could receive services from the regular WIN agency, and 3.7 percent of them did.

The program goal in Baltimore was economic security for enrollees rather than rapid job entry as it was in the other programs. The hallmark of the Baltimore program was individualization of services. Unlike the other programs, Baltimore staff were expected to assess each enrollee and prescribe a regimen of activities best suited to that person's abilities and interests. There was no fixed sequence of activities, and job search was not necessarily the first assignment. This "assessment first" approach—as contrasted with a "job search first" approach—is now found in many JOBS programs. In Baltimore, managers intended to encourage enrollees who needed education and training to participate in those activities to help them obtain higher-paying jobs than they would otherwise find, even if that meant staying on AFDC longer. Education and training were usually provided by administrative units under the direct authority of the program or by providers under contract with the program, rather than by referral of enrollees to community institutions open to all Baltimore residents.

Enrollees in Baltimore were offered some choice among several activities, where openings in particular classes or groups permitted. Although participation was mandatory, sanctioning was rare, and staff tended to secure enrollee compliance through persuasion.[9] As shown in Table 3-1, job search was the most common activity, but unpaid work and education and training were also used to a significant extent. In line with the relatively greater intensity of participation in Baltimore, the three-month unpaid work assignments in public or nonprofit agencies could be full-time rather than part-time.[10] Overall, 45 percent of the

[9] In a sample of seventy for whom case records were examined, no evidence could be found of an actual AFDC grant reduction associated with sanctioning.

[10] Two kinds of unpaid work activities could be used by welfare-to-work programs during the 1980s. CWEP, which was permitted under 1981 law, limited a partici-

experimental sample participated in some activity, but only a little more than half of the participants were active in a formal job search activity, a lower proportion than in any of the other programs. Average net costs were $953 per sample member and were substantially above costs in Virginia and Arkansas. The short-term data show that about a quarter of experimentals remained on AFDC and enrolled in the program without having participated in any program activity.

San Diego SWIM took an approach opposite of Baltimore's. Program goals in SWIM emphasized maximum participation, rapid job entry, and reduction of AFDC receipt. Endowed with special funding, SWIM was designed to test a particular approach to employment and training services for the AFDC population, the so-called "caseload saturation" approach. This approach has two objectives: (a) to require participation (or employment) for the entire time an individual remains on AFDC and (b) to impose this requirement on all targeted AFDC applicants and recipients.[11] This strategy represents one popular approach to welfare reform, an approach that stresses program participation and work obligations for persons on public assistance.

In several respects, San Diego was an ideal site for testing the caseload saturation approach. Like the Baltimore program, San Diego SWIM was run by an agency known nationally for its management expertise. Line staff were experienced with the format and content of program activities. Staff members by and

---

pant's work hours to the monthly AFDC grant divided by the minimum wage. The client's work in CWEP was seen as a way to "pay back" the value of the AFDC grant through community service. CWEP assignments were often part-time, depending on a state's AFDC grant level and a family's monthly benefit amount. Baltimore elected to operate its unpaid work activity under the rules in effect for WIN prior to 1981. Those rules permitted unpaid work assignments to be full-time, without regard to the amount of the monthly AFDC grant. Unpaid work assignments were formally titled "Work Experience," and the format stressed skill enhancement on the job as a benefit to participants rather than payback of the welfare grant.

[11] SWIM had a target of 75 percent participation among enrollees in each month. The actual rate was 52 percent, which included program-arranged participation, employment while on AFDC, and enrollee-arranged education and training. Although the observed rate fell short of the target rate, researchers found that 90 percent of those eligible for SWIM services in a month were either active or otherwise in compliance with program requirements during the month, even if they did not participate. Among those who were not participating but were in compliance with program rules, many were assigned to activities that had not yet begun; others were temporarily excused owing to illness or other situational factors; and still others were awaiting removal from the list of program enrollees (a process known as *deregistration*). Thus, the achieved rate was considered by researchers to be near the maximum possible under existing program rules and resources.

large agreed with the program's philosophy and goals. The San Diego environment was rich in education and training opportunities available through the city's community college system. The two areas of San Diego selected for the demonstration were inner-city areas, with heavy concentrations of low-income, relatively disadvantaged families. It is also important to note that California is a high-grant state, and many program enrollees were able to fulfill their participation requirement by working part-time while remaining on AFDC (i.e., without their part-time earnings reducing their grant amount to zero). This combination of part-time employment and continued welfare receipt is virtually impossible in a low-grant state like Arkansas, since even part-time employment can produce enough earnings to make a family ineligible to remain on AFDC.

As a test of the saturation approach, SWIM was implemented on a large scale. The large number of enrollees is a distinctive feature of San Diego SWIM. The demonstration was intended to work with all mandatory AFDC applicants and recipients in its inner-city target area, and it enrolled more than ten thousand individuals during its two years of intake. To boost participation, activities were assigned in a fixed sequence, with little scope for enrollee choice.[12] In line with the aim of rapid job entry, job search was first. This was followed by unpaid work assignments, then education and training, which was offered by referral to community providers rather than provided directly by program staff. Because participation was intended to last for as long as an enrollee remained on AFDC, activities could be assigned again after the sequence was completed.

As shown in Table 3-1, 64.4 percent of the experimental sample participated in some SWIM activity. Job search was the most common activity, with just over half of the experimental sample participating. Unpaid work assignments were also used extensively, as were education and training. Not surprisingly, financial penalties were applied at a rate that was among the highest for any experimentally evaluated welfare-to-work program, with more than 10 percent of all enrollees sanctioned. Program net costs were $920 per sample member, about the same as in Baltimore. Investigation of the records of community education and

---

[12] For some individuals this sequence could be delayed or modified. Enrollees who were employed fifteen hours or more per week while on AFDC could be excused from other participation. Also, enrollees who were already engaged in SWIM-approved community education and training programs at the time they entered SWIM could continue those activities in fulfillment of their SWIM obligation.

training agencies revealed that many people in the control group
sought out and participated in education and training activities
on their own, outside SWIM.

THE DURATION ISSUE

An important issue affecting the interpretation of the empirical results concerns the duration of each experiment. After randomization occurred, experimentals were assigned to program
services and became subject to program participation requirements. Members of the control group were neither assigned to
special services nor subject to sanctions for failure to comply
with program rules.[13] In Virginia, Arkansas, and Baltimore, the
program embargo against working with a control was planned
to last for two years from the date each individual was randomly
assigned. In San Diego SWIM, the embargo lasted for two years
after the last sample member was randomly assigned. It was
during this embargo period, which defines the evaluation proper,
that all data on program activity were collected and the initial
impacts of the program were estimated. The original evaluation
designs called for no further collection of activity data or outcome data on earnings or AFDC payments after the embargo
period. For the present study, outcome data were collected for
the period after the original evaluation ended. In all four of these
evaluation sites it is possible that some controls who remained
on AFDC after the embargo period may eventually have been
required to participate in program activities. This possibility has
important implications for our interpretation of the experimental estimates of program impact.

An ideal five-year experimental study of a permanent program
would maintain the treatment protocols for experimentals and
controls for five full years of data collection. Experimentals
would continue to be subject to the program mandate and to
receive program services, whether they remained on AFDC the
whole time or returned to AFDC after an exit from the rolls.
Thus, behavior in the treatment group would continue to be
influenced by the program over the full five years. With the ex-

---

[13] In the case of Baltimore, controls remained enrolled in the existing WIN program, where a small number participated in employment-directed activities. During
the first twelve months of follow-up, 2.0 percent of controls participated in job
search, 0.7 percent participated in work experience, and 1.0 percent participated in
education or training. See Friedlander, Hoerz, Long, and Quint (1985, Table 4.1).

ception of SWIM, discussed in detail below, the programs evaluated in the experiments continued to exist and may well have gone on working with experimentals after the end of the experiment period proper. However, in a five-year experiment, controls would have been prevented from receiving program services and would have been exempted from the participation mandate for the full five years. This was not the case in the experiments we are examining. After about two years, some controls who remained on AFDC or who returned to AFDC after having left may have received the program treatment.

Any experimental treatment received by controls after the end of the embargo period may have affected control-group earnings and AFDC payments. Such program effects on controls would presumably narrow the measured differences in earnings and AFDC payments between experimentals and controls near the end of the five-year follow-up. In the absence of participation data after the experiment period proper, it is not possible to state definitely whether controls actually participated in the experimental treatment in significant numbers. It is reasonable, however, to assume that the impact estimates presented in this study understate the impacts of permanent programs for the late part of the five-year follow-up. Had the control embargoes remained in effect the full five years, late-period estimates of impacts on earnings and AFDC may well have been larger and longer lasting.

The case of SWIM in San Diego differs in some respects from those of the other three programs. SWIM was a time-limited demonstration, not a permanent program. When the demonstration came to an end, SWIM was replaced by California's current JOBS program, the Greater Avenues for Independence (GAIN) Program. SWIM controls as well as experimentals were eligible for GAIN. A recently issued report on early GAIN impacts indicates that, in San Diego, GAIN increased earnings and decreased AFDC payments of enrollees over the first two years following their entry into the program.[14] These GAIN impact findings imply that any GAIN participation by SWIM controls would likely have affected their employment and AFDC behavior.

In order to examine the potential importance of post-SWIM

---

[14]Friedlander, Riccio, and Freedman (1993, Table 2.1) report two-year GAIN impacts for six California counties. In San Diego County, individuals randomly assigned to an experimental group required to enroll in GAIN experienced two-year earnings that were $1,058 greater than a randomly assigned control group not eligible for GAIN. Two-year AFDC payments were $783 less for experimentals than for controls. Both impact estimates were statistically significant.

GAIN activity, researchers recently returned to San Diego to search GAIN program files for any records of GAIN participation among a random sample of former SWIM experimentals and controls.[15] The data reveal that participation among many SWIM experimentals did extend into GAIN. The data also show that a significant percentage of controls came under the GAIN mandate and participated in GAIN during the latter part of the five-year follow-up period. In fact, the rate of GAIN participation was similar for SWIM experimentals and controls: just under one-fifth of each group (a much higher percentage of those still on AFDC) participated in a GAIN activity. This level of participation among controls, together with the early impacts reported for GAIN, imply that the apparent impacts of SWIM in the last years of the five-year follow-up are almost certainly less than those that would have occurred had the control group embargo been maintained for the full five years of follow-up.

Only in SWIM did researchers return to collect data on participation after the short-term follow-up period. The SWIM/GAIN participation experience of controls may not be typical of the experience of controls in the other three evaluations. GAIN was a new program making special outreach efforts. It is clear, however, that in this study estimates covering the end of the five-year follow-up probably represent lower-bound estimates of the long-term impacts of a permanent program. This limitation introduces a degree of uncertainty about some of the results we present in this study. But the interpretation of many results will be unaffected. Findings about the quality of initial employment, the importance of more rapid AFDC case closure, and other events occurring in the first two years of follow-up are unaffected. In addition, when we observe small impacts in the first few years of follow-up and small impacts at the end, we can be reasonably certain that extending the control embargo would still have yielded small impacts, too. When we observe large impacts at the end of the five-year follow-up, we can be fairly confident that extending the control embargo would have yielded still larger impacts. In those cases where impacts were large at the beginning and smaller at the end we have reason to speculate whether a five-year embargo would have increased

---

[15] Details of the records search may be found in Friedlander and Hamilton (1993). The findings we cite in the text pertain to the single-parent AFDC sample members. SWIM and GAIN also worked with two-parent AFDC-U enrollees, but impact and GAIN participation results for that assistance category are not discussed here.

observed treatment effect towards the end of the follow-up period.

DATA

The main data available from the experiments include background demographic characteristics of sample members plus records of earnings and AFDC payments for several years following random assignment. Background characteristics were obtained from a one-page questionnaire administered to sample members just before random assignment. The baseline questionnaire provided information about gender, age, education, welfare history, marital status, number and age of children, and ethnicity.

Quarterly earnings for the year before random assignment and for the follow-up period were obtained from the computerized tapes of state unemployment insurance (UI) systems, matched for the individuals in the samples using Social Security numbers. AFDC payments data for sample members were assembled in a similar fashion from automated payment ledgers maintained by the state or local welfare agencies. The use of administrative records data of this kind provides several advantages for the researcher. Administrative records are considerably less costly for large samples than survey data because sample members do not have to be contacted during the follow-up period. Once programs to access the records systems have been written and verified, large samples can be supported with virtually no cost per additional sample member. Adding more follow-up periods for each sample member is also relatively inexpensive, provided the source reporting systems have not changed. Records may, in some respects, be more accurate than individual reports of earnings or AFDC payments in surveys, since they do not depend on recall from memory of past dollar amounts and dates. Finally, the use of administrative records permits the analyst to avoid the problem of nonrandom attrition. Phone or in-person interviews are often afflicted by differential rates of responding to survey questions for experimental and control groups, which can severely bias impact estimates. This statistical problem is avoided with records data. Records data do have certain disadvantages, however, which are discussed later in this section.

Earnings were obtained for calendar (or "fiscal") quarters: January through March, April through June, and so on. These data were then organized for each individual sample member relative to the date of random assignment. Thus, "quarter one" earnings are those for the quarter in which a sample member was randomly assigned, quarter two earnings are for the quarter following random assignment, quarter three for the quarter after that, and so forth. The sum of earnings over quarters one through four is annual earnings for "year one," quarters five through eight for "year two," and so on. Sample members with earnings in a particular period were classed as "employed," and those without earnings were classed as "not employed."

Unemployment insurance earnings are subject to a peculiarity that affects our estimates of earnings impacts. For some sample members, quarter one may include as many as two months of wages earned before the month of random assignment. To prevent these pre-program earnings from contaminating some of the impact estimates, previous MDRC research reports have defined certain summary variables with quarter one omitted. For example, total earnings during the follow-up period may be given as "the sum of earnings from quarters two through twenty." The practice is followed where appropriate in this study.

Data on AFDC payments were available on a month-by-month basis, permitting a somewhat more detailed analysis of behavior patterns over time. The AFDC data were organized so that month one would be the month of random assignment for a sample member, month two the next month, and so forth. For some purposes, these months could be summed into quarterly or annual amounts. It should be noted, however, that a "quarter" for AFDC payments data does not usually overlap exactly the same "quarter" of earnings data. For example, an individual randomly assigned in March would have a first quarter of AFDC payments covering March, April, and May. The first quarter of earnings for this same individual would cover January, February, and March. This discrepancy between periods for earnings and AFDC payments is of no practical consequence for the analysis.

Administrative records data have some drawbacks. These data are limited in the kinds of information they can provide. For example, UI systems provide records of total earnings in a particular calendar quarter, but they do not give hourly rates of pay, weekly hours worked, number of weeks employed, fringe benefits, or other information about workers' terms of employment. In addition, the administrative records utilized in this study provide earnings information only for the sample member and not for other members of a family. Contributions to income from the earnings of these others can be critical determinants of family poverty status and well-being.

There will be cases in which received earnings or AFDC payments do not show up in the records systems. For example, UI records do not show earnings for sample members working off the books, which, in these samples, may be particularly common among domestic workers. Also, UI records do not include earnings for occupations not covered by UI, such as certain agricultural occupations. Nor will UI records show earnings for individuals who move to a different state. The UI system cannot distinguish persons who have zero actual earnings from those who have earnings which are not reported: both kinds of people will be described in the research data sets as non-earners. Similarly, AFDC ledgers do not show AFDC payments to individuals who move outside the state or local AFDC jurisdiction. Consequently, sample members who actually received no AFDC and those who collect AFDC in a different jurisdiction after moving will both be counted in the research data sets as having zero AFDC payments.

Nonreporting and misreporting will tend to reduce the averages of both earnings and AFDC payments in the research samples. Reductions in averages should occur to a similar degree for both experimental and control groups, however, implying only minor biases in estimates of experimental-control *differences*. It is these differences that are the estimates of program impact. To see why the effects of mobility on impacts should be minor, it is worth considering an extended illustration. Suppose the *true* employment rate for an experimental group in quarter twelve is 39.0 percent and for controls is 30.0 percent. The difference of 9.0 percentage points is the true impact of the program in the quarter. Further, suppose that employed sample members in both research groups actually earn, on average, $2,200 for the quarter. Then average earnings would be $858 for experimentals ($2,200 × .390) and $660 for controls ($2,200 × .300), for a true difference or impact of $198 for the quarter. This dollar impact can also be stated as a 30.0 percent impact relative to the control mean (100 × $198/$660).

Suppose that a large number of sample members—20 percent—move to a different state. We would expect that measured employment rates would be reduced by 20.0 percent. Thus, experimental and control measured employment rates would be 31.2 percent and 24.0 percent, respectively, for a measured employment impact of 7.2 percentage points. At the same time, we would expect that the earnings reported for individuals employed within the state would be unaffected. Average earnings would therefore be measured as $686.40 and $528.00, with a difference or impact of $158.40, still 30.0 percent of the new control mean.

The effect of cross-state mobility, shown by this example, is to reduce somewhat the measured impacts on the employment rate and on dollar earnings but to leave unaffected the impact as stated in percentage terms relative to the control level. The number of movers will naturally increase over time, so any effects of mobility would tend to grow larger near the end of follow-up. In preparing the basic five-year impact estimates for the next chapter, we examined both dollar and percentage point impact estimates to see whether mobility might be a significant factor in determining the time patterns of earnings gains and AFDC reductions. In general, dollar impacts and percentage point impacts tend to increase or decrease over time in the same direction as impacts stated as a percent of the control mean. Although not conclusive, this implies that mobility does not seriously bias our conclusions about the changes in impacts from early to late during the follow-up period.

One peculiarity of the outcome data affects estimates from the Baltimore experiment. The UI earnings for Baltimore are available up through quarter twelve and then again from quarter nineteen through quarter twenty-one: Quarters thirteen through eighteen are missing.[16] This gap in the data reduces our certainty about the shape of earnings impacts in that site. In addition, AFDC data could not be obtained for Baltimore after month thirty-six (quarter twelve), the end of follow-up year three. As we will see, however, the truncated AFDC follow-up does not represent a significant analysis problem, since the impact of the Baltimore program on AFDC benefits appears quite small even before the thirty-sixth month.

A final data issue concerns the comparability of estimates presented in this study and in prior studies using earlier versions of the same data bases. Our current estimates for the early

---

[16] The additional data collection in Baltimore was undertaken after a hiatus, during which time some earnings records were purged by UI bookkeeping routines in the normal process of updating old information as claims for UI benefits are made. This process affected follow-up quarters thirteen through eighteen. These contained only partial data, which could not be used for impact analysis. Quarters nineteen through twenty-one are complete, however, and provide important new data on the longer-term impacts of the Baltimore program.

follow-up years may differ slightly from estimates for the same periods published previously, owing to updating or correction of historical records by local UI and AFDC systems.[17] In addition, small discrepancies may be noted specifically between SWIM AFDC impacts given here and those reported elsewhere. In order to match the format used in the other three evaluation samples, we organized monthly SWIM AFDC data with month one as the month of random assignment. In other SWIM reports, however, AFDC months have been organized so that quarters exactly coincide with UI earnings quarters. Thus, "quarters," "years," and summary measures covering the full follow-up for SWIM AFDC data do not have precisely the same definitions in this study as in others.

THE RESEARCH SAMPLES

The demographic characteristics of the research samples for the four programs are shown in Table 3-2.[18] The composition of these samples is, in several respects, similar across programs. As groups of individuals, however, the samples for each program are heterogeneous with respect to prior work and AFDC history, education level, numbers of children, and other characteristics. For example, about 10 to 35 percent had never received AFDC on their own case before, whereas another 30 to 70 percent had had their own case for two years or more. Half to three-quarters of the sample members had not worked at all in the year prior to random assignment. About half had no high school diploma. Child care needs differed as well, with 40 to 50 percent having only one child and the rest more than one.

Some cross-site differences are worth noting. Arkansas, in particular, is unique in several ways. The Arkansas program differed from those in the other sites by including as mandatory those single parents who had a youngest child three to five years old, a group which made up about half the research sample there.

---

[17] Additions or deletions of small numbers of cases to the samples, noted in the next section, may also contribute to small discrepancies in impact estimates.

[18] Sample sizes in this study may differ slightly from those in the original studies. An attempt was made here to assign values to demographic data where these were missing. If missing data could not be inferred with reasonable certainty, the cases were dropped from the analysis. The effect of this strategy on sample size was the gain of fifty-four cases in Baltimore and eight in Arkansas but a loss of thirty-two cases in Virginia.

TABLE 3-2

Characteristics of Enrollees

Characteristic	Virginia ESP	Arkansas WORK Program	Baltimore Options Program	San Diego SWIM
Research Group (%)				
Experimental	67.3	49.7	49.4	50.0
Control	32.7	50.3	50.6	50.0
AFDC Status (%)				
Applicant	40.3	59.4	50.1	39.2
Recipient	59.7	40.6	49.9	60.8
Prior Earnings (%)				
$3,000 or more	13.7	8.0	19.3	17.7
$1–2,999	23.2	16.3	24.9	21.6
None	63.0	75.7	55.8	60.7
Had Own AFDC Case (%)				
Never	12.0	36.7	14.0	11.2
Two years or less	28.1	32.7	31.4	20.2
More than two years	59.8	30.5	54.6	68.6
High School Diploma or GED (%)	43.6	49.8	43.5	56.1
More Than One Child (%)	55.0	60.6	53.2	54.3
Never Married (%)	31.1	49.2	40.5	30.1
Age 30 or Over (%)	65.1	38.3	54.0	68.3
Ethnicity (%)[a]				
White	32.8	13.4	29.5	27.3
Black	67.2	86.6	70.5	42.4
Hispanic	—	—	—	25.4
Asian	—	—	—	4.9

SOURCES: Demographic information is from MDRC Client Information Sheets. Prior earnings were calculated from the UI records of the Commonwealth of Virginia, the State of Arkansas, the State of Maryland, and the State of California.

NOTES: Distributions may not sum exactly to 100 percent owing to rounding. Categories not applicable for particular program samples are indicated with a dash.

[a] For Virginia, Arkansas, and Baltimore, the category "black" includes a small number of individuals in other nonwhite groups. In San Diego, the category "Asian" includes a small number of individuals in other nonwhite, nonblack, non-Hispanic groups.

Arkansas also had AFDC grant levels substantially below those of the other states, with AFDC payments for a family of three at $140 per month during the research period. Given these grant levels, it is likely that individuals applying for or receiving AFDC in Arkansas would usually be individuals with few opportunities for earnings. As a consequence, rates of employment, both before and after random assignment, tended to be lower for the Arkansas sample than for the others. Finally, the rate of approval for AFDC among applicants in Arkansas was lower than elsewhere. The urban/rural composition of the samples differed. The Baltimore and San Diego samples were entirely urban, whereas the Arkansas and Virginia samples contained less urbanized and rural areas. Ethnic makeup differed as well. The samples in three sites were predominantly black, but San Diego had a significant Hispanic minority of 25 percent with only 42 percent black.[19]

[19] Differences in demographic characteristics between experimental and control groups within each study are minor. In Baltimore and Virginia, small differences are apparent in measures of education and prior employment and earnings.

4

Program Impacts on Earnings and AFDC

This chapter presents estimates of impacts on employment, earnings, AFDC receipt, and AFDC payments for the four programs. These estimates of "average impact per experimental sample member" constitute the basic findings for these programs. The first section contains a discussion of the program goals against which the program effects must be assessed. After that, we describe the typical patterns of employment and AFDC receipt in the absence of the programs. This preliminary analysis suggests what kinds of changes in behavior might be possible or important. We then look at a set of impact estimates covering the full follow-up period available for each program. These estimates show the overall magnitude of observed program impacts, on average, for a representative group of sample members in each program. They allow us to make some comparisons of impacts with costs and of earnings impacts with AFDC impacts. They also permit some preliminary comparisons across programs.

We next examine the detailed five-year time pattern of treatment effects. We look for several distinct phases in the development of differences between experimentals and controls over time. We expect, first of all, that there will be very little difference between experimentals and controls around the date of random assignment, before the program begins to work with experimentals. During the initial part of follow-up, when experimentals are in the program, differences between the research groups may continue to be small. Then, as program experiences start to affect enrollees, we expect to see employment and earnings for experimentals begin to climb above those for controls. At the same time, AFDC receipt for experimentals should begin to fall faster. The difference between experimentals and controls provides the estimate of program impact. This gap may last for several years; for employment and earnings, it may persist indefinitely. In each new year in which the gap is observed, the experimental-control difference is added to the total or *cumulative* impact of the program.

The impact of the treatment towards the end of the follow-up period is suggestive of the program's long-term effect. During this phase, we may see the experimental-control gap remain constant from one year to the next for as long as data are available. Or we may see a narrowing of the gap over time. Many controls sooner or later find jobs on their own, and all eventually leave AFDC. Thus, a number of quarters or years into the follow-up period we may see control employment and AFDC receipt rates begin to overtake those of experimentals as controls start to catch up. Controls may also begin to overtake experimentals if the treatment effect starts to wear off, which may occur, for example, if the jobs experimentals initially obtain with program help do not last very long. Impacts that have accumulated before the onset of the narrowing remain real and "bankable," but *additions* to the cumulative impact of the program will continue at a slower rate or will stop altogether if the gap goes to zero. Narrowing of the experimental-control differential is typically referred to as impact *decay*. For some, this term will connote a wearing-off of treatment effect, but it should be understood that wearing-off is only one possible cause of the narrowing, with control-group catch-up as the other possibility. A more neutral term than "decay" would be *convergence* of experimental and control outcomes.

HOW SHOULD WE ASSESS PROGRAM IMPACTS?

Estimates of program impacts should be assessed with reference to the goals the program is intended to achieve. A variety of goals have been put forward for welfare-to-work programs, and different policymakers assign different emphasis to each. In the main, welfare-to-work programs are intended to

Increase employment among AFDC recipients.[1]

Reduce AFDC receipt.

---

[1] Some policymakers set a high priority on increasing general productive activity among AFDC recipients, and they include unpaid work assignments along with regular unsubsidized employment in defining the program employment goal.

Increase self-reliance and self-sufficiency (e.g., increase the share of income that comes from earnings and decrease the share that comes from welfare).

Save money for government budgets by reducing AFDC and other transfer expenditures more than the program costs.

Reduce poverty.

Increase employment of AFDC recipients in "good" jobs (i.e., high-wage, full-time, stable jobs).

Make families substantially better off financially.

Despite apparent similarities, these goals are not the same, and some of them may be in conflict. For example, a reduction in poverty may be inconsistent with a reduction in AFDC expenditures. Increased employment may be achieved without reducing poverty, if the employment is low-wage or intermittent. An increase in "self-sufficiency" may imply replacement of the AFDC grant with a similar amount of earnings, which may not lead to an improvement in family well-being or a reduction in poverty. Employment in high-wage jobs may be consistent with making a family better off financially, but it may be at odds with reducing AFDC expenditures if it means focusing resources narrowly and providing intensive (and expensive) training for a small number of program enrollees.

Along with these specific goals, programs have two cross-cutting goals. The first is cost-effectiveness, which means achieving the specific goals with the least expenditure of program resources. Cost-effectiveness is impact per dollar spent, or "bang for the buck." The more cost-effective a program is, the more it can achieve under a given budget and, hence, the larger the aggregate or total impact. Thus, in comparing two programs with the same average impact per enrollee, the one with the lower cost per enrollee will usually be judged superior.

The second cross-cutting goal concerns program target groups. For each specific goal listed above, it may be deemed important to achieve results for the more disadvantaged in the program-eligible population. For example, in reducing AFDC receipt, the JOBS legislation has assigned an explicit priority to reducing *long-term* AFDC receipt. Producing results for long-term or potential long-term AFDC recipients may also be crucial in achieving other goals, such as reduced AFDC expenditures. A program achieving large effects for long-term AFDC recipients or other disadvantaged groups may be assessed favorably even though it performs less well on other criteria.

WHAT CHANGES IN EMPLOYMENT
AND AFDC RECEIPT SHOULD WE LOOK FOR?

In this chapter, we examine the overall or "average" impacts of the four programs. We should be mindful, however, that the averages can obscure details that are crucial for understanding what the programs actually accomplished. These details are examined in succeeding chapters. As preparation for the overall results and as a foundation for the deeper analysis to follow, we begin by describing the employment and AFDC behavior occurring in the absence of program intervention. This behavior is reflected by the actual behavior of controls, who were not given the special program treatment.

Employment and Earnings

We examine the control group in Virginia. The Virginia sample is emphasized here because it has a full five years of follow-up data on both earnings and AFDC payments and because its wage and AFDC grant levels were close to national medians. Figure 4-1(a) shows the quarter-by-quarter rates of employment and average quarterly earnings per control sample member in Virginia. Figure 4-1(b) shows the corresponding rates of AFDC receipt and average quarterly AFDC payments. The quarter of random assignment is the quarter in which sample members joined the sample and were referred to the Virginia Employment Services Program. Percent and dollar amounts for the quarter of random assignment and the final quarter of follow-up are written into the figures near the appropriate points on the curves.

Average earnings in each quarter are calculated by including estimates of the earnings of *each* member of the control sample, counting zeroes for those with no earnings. Thus, in quarter twenty, controls who were employed earned an average of $2,170; but only 43 percent of controls were employed. The average earnings among all controls was equal to $2,170 × .43 or $933, as shown in the figure. Likewise, the averages for AFDC payments count zeroes for sample members not receiving AFDC in a quarter. This convention of including zeroes in averages for dollar-denominated variables is observed throughout this study, except where noted.

The patterns displayed in the figure for Virginia controls are typical for groups of individuals eligible to enroll in a welfare-to-

FIGURE 4-1

Virginia: Control-Group Employment, Earnings, AFDC Receipt,
and AFDC Payments

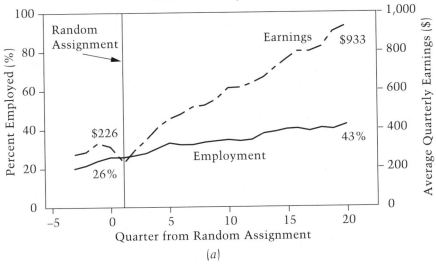

(a)

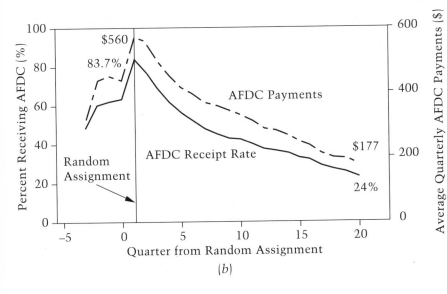

(b)

work program. There is a pronounced decrease in earnings beginning just before program enrollment. This "pre-program dip" occurs because application for AFDC (and entry into the employment and training program) follows loss of a job for some individuals.[2] Immediately after random assignment, however, earnings and employment begin to increase. Some individuals find jobs to replace the jobs they have recently lost. Others, whose constraints on jobholding have eased as their youngest child enters school for the first time or who experience other changes in home circumstances, start to work as time goes on. In Virginia, the control group employment rate climbs steadily throughout the follow-up period. Earnings grow faster than employment because earnings on the job increase with promotions and pay raises, with mobility to higher-paying or more stable jobs, and with increases in weekly hours of work.

It is immediately clear that simple outcomes such as "rate of job entry" or "post-program earnings" will not serve as valid measures of program impact, since a substantial amount of employment would have occurred even without the special program. In order to achieve an impact, the program must raise outcomes for enrollees above the levels shown in the figure for controls. The employment and earnings figure points up the heterogeneity of the program population, which contains some people who will find jobs quickly on their own, some who will take longer but will still become employed in the short run, and some who will not find jobs at all during the five years we can observe them. In order to achieve its goals, a program will have to work towards different objectives with the different kinds of enrollees. For the short-term jobless, the program can try to increase the speed at which individuals find jobs through job search assistance. It might also attempt to increase the earnings they receive once they find work. Helping them locate higher-paying, full-time, stable jobs, given their existing work skills, might accomplish this for some enrollees. Upgrading skills through training might be an effective supplemental approach for others. But problems of illiteracy, lack of work experience, and poor motivation are probably less severe with the short-term jobless than with other parts of the program population.

---

[2]Employment often shows a pre-program dip, too. This is not seen in Virginia possibly because employment is reported quarterly: individuals losing jobs in the middle of a quarter still show employment in the quarter, even though earnings for the quarter show the characteristic drop.

Among enrollees who would never have worked in the absence of intervention, program options are somewhat different. For many, their ability to earn—their so-called "earnings potential"—will be quite low. Efforts at job search assistance and occupational training may be ineffective for individuals with severe basic skill deficits; extensive remediation may be needed before specific job skills can be learned. Many may have barriers to employment, such as child care problems, which they cannot remove without assistance. Anxiety about working, low self-esteem and self-confidence, and lack of work ethic are additional psychological and motivational barriers that might not yield readily to program services. However, the potential for employment and earnings effects in this group is large relative to enrollees who would eventually find jobs on their own. The change from no employment to a regular job is a bigger change (i.e., impact) than speeding up job finding. The move from no earnings to entry-level employment is usually a bigger change than the move from one earnings level to another. In view of the large number of enrollees who would not work even after five years, the *potential* increase in employment and earnings from working with this severely disadvantaged group could be substantial. It is an empirical question whether available services and program participation requirements can achieve much *actual* improvement in employment at a feasible cost.

When we examine program impacts later in this chapter, we begin with rather simple measures: employment rates and average earnings per sample member. We compare experimental and control groups on these measures, and the differences between the two groups are our estimates of program impact. But the heterogeneity in the control group just mentioned implies that the mechanisms of program impact are complex and diverse rather than simple. The ideal program should produce not just one effect, but should produce different kinds of effects for different kinds of enrollees. As a consequence, in analyzing the details of employment and earnings in the next chapter, we look for a variety of employment and earnings effects: (*a*) speedier job finding, (*b*) higher earnings on the job, (*c*) greater employment stability, and (*d*) new employment among those who would not have worked. Patterns of effects may show improvements for some measures and not for others.

It may be noted that it is the first of these effects, speedier job finding among program enrollees who would have worked eventually anyway, that is the one most likely to be associated with convergence over time in experimental and control employment and earnings levels. Faster job finding by some experimentals, by definition, implies that about the same number of controls will sooner or later find jobs without program assistance and that those jobs will be of similar pay and duration. The employment and earnings of controls must therefore eventually catch up to those of experimentals if the program produces no other labor market effects than more rapid job finding. If, on the other hand, faster job finding is not the only program effect but is combined, for example, with employment in *better* jobs (i.e., more stable and higher-paying jobs), then experimental-control differences in earnings need not converge.

AFDC Receipt and AFDC Payments

AFDC receipt among Virginia controls declines over time at a faster rate than employment increases (see Figure 4-1(b)). Entering employment is, in fact, only one of the reasons people exit from AFDC. Changes in family circumstances—marriage or reconciliation, and children aging out of AFDC eligibility—are the main routes off the rolls. For the great majority of control sample members in Virginia, AFDC receipt was not a permanent or even a long-term condition.

For a welfare-to-work program, the normal processes of AFDC turnover imply that counting numbers of "case closures" or adding up the value of grants for closed cases as "AFDC savings" will not paint a true picture of program impact on AFDC. To claim a real impact on AFDC receipt, a program cannot just close cases; it must close them faster than they would have been closed without the program. And speeding up case closures may still not produce AFDC impacts if people return to welfare after only a few months off. A high normal rate of return to AFDC—that is, a high rate of *AFDC recidivism*—will tend to offset the effects of faster case closure, and any increase from the normal rate will create an even larger offset. On the other hand, if AFDC recidivism decreases, if more of those who leave the rolls do not return, then impacts on AFDC receipt will be larger.[3] Impacts on AFDC receipt will, in turn, result in impacts on AFDC payments. Additional impacts on payments may come

---

[3] Ongoing programs may also have an impact on AFDC receipt by discouraging the filing of initial AFDC applications. Effects of this sort cannot be captured by the research designs for the four programs in this study because the samples do not track people before their initial AFDC application.

about through reductions in the monthly amounts paid to families remaining on AFDC, whether from sanctions or from grant adjustments for earnings from part-time employment. It seems likely, however, that any impacts on AFDC payments resulting from partial changes in monthly grant amounts would be small compared with impacts from complete case closures.[4]

The rapid decline in AFDC receipt over time in Virginia does not mean that everyone in the control group left AFDC within a few years. Just as there are short-term and long-term jobless, so there are short-term and long-term AFDC "stayers." About 24 percent of Virginia controls were still receiving AFDC at the end of five years. This is not a large proportion of the program population, but these long-term AFDC recipients account for a disproportionately large share of total time on AFDC and total AFDC expenditures. It follows, then, that impacts on long-term AFDC recipients would have a disproportionate impact on the aggregate AFDC receipt and expenditures for the program population.[5] As an illustration, we can compare the impact of closing a short-term case and a long-term case in Virginia. Suppose the short-term case would have left AFDC within two years, but the program reduces that spell to one year. Assuming an average monthly grant amount of $270, the AFDC saving would be $3,240 (12 × 270). Let us now say that the long-term case would have remained on AFDC six years but, as with the short-term case, leaves after one year following enrollment in the program. The total AFDC saving would now be $16,200 (5 × 12 × 270), enough to pay the net cost of program services for nearly thirty-eight enrollees. Thus, the percentage of successes achieved in working with potential long-term AFDC recipients need not be large for a program costing as much as Virginia's to produce government budget savings. Conversely, the relatively large payoff for each success may justify use of more costly services with long-term groups, including intensive, possibly lengthy, basic education and job-specific skills development.

---

[4] At the time of the four evaluations, sanctions reduced the AFDC grant only temporarily. With regard to part-time earnings, only a small proportion of AFDC recipients report earnings while they are on the rolls.

[5] Although the majority of families that ever use AFDC do not stay a long time, the majority of families on the rolls at any given time are in the midst of long spells. Reductions in long-term AFDC receipt would therefore have more impact on caseloads and expenditures than reductions in short-term receipt. Documentation of the distribution of AFDC spell lengths and a discussion of the implications for employment program targeting may be found in the seminal work of Bane and Ellwood (1983) and Ellwood (1986).

Our first look at welfare impacts, later in this chapter, consists of a comparison of AFDC receipt rates and average AFDC payments for experimentals and controls. But, as the discussion in this section indicates, when we analyze the details of the AFDC impacts in later chapters, we are looking for (a) faster case closure, (b) reduced recidivism, and (c) impacts on potential long-term AFDC recipients. As with employment and earnings, programs may achieve success on one measure but not on another.

It is important to note, too, that AFDC receipt for any group of individuals—long-term stayers included—must eventually fall all the way to zero, even without intervention. When all the children on a case become too old to qualify for AFDC, the AFDC grant ends. This ultimately occurs for everyone if nothing else happens to close a case first. In the Virginia figure, this means that the AFDC receipt curve for a group of program enrollees might initially fall faster than the control group curve, perhaps for several years, but would eventually have to flatten out towards the right, letting the control group catch up. This inevitable catch-up for AFDC impacts will not imply a program failure. It is a natural result of the time limit placed on all AFDC eligibility, which ensures that AFDC levels for experimentals and controls must converge eventually. Moreover, any savings or reductions in receipt achieved within the time limit will be real and may well be substantial. As the time limit approaches, the *additions* to AFDC impacts in each period will become smaller, but the impacts on months of receipt or on dollars that have accumulated to that point will not be lost.[6]

The Relationship Between Impacts on Earnings and AFDC Payments

The relationship between impacts on earnings and AFDC is complex. This complexity makes it difficult to form prior expectations about the relative magnitude of earnings impact and AFDC impact for any given program or about differences in the ratio of AFDC impact to earnings impact across programs. On one hand, several factors tend to make the potential for long-

[6]If we consider the unit of treatment as an "AFDC family" rather than a single person on a case, the potential for "permanent" AFDC impacts arises through the possibility of intergenerational effects on AFDC receipt. For example, if a parent leaves the AFDC system, the children on the AFDC case may have lower propensity to become AFDC recipients themselves when they grow up. Such effects cannot be captured with the data at hand.

term impacts greater for earnings than for AFDC. There is no strict upper bound to the dollar amount of earnings impact for an enrollee in a particular follow-up year, whereas the AFDC impact can be no larger than the AFDC grant amount. Earnings on a new job, found with the help of the program, can be larger than the amount needed to close the AFDC case—larger, in fact, than the amount of the grant that is terminated. In addition, earnings effects may endure for an individual's entire working life. In contrast, AFDC payments go to zero for all recipients, even without the program, as the children on a case "age out," thereby placing a shorter time limit on the duration of an AFDC impact. Thus, earnings impacts may not only exceed AFDC impacts at any point in time, but they may last longer as well. Added to this, the share of program enrollees that could potentially obtain large earnings gains is larger than the share that could obtain large AFDC reductions. In particular, substantial increases in earnings might be achieved either by potential long-term recipients or by short-termers or by both. The magnitude of AFDC impacts is, however, limited for short-termers, a group which, as shown in the Virginia figures, makes up the bulk of all people eligible for services under the program. Thus, relatively large earnings gains may be found for some groups for whom there are only small AFDC reductions or none at all. For these several reasons, it would not be surprising to see earnings gains larger than AFDC reductions.

At the same time, however, certain program features, such as sanctioning, can magnify the relative size of AFDC impacts in comparison with earnings impacts. Sanctioning an AFDC recipient reduces the AFDC grant without directly affecting earnings. More generally, some enrollees will find enforced participation requirements to be inconvenient or onerous, and they may move off the rolls without obtaining any improvement in their earning power. Shifts in enrollee preferences favoring work over welfare, which might result from program experiences or from the experience of working, may produce similar behavioral effects. These hypothetical effects are associated with the "mandatory" aspect of welfare-to-work programs, not with the services aspect. Their potential existence raises the possibility that some programs or groups may obtain sizable AFDC reductions with small or zero earnings gains. Whether or not program mandatoriness actually does increase the ratio of AFDC impact to earnings impact is an empirical question, however. In actuality, it may turn out that enrollees who are induced to leave AFDC by the mandatory aspects of a program go to work afterwards and obtain earnings exceeding their lost AFDC grants.

These considerations suggest that there may be conflict between the program goals of reducing poverty and decreasing welfare receipt. For example, it is possible that one program approach may increase earnings enough among short-term AFDC recipients to reduce their poverty rate after they leave AFDC. The same approach may leave longer-term recipients, with their greater potential AFDC impacts, largely unaffected. A different approach might be more successful in reducing long-term welfare receipt, but might perhaps do so with earnings gains only just large enough for case closure, not large enough to affect the prevalence of poverty (in the absence of other changes). We examine the relative magnitudes of earnings gains and AFDC reductions later in this chapter.

PROGRAM IMPACTS ON EMPLOYMENT, EARNINGS, AFDC RECEIPT, AND AFDC PAYMENTS

In this section, we examine program impacts twice. We begin by looking at the total impact of each program, summing effects for as much of the follow-up period as we have data for in each evaluation. These "observed total" estimates constitute the raw data on impacts, the natural starting point for more detailed analyses. They do, however, fall short of providing us with a complete perspective on program accomplishments during the five-year follow-up period and afterwards. To obtain a more complete picture, our second look at impacts focuses on the year-by-year estimates of experimental-control differences.

Observed Total Impact on Earnings and AFDC Payments

Table 4-1 shows the sum of observed quarterly earnings and monthly AFDC payments for experimentals and controls in the four evaluation samples. For both earnings and AFDC payments, the sums run through the last period observed for all members of a particular evaluation sample. For earnings, these sums begin with the quarter immediately after the quarter of random assignment. The quarter of random assignment, which we designate "quarter one," has not been included in the sums for earnings because this quarter may contain some earnings prior to the actual date of random assignment. "Month one" of the first quar-

TABLE 4-1
Total Observed Impacts on Earnings and AFDC Payments

Program and Outcome	Experimentals	Controls	Difference	100 × Diff/Ctls
Virginia				
Sample size: 3,150				
Net program cost: $430				
Average total earnings, quarters 2–20 ($)	13,098	11,919	1,179*	9.9%
Average total AFDC payments, months 1–60 ($)	6,318	6,641	−323	−4.9%
Arkansas				
Sample size: 1,127				
Net program cost: $118				
Average total earnings, quarters 2–22 ($)	7,823	6,744	1,079	16.0%
Average total AFDC payments, months 1–66 ($)	4,390	5,125	−735***	−14.3%
Baltimore				
Sample size: 2,757				
Net program cost: $953				
Average total earnings, quarters 2–12, 19–21 ($)	11,609	10,229	1,380***	13.5%
Average total AFDC payments, months 1–36 ($)	6,361	6,424	−62	−1.0%
San Diego SWIM				
Sample size: 3,210				
Net program cost: $920				
Average total earnings, quarters 2–21 ($)	16,109	14,033	2,076**	14.8%
Average total AFDC payments, months 1–63 ($)	16,758	18,688	−1,930***	−10.3%

NOTES: Net costs are taken from Gueron and Pauly (1991), pp. 85–92. Net cost estimates are reported per experimental and are given in nominal dollars. Net cost estimates include all expenditures by the operating agency specifically for the program under study, plus expenditures by other organizations for services that were considered an essential part of the program treatment. Costs to operating agencies and to other organizations for serving control sample members have been subtracted in order to arrive at the net cost estimates.

Details may not sum to totals owing to rounding.

A two-tailed t-test was applied to experimental differences. Statistical significance levels are indicated as: * = 10 percent; ** = 5 percent; *** = 1 percent.

ter of AFDC payments is the month of random assignment, and the AFDC sums may therefore include quarter one without including any pre-random assignment AFDC payment months.

These summary estimates cover somewhat different time periods for different evaluation samples. Virginia follow-up runs through quarter twenty (month sixty); Arkansas follow-up ends in quarter twenty-two (month sixty-six); and San Diego SWIM follow-up lasts through quarter twenty-one (month sixty-three). Baltimore has a gap in earnings from quarter thirteen through quarter eighteen (as explained earlier), but earnings for quarters nineteen through twenty-one are available. In addition, Baltimore AFDC data end in month thirty-six. San Diego SWIM has three additional months of AFDC data (months sixty-four through sixty-six) which are not used in this table to allow earnings and AFDC follow-up to end at the same quarter. Because of the cross-site differences in follow-up periods, assessment of these raw results, particularly comparisons across sites, should be made with caution. The gaps in Baltimore, for example, imply that impacts shown in the table do not represent total program impact during the first five years of follow-up.

The table presents the fundamental comparison between experimentals and controls that is the basis for estimates of program impact. All estimates in this table and those that follow are regression-adjusted. The first column of the table shows the average dollar amount of earnings or AFDC payments for experimental sample members. The second column shows the same dollar average for control sample members. The third column shows the difference between the two, which is the estimate of program impact per sample member. Next to this estimate is the statistical significance level of the impact estimate. Finally, the table shows the "percentage impact" or "relative gain," which is simply the dollar impact estimate divided by the control average and multiplied by 100.

Table 4-1 also shows sample size and the net cost estimate for each program evaluation. Sample size is important in interpreting the impact estimates, since larger samples produce more accurate estimates. Among these four programs, the Arkansas sample is the smallest, and the estimates for that sample are the least precise. This means that impact estimates of any given magnitude in Arkansas are less likely to be statistically significant than estimates of the same magnitude for another sample.

Net cost is calculated in a fashion analogous to impact estimates. Costs paid by the program agency and costs to other institutions for services deemed to be an integral part of the program are summed and averaged over the experimental group. Any costs for the same activities—for example, for participation in education or training in a community college—for controls are averaged over the control sample. The difference between average cost per experimental and average cost per control is the net cost.

All programs produced impacts on earnings. We begin with the results for Virginia, which we will consider to be the representative program, characterized by a middle level of cost, intensity of effort, and mandatoriness. Virginia has a full five years' data, without gaps, an addition of about two years to previously reported information. As shown in the table, over the five years, experimentals produced, on average, $13,098 in earnings, according to the UI records (including zeroes for nonearners). Controls produced an average of $11,919 in earnings. The difference of $1,179 is the impact of the Virginia program. The estimate is statistically significant and represents a 9.9 percent gain over the control mean earnings level.

Is this impact large or small? The absolute dollar amount of the earnings impact appears modest. The dollar impact is nevertheless large relative to net costs. The observed dollar impact is, in fact, nearly triple the net cost of the program. Moreover, we have not taken into account possible additional earnings impacts for years after year five, which could increase the total earnings impact. Viewed in this light, the cost-effectiveness of the Virginia program is quite high. It is a relevant question whether an increase in program resources would increase impacts in the same proportion to effort.

Arkansas also has new data without gaps, extending the previously available follow-up period from the end of year three to the middle of year six. At less than half the cost of the Virginia program, Arkansas was the least costly and least intensive effort. Despite its low net cost per experimental, the Arkansas program produced earnings impacts amounting to 16.0 percent of the control mean, although the total amount was not statistically significant, possibly owing to the small sample size. The ratio of earnings impact to net cost was even larger than in Virginia, indicating that the program was highly cost-effective in raising earnings. It is worth noting that the earnings levels for both controls and experimentals were much lower in Arkansas than in Virginia, despite the similarity in the number of quarters observed. Earnings prospects for members of the Arkansas sample may have been lower because the AFDC grant levels were relatively low: individuals with almost any employment opportunity would be unlikely to enter the AFDC system in that state.

Baltimore and San Diego SWIM represent moderate-cost efforts, somewhat more than twice the cost of Virginia. Both produced statistically significant total earnings impacts, 13.5 percent of the control mean for Baltimore and 14.8 percent of the control mean for San Diego SWIM. At $2,076, the observed earnings impact for SWIM is more than twice program net costs. For Baltimore, the impact estimate of $1,380 is missing a full six quarters of earnings; with those added, and given the pattern of impacts over time, the total earnings gain would be $2,119 for the five years plus one quarter.[7] This is an amount more than twice net costs and quite similar to the earnings impact for San Diego SWIM over the same period.

Precise comparisons of impact results across programs are problematic. Indeed, cursory comparisons can be quite misleading. One example will illustrate this point. The observed total earnings impact from our representative program, Virginia, is considerably less than that for San Diego SWIM. We might therefore be tempted to conclude that the Virginia program was substantially less effective. But our assessment would change if we factor in the net costs of the two programs. Net costs in Virginia were less than half those for San Diego SWIM. Cost-effectiveness—the dollar amount of earnings impact per dollar of net cost—was greater in Virginia than in San Diego SWIM.[8] For a given amount of total resources, Virginia could enroll more than twice as many AFDC recipients as SWIM. The *aggregate* earnings impact, which is the impact per enrollee times the number of enrollees, might therefore actually be just as large in Virginia, and possibly even larger. The average impact per enrollee would be smaller, but the total number of enrollees would be much greater.[9] With this in mind, our judgment about which program was more effective could change. The same point can be made for Arkansas. As with Virginia, the lower dollar magnitude of impacts in a particular year or overall does not necessarily mean that the Arkansas program was less effective than Baltimore's or San Diego SWIM. In fact, the extremely modest average net cost in Arkansas made that program very cost-effective.

[7] To obtain a five-year estimate for Baltimore, we imputed the earnings impact for each of the missing six quarters as the average quarterly earnings impact for the year preceding the gap and the year (three quarters) following the gap.

[8] One use of the cost-effectiveness concept is to address the question, How much total impact on earnings can be obtained from a given expenditure? This version of cost-effectiveness does not take into account recovery of costs through AFDC savings. Moreover, it ignores the effects of increasing the budget allocation to the point where resources are still available even after low-cost services have been provided for all enrollees. Finally, it assumes that earnings impacts do not extend beyond the observed follow-up period.

[9] Naturally, if a program were richly enough endowed to enroll everyone in an area in a lower-cost program like Virginia's, the only way to further increase aggregate impacts would be to spend more per enrollee. For a fuller discussion of several measures of comparative effectiveness for low- and higher-cost programs, see Friedlander and Gueron (1992).

In turning to AFDC payments, we first examine the payments made to the control samples. We begin by noting the differences across programs. Virginia and Arkansas controls received the least in dollar payments. Baltimore, if allowance is made for the missing years four and five, came in next highest. San Diego SWIM controls received by far the largest total payments, in part because of the relatively high monthly grant levels in California and in part because members of the SWIM control sample were more likely to remain on AFDC in the absence of special program services.

Average AFDC payments to controls may also be used as a benchmark to judge the size of the program investments. In Virginia, net costs were 6.5 percent of observed control-group AFDC payments. Arkansas was much lower at 2.3 percent, and SWIM was a bit lower at 4.9 percent. We obtain an estimate for Baltimore by projecting payments for years four and five, yielding a ratio of program costs to AFDC benefits of approximately 10 percent.[10] Thus, the program investment ranged from 2–10 percent of average five-year AFDC cash expenditures for family support. Had we been able to include payments to be made after year five, and had we included expenditures on Medicaid and food stamps, these percentages would have been even lower.

AFDC impacts were, in general, smaller than earnings gains and were not found in every program. We begin, as before, with Virginia. AFDC impacts there were in the middle range among those of the four programs. Total AFDC benefits paid to controls over the five-year period amounted to $6,641 (including zeroes for periods off AFDC); experimentals received total payments of $6,318. The difference of $323 represents a 4.9 percent reduction relative to payments to controls, although the difference was not statistically significant. From the point of view of government budgets, the saving was three-quarters of program net cost. From the point of view of the experimental sample members, AFDC reductions offset less than a third of the earnings impact.

AFDC impacts were larger in Arkansas than Virginia. The dollar amount of savings, $735, covers a slightly longer follow-up period but is more than twice as large; it also substantially exceeded net program costs. The impact is statistically significant and represents a 14.3 percent reduction relative to the control

[10] We estimated five-year AFDC payments for Baltimore controls by assuming that the rate of decline in payments from year two to year three would continue for years four and five. This gave us a five-year AFDC payments total of $9,365 per control sample member. Net costs are 10.2 percent of this amount.

mean. The AFDC reduction offset more than two-thirds the increase in earnings.

The AFDC impacts in Baltimore were the smallest of the four programs, even accounting for the absence of information from years four and five. The dollar amount of payment reduction was close to zero and represents only 1.0 percent of control-group payments. AFDC savings alone were clearly insufficient to pay the net costs of the Baltimore program. Enrollees, on the other hand, obtained the benefit of increased earnings without much of an offset from reduced AFDC income. Why a program with some of the largest earnings impacts should produce so little welfare savings has been a subject of speculation. Researchers found no evidence of administrative problems in reducing monthly payments in response to earnings. It may be that earnings gains were obtained mostly among short-term AFDC recipients; that earnings gains were larger than the minimum amount needed to close cases; or that an increase in case closures was offset by lengthened AFDC stays among program enrollees participating in education or training or waiting for education or training assignments to begin.

AFDC results for San Diego SWIM were quite different from those for Baltimore, despite the similarities in program cost. AFDC reductions over the initial thirty months of follow-up, as previously published,[11] were already the largest found for an experimentally evaluated broad-coverage program up to that time. The additional follow-up data do not change this result.[12] The dollar reduction of $1,930 was statistically significant and amounted to 10.3 percent of average payments to controls over the observation period (five years plus one quarter). This impact was more than twice net program costs. On balance, the incomes of people enrolled in the SWIM program did not change much as a result of the program: reduced AFDC receipts offset nearly the full amount of the earnings gain.

[11] The AFDC results for SWIM presented in this chapter may differ slightly from those presented elsewhere. AFDC data analyzed in other San Diego SWIM reports (Hamilton and Friedlander, 1989, and Friedlander and Hamilton, 1993) were organized in fiscal quarters to match the organization of UI earnings data. In this chapter, these same data were reorganized to match the format of AFDC payments in the other three samples. That is, the months were restructured so that "month one" would always be the month of random assignment.

[12] More recently, two-year impacts for several counties in the California GAIN evaluation showed AFDC savings of $1,397 per experimental sample member in Riverside County, an impact larger than dollar savings for the first two years in SWIM. See Friedlander, Riccio, and Freedman (1993), Table 2.1.

Why were the AFDC results for San Diego SWIM so different from those of Baltimore even though the five-year earnings impacts were probably similar? The much greater degree of "mandatoriness" of San Diego SWIM is probably the best explanation. One aspect of mandatoriness is the higher sanctioning rate for San Diego SWIM. But, as we have already argued, it seems unlikely that the temporary and partial reduction of AFDC grants by sanctioning could account for more than a small share of the total AFDC savings. There are aspects of mandatoriness other than sanctioning, however, and the ability of these to explain the difference in AFDC impacts between Baltimore and San Diego SWIM is considered later.

In summary, the impacts of these programs were in line with the effort committed to them, if that effort is measured by program net cost. This is true even when we limit ourselves only to the earnings and AFDC payments within the five-year follow-up period, although the conclusion holds more for earnings than for AFDC payments. All four programs obtained earnings gains that were a multiple of net cost. In two of the four programs, AFDC impacts were also substantially larger than net costs, and in a third they were of similar magnitude. The only instance of an observed dollar impact substantially below net cost was AFDC savings for Baltimore. Would our estimates of these positive effects increase if we look beyond the available data to fill in gaps and project into the future beyond five years? To answer this question, we must consider the more detailed year-by-year pattern of impacts.

Year-by-Year Impact Estimates

To obtain a more precise description of program impacts, we have grouped the quarterly earnings and monthly AFDC data into "years." The impact estimates are shown in Table 4-2. The estimates reflect the average experience of sample members randomly assigned during the first quarter of "year one." (Thus, the first year of earnings impacts may include up to two months of pre-program information.) The table shows the outcomes for each year of follow-up, first for the experimental group and then for the control group, followed by the difference between experimental and control means, the estimate of program impact.

Our particular interest in examining year-by-year impact estimates is to understand what might have happened *after* the end of the observation period. The year-by-year movement of im-

TABLE 4-2
Impacts on Employment, Earnings, and AFDC Receipt

Program and Outcome	Average Employment Rate (%)			Average Annual Earnings ($)		
	Experimentals	Controls	Difference	Experimentals	Controls	Difference
Virginia						
Year 1: Qtrs 1–4	30.4	27.9	2.6**	1,352	1,282	70
Year 2: Qtrs 5–8	36.7	32.7	4.0***	2,269	1,987	282**
Year 3: Qtrs 9–12	39.0	34.3	4.7***	2,740	2,436	304*
Year 4: Qtrs 13–16	41.0	39.4	1.6	3,286	2,968	318*
Year 5: Qtrs 17–20	41.8	40.7	1.1	3,674	3,473	201
Year 6: not available	—	—		—	—	
Arkansas						
Year 1: Qtrs 1–4	18.5	13.5	5.0***	675	505	170**
Year 2: Qtrs 5–8	22.4	17.7	4.6**	1,181	956	224
Year 3: Qtrs 9–12	25.1	19.0	6.1***	1,440	1,122	319**
Year 4: Qtrs 13–16	27.5	22.4	5.1*	1,693	1,443	250
Year 5: Qtrs 17–20	27.7	25.2	2.5	1,890	1,800	90
Year 6: Qtrs 21–22 × 2	29.3	24.4	4.9**	2,108	1,995	114
Baltimore						
Year 1: Qtrs 1–4	30.5	27.1	3.4***	1,607	1,476	131
Year 2: Qtrs 5–8	38.3	34.3	4.0***	2,784	2,389	395***
Year 3: Qtrs 9–12	40.8	38.4	2.4*	3,497	2,991	506***
Year 4: not available	—	—		—	—	
Year 5: Qtrs 19–21 × 4/3	48.7	47.2	1.5	5,307	4,832	475*
Year 6: not available	—	—		—	—	
San Diego SWIM						
Year 1: Qtrs 1–4	31.3	25.3	6.0***	1,694	1,466	228**
Year 2: Qtrs 5–8	35.1	27.4	7.8***	2,735	2,109	626***
Year 3: Qtrs 9–12	34.5	28.3	6.2***	3,205	2,623	582***
Year 4: Qtrs 13–16	33.6	30.5	3.1**	3,653	3,227	426*
Year 5: Qtrs 17–20	33.7	32.0	1.7	4,069	3,850	219
Year 6: not available	—	—		—	—	

TABLE 4-2 (continued)

Program and Outcome	Average AFDC Receipt Rate (%)			Average Annual AFDC Payments ($)		
	Experimentals	Controls	Difference	Experimentals	Controls	Difference
Virginia						
Year 1: Qtrs 1–4	65.2	66.4	−1.1	1,971	2,050	−79*
Year 2: Qtrs 5–8	46.9	47.0	−0.1	1,488	1,528	−40
Year 3: Qtrs 9–12	35.5	38.1	−2.5*	1,157	1,270	−113**
Year 4: Qtrs 13–16	29.3	31.6	−2.3	942	1,024	−82
Year 5: Qtrs 17–20	23.6	24.1	−0.4	760	769	−9
Year 6: not available	—	—	—	—	—	—
Arkansas						
Year 1: Qtrs 1–4	54.7	61.0	−6.3***	1,021	1,169	−148***
Year 2: Qtrs 5–8	40.9	48.9	−8.0***	812	1,004	−192***
Year 3: Qtrs 9–12	33.6	41.2	−7.6***	757	932	−175***
Year 4: Qtrs 13–16	31.8	36.5	−4.7*	725	839	−114*
Year 5: Qtrs 17–20	31.4	34.3	−2.9	733	810	−77
Year 6: Qtrs 21–22 × 2	28.6	30.8	−2.2	682	740	−57
Baltimore						
Year 1: Qtrs 1–4	76.9	77.4	−0.5	2,520	2,517	4
Year 2: Qtrs 5–8	59.6	61.2	−1.6	2,057	2,092	−35
Year 3: Qtrs 9–12	48.6	50.0	−1.4	1,783	1,815	−31
Year 4: not available	—	—	—	—	—	—
Year 5: not available	—	—	—	—	—	—
Year 6: not available	—	—	—	—	—	—
San Diego SWIM						
Year 1: Qtrs 1–4	76.1	79.6	−3.5***	4,625	4,964	−339***
Year 2: Qtrs 5–8	55.0	62.4	−7.4***	3,523	4,088	−565***
Year 3: Qtrs 9–12	44.7	51.0	−6.3***	3,004	3,496	−492***
Year 4: Qtrs 13–16	37.9	41.8	−3.9***	2,676	2,982	−306***
Year 5: Qtrs 17–20	33.0	35.5	−2.5*	2,386	2,580	−194*
Year 6: Qtrs 21–22 × 2	30.2	31.4	−1.2	2,137	2,276	−140

NOTES: "Average employment rate" is the average percent employed in each quarter. "Average AFDC receipt rate" is the average percent receiving AFDC in each month. Earnings and AFDC payments for the last year are often based on data for part of the year; if so, annualization is performed by dividing by the number of quarters and multiplying by four, as indicated in the row label.

Details may not sum to totals owing to rounding.

A two-tailed t-test was applied to experimental differences. Statistical significance levels are indicated as: * = 10 percent; ** = 5 percent; *** = 1 percent.

pacts, either up or down or remaining at a constant level, should help us project treatment effects into the future. Impacts occurring in subsequent years will add to the accumulated five-year impact amounts we have already examined. Predicting those future effects can help us complete our assessment of overall program impacts.

Estimates in the table that cover early years already reported elsewhere may differ slightly from the previous estimates for reasons noted earlier. In no case, however, are the discrepancies large enough to change previous conclusions about the effects of the programs.

Year-by-Year Impacts: Employment and Earnings

The average employment rate in Table 4-2 is defined as the percent of a research group with earnings in a quarter, averaged over the four quarters in a year. Annual earnings are the sum of earnings for the four quarters. Where the amount of follow-up data differs across programs, we use dashes to indicate years not available. As noted in the table, some years do not have a full four quarters available. Thus, for example, Baltimore year five is based on only quarters nineteen through twenty-one, since complete data for quarters seventeen and eighteen for year five could not be obtained and no data for quarters twenty-two through twenty-four were available for year six. Similarly, the last year in Arkansas is based on only two quarters, as is the last year of AFDC payments in San Diego SWIM.[13] Estimates for incomplete years are less accurate than those for years in which all quarters are available. One extra quarter of earnings (quarter twenty-one) is available for SWIM, but the single quarter was deemed insufficient basis to form an impact estimate for an entire year. It should be noted that year four is missing in Baltimore, owing to the absence of quarters thirteen through sixteen. This data gap reduces our certainty about the time pattern of impacts in that site.

As before, we begin with Virginia as the representative program. Employment rates for Virginia experimentals exceeded those for controls by 4 to 5 percentage points by years two and

---

[13] The last *month* of AFDC data in San Diego SWIM was not available for the 263 individuals who entered the research sample during the final month of random assignment. For these persons, AFDC payment amounts from the previous month were carried over.

three. After that point, the employment rate among controls began to overtake that among experimentals. By the last two years, controls had almost attained the employment levels of experimentals, and little difference in employment remained. Earnings behaved differently. The average earnings impact peaked later and lasted longer. The peak earnings impact of $318 was not reached until year four. This impact represents a 10.7 percent increase over the fourth year earnings of the control group ($2,968). The peak annual impact also amounts to about three-quarters of program net costs just in one year alone. The earnings impact for year five was still $201, although this amount was not statistically significant. This estimate indicates that the "observed total" earnings impact of the previous section was, as we expected, an underestimate of the total long-term earnings impact of the program. Adding projected dollar effects for years after year five to the observed total would undoubtedly raise our already favorable assessment of the cost-effectiveness of the Virginia program. We do, however, expect that additions to cumulative earnings gains made for each year after year five will become smaller, eventually approaching zero as experimental and control earnings levels converge over time. It should be noted also that the dollar estimates in Table 4-2 are not indexed for inflation. The rate of decline of the impact on *real* earnings (i.e., inflation-adjusted earnings) is therefore somewhat faster than the reported estimates might suggest.

The Arkansas program produced employment increases from 5 to 6 percentage points in almost all years. Both employment and earnings impacts peaked in year three. Earnings in that year increased $319 above the control mean of $1,122. Average earnings in Arkansas, as indicated earlier, were low compared to the other states, and the dollar effect amounted to a 28 percent increase relative to the control mean. The dollar impacts compare well with Virginia for years one, two, and three, but they declined more in succeeding years and by the end of the follow-up period were about a third of the peak-year amount. As in Virginia, we expect additions to earnings gains for each year after year five to become smaller and to approach zero.

The pattern of employment impacts in Baltimore was similar to that in Virginia. The experimental-control difference peaked at 4.0 percentage points in year two and decreased rapidly thereafter. As in Virginia, earnings impacts lagged somewhat, peaking in year three. The peak-year gain of $506 is relatively large for an experimental evaluation of a broad-coverage program and amounts to a 16.9 percent increase over the control mean. And, unlike Virginia, it is not clear that the experimental-control differential in earnings is actually declining through the end of follow-up. The earnings impact calculated for year five is still $475, not much below the peak effect and still statistically significant. The magnitude of this estimate, averaged with the estimate for year three, suggests that the missing year earnings impact may be close to $500.

The year-five earnings gain for Baltimore is more than twice the earnings impact in the same year for any of the other programs. Should the experimental-control differential in earnings continue at the year-five level for several more years, then our estimate of total earnings impact from the previous section would have to be revised upward substantially. There would also be a substantial increase in the ratio of total earnings impact to program net cost. The absence of data for year four makes it difficult to plot the movement of the earnings impact over the latter half of the follow-up period, however, and makes it difficult to project program effects into future years. Additional follow-up would be particularly helpful for assessing the Baltimore program.

The results for San Diego SWIM add three years to those previously presented in the final report on that demonstration. As in Baltimore, a peak in the experimental-control employment differential occurred in year two. The peak-year impact on employment was, however, nearly twice the corresponding estimate for Baltimore. At nearly 8 percentage points, this employment effect is among the largest measured in an experimental evaluation of a broad-coverage welfare-to-work program. Earnings impacts also peaked in year two and are also relatively large for the scale of program and type of evaluation. The estimated year-two earnings impact of $626 is 29.7 percent of the average earnings among control-group members ($2,109). Both employment impacts and earnings impacts decline after year two, however. The one extra quarter of earnings data, not used in the table, shows approximately zero impact on employment and earnings, indicating that the differential between experimentals and controls may have disappeared entirely by quarter twenty-one. If so, we would not expect any additions to the observed total earnings impact we have already calculated. Since net costs for San Diego SWIM and Baltimore were similar, the latter may have had greater overall cost-effectiveness in increasing long-term earnings, although we cannot be sure how long the Baltimore earnings impacts will continue beyond the available follow-up period.

Some preliminary conclusions from these year-by-year earnings estimates are now possible. Although we are uncertain about the precise magnitude of the ultimate long-term earnings impacts—that is, the experimental-control earnings differences after ten or fifteen years—the weight of the evidence supports three findings: the earnings gain among experimentals relative to controls lasted in all cases for at least several years; it often lasted longer than the employment effect; and the increase in the size of the experimental-control differential did not usually continue to increase year-by-year indefinitely. This last would have been a highly desirable result, which might have occurred if the program had succeeded in placing enrollees in jobs with continually rising "career ladders," where their wages might show year-by-year increases that added cumulatively to their advantage over controls. Instead, in three of the four programs, it appears likely that each additional year after the follow-up period will add smaller and smaller amounts to the total, and the additions may soon approach zero. The notable exception may be Baltimore, which had earnings impacts at the end of the follow-up period that were almost as large as in the peak year.

We can obtain some additional information about longer-term earnings impacts in Baltimore by splitting the sample into two mutually exclusive subgroups. The first subgroup we call *applicants*, whom we identify as sample members who were referred to the welfare-to-work program (and randomly assigned) while they were in the process of applying for AFDC. The second subgroup, which we designate *recipients*, are sample members who were already receiving AFDC and were referred to the welfare-to-work program (and randomly assigned) when a change in their family circumstances made them no longer exempt from the participation requirement. Table 4-3 gives year-by-year employment and earnings impacts for applicant and recipient subgroups in Baltimore.

This table permits a comparison of the size of subgroup earnings impacts and their patterns over time. Baltimore applicants had much larger earnings impacts than recipients. This latter subgroup obtained a peak annual earnings gain of only $204 (not statistically significant), which came in year two. The next year this had declined to only $92. By the final follow-up year, their annual earnings impact was essentially zero (a negative differential of $9). In contrast, Baltimore applicants in year two had

TABLE 4-3

Baltimore AFDC Applicant and Recipient Subgroups: Impacts on Employment and Earnings

Program and Outcome	Average Employment Rate (%)			Average Annual Earnings ($)		
	Experimentals	Controls	Difference	Experimentals	Controls	Difference
Baltimore Applicants						
Year 1: Qtrs 1–4	38.9	35.2	3.8**	2,267	2,080	187
Year 2: Qtrs 5–8	46.0	40.8	5.3***	3,799	3,142	657***
Year 3: Qtrs 9–12	48.5	45.1	3.5	4,796	3,830	966***
Year 4: not available	—	—		—	—	
Year 5: Qtrs 19–21 × 4/3	53.4	50.4	2.9	6,569	5,534	1,034**
Year 6: not available	—	—	—	—	—	—
Baltimore Recipients						
Year 1: Qtrs 1–4	22.2	18.8	3.4***	975	844	131
Year 2: Qtrs 5–8	30.6	27.6	3.0	1,806	1,603	204
Year 3: Qtrs 9–12	32.9	31.7	1.2	2,226	2,134	92
Year 4: not available	—	—		—	—	
Year 5: Qtrs 19–21 × 4/3	44.1	43.9	0.2	4,090	4,099	−9
Year 6: not available	—	—	—	—	—	—

NOTES: "Average employment rate" is the average percent employed in each quarter. Earnings and AFDC payments for the last year are based on data for part of the year; annualization is performed by dividing by the number of quarters and multiplying by four, as indicated in the row label.

Details may not sum to totals owing to rounding.

A two-tailed t-test was applied to experimental differences. Statistical significance levels are indicated as: * = 10 percent; ** = 5 percent; *** = 1 percent.

earnings impacts of $657 (statistically significant), more than three times the earnings impacts for recipients in the same year. Instead of decreasing at that point, the experimental-control differential for applicants increased by half over the next year, bringing the year-three impact to $966 (statistically significant). By the final year, instead of declining, the impact for applicants had actually *grown* to $1,034 (statistically significant).

The combination of these two quite opposite results for the major subgroups in Baltimore yields a full-sample impact that gives the appearance of only a modest change in the experimental-control differential from year three to year five. If the experimental-control differential for recipients continues at around zero, however, the total program earnings impact after year five will be determined exclusively by impacts on applicants. Because the applicant impact does not appear to be decreasing, the full-sample program impact on earnings may not decrease after year five. The total program earnings impact may therefore increase considerably over the long run, along with the program's cost-effectiveness relative to the other programs.

Year-by-Year Impacts: AFDC Receipt and AFDC Payments

Impacts on employment and earnings are intended to produce impacts on AFDC receipt. Work, it is hoped, will enable program enrollees to get off AFDC and stay off. In this sense, AFDC impacts are secondary effects, following as a consequence of the primary program impacts on work. To a great extent, then, AFDC impacts should be determined by the magnitude, distribution, and timing of impacts on employment and earnings. AFDC impacts could, however, also come about directly through monetary sanctions or from client reaction to the participation requirement itself. This multiplicity of potential causes makes AFDC impacts difficult to explain fully.

A second issue in studying AFDC impacts stems from the fact that AFDC impacts may have to be considered in relation to a number of other program effects, depending on which program goal is being considered. One program goal given high priority by many administrators is reduced use of public assistance. In assessing how well this goal may have been achieved by any particular program, it may well be sufficient to examine only the AFDC impacts themselves. Another program goal is expenditure reductions for government budgets that are large enough to pay for most if not all the costs of running the welfare-to-work program. For that goal, reductions in AFDC payments are "welfare savings" accruing to government budgets and taxpayers. Such savings, which include reductions in AFDC proper and accompanying reductions in food stamps, Medicaid, and associated transfers, are necessary if a welfare-to-work program is to pay for itself.[14] In assessing how well this goal may have been achieved, information beyond the basic AFDC impacts—information on program costs and various budgetary effects—must be examined.

A full assessment of the magnitude of budgetary gains relative to program costs is a complicated and highly specialized undertaking. It is the traditional domain of benefit-cost analysis. In the discussion below, we rely on MDRC's previously published benefit-cost studies of the four programs. The government budget analyses for those studies asked the question, How much would the budgetary benefits and costs for a typical group of program enrollees total over a five-year period beginning with entry of that group into the program? Since these studies were carried out with only short-term follow-up data (sometimes only a year or less), answers to this question required projection of impact estimates a few years into the future, which involved a high degree of uncertainty. Using our additional follow-up data, we will indicate whether the new estimates of AFDC impacts change previous benefit-cost conclusions. Producing exact revised dollar estimates is beyond the scope of this study, however.[15]

We look at Virginia impacts first. As shown in Table 4-2, AFDC receipt of both experimentals and controls fell steadily throughout the five-year follow-up. Experimentals fell faster, and by year three the differential receipt rate was 2.5 percentage

---

[14]Closely associated with savings in transfers is any saving on administrative costs of AFDC, food stamps, Medicaid, and the other transfer programs. There are also nonwelfare effects that can help defray program costs. Primary among these are income taxes from increased earnings and sales taxes from increased spending by enrollees. The total of these additional cost savings and revenues alone has not proved sufficient to pay back program costs where AFDC savings were not significant.

[15]The original benefit-cost studies predicted program effects on various government budget items. They did so, however, by using only data on employment, earnings, AFDC receipt, and AFDC payments, imputing rather than directly measuring the accompanying changes in food stamps, Medicaid, other transfers, cost of administering transfer programs, and tax payments. For this study, we therefore find it sufficient to compare the present values of earnings gains and AFDC savings, calculated using the additional follow-up data, to the previously predicted present values. If the new numbers are at least as great as the old numbers, we can conclude that the net budgetary impact must turn out to be at least as large as before.

points, which was statistically significant. This was the peak effect and was paralleled by a difference of $113 (statistically significant) in AFDC payments for the year, also a peak effect. This dollar amount represents an 8.9 percent saving relative to the control mean of $1,270 (including zeroes for sample members not receiving AFDC). The new follow-up data (part of year three and all of years four and five) reveal that AFDC for controls eventually fell as far as that of experimentals, and the experimental-control difference faded by year five. Thus, the observed five-year AFDC impact of the previous section probably captured the full AFDC impact of the Virginia program. Additional follow-up years would not increase the total effect.

A previously published benefit-cost analysis for Virginia predicted that AFDC reductions and other budgetary effects over the five-year horizon would be sufficient to cover program costs. That prediction was made on the basis of one year of follow-up data by projecting those short-term results for four more years. These projections rested on assumptions about the growth and decline of AFDC impacts over time. Using the actual longer-term estimates, the original conclusion appears still to hold. The peak amount of savings for year three is higher than originally projected, compensating for a faster-than-expected decline after the peak.[16]

AFDC impacts in Arkansas were evident even in year one. By year two, the experimental-control difference in AFDC receipt was 8.0 percentage points, the largest in any year in any of the four programs. The peak annual saving of $192 (year two) amounts to 19.2 percent of the control mean of $1,004 for that year, the largest percentage reduction found in these data. The addition of new follow-up data indicates that experimental-control differentials for both AFDC receipt and AFDC payments narrowed from year two onward. Dollar impacts eventually fell

---

[16] The original benefit-cost study in Virginia estimated the excess of benefits over costs to government budgets during the five-year projection period to be in the range of $159 to $336 per experimental sample member (Riccio, Cave, Freedman, and Price, 1986, p. 152). We calculate the present values of earnings gains and AFDC reductions to be quite close to those that produced the lower end of this range. Our present value estimates over a five-year follow-up were obtained by deflating and multiplying each year's impact by $(1 + d)^{-(y-1)}$, where $d = 0.05$ and y is the year, and summing. For impacts on earnings, this gives us a net present value of $990, compared to the original published estimate of $999 obtained with four quarters of follow-up and assuming a subsequent 22 percent annual decay rate. For impacts on AFDC payments we get a net present value estimate of $-$284, compared to the original estimate of $-$290.

by more than two-thirds from the peak to year six, and we should expect them to decrease further beyond that point. Five years of follow-up probably captures the bulk of the AFDC impact of the Arkansas program, although there may be some additions after that point.

The gradual fading of the AFDC effect with convergence over time does not wipe out the savings that accrued during the observation period. The total amount of AFDC savings in Arkansas was large relative to the modest cost of the program, and the new estimates confirm the previously published benefit-cost finding (based on projected effects from year one onward) that the program easily paid for itself several times over within five years.[17] Moreover, the $57 dollar difference between experimentals and controls in the last year of follow-up, though apparently small (and not statistically significant), was still 7.7 percent of outlays to the control group in that year.

In Baltimore, the thirty-six-month follow-up results (presented in a previous report) show no significant AFDC reductions, either in percent receiving or in the amounts received. The maximum dollar saving for a year is estimated as only $35 per experimental sample member (year two). The $31 saving for year three, which we can use for comparison across programs, was less than 2 percent of the control mean of $1,815 for the year. These savings were not sufficient to cover the program's cost, although other budgetary effects limited the estimated shortfall. Still more earnings data would not change this result; and it is quite unlikely that longer AFDC follow-up would change it either.[18]

As in Arkansas, AFDC impacts in SWIM appeared in year one. By year two, the average AFDC receipt rate was down 7.4

[17] Friedlander, Hoerz, Quint, and Riccio (1985, p. 140) estimated net budgetary benefits over costs in the range of $691 to $1,157 per experimental for the Arkansas program. Using the formula in the previous footnote, we calculate the present value of earnings impacts over five years (not counting year six) to be substantially greater than the original five-year projections ($943 versus the original range of $344 to $570); our estimated net present value of AFDC impacts is within the original projected range (−$642 versus the range −$535 to −$836). Thus, we expect that a revision of the benefit-cost calculations would yield a benefit exceeding cost for government budgets, with the net difference within the original range given above.

[18] A study of the Baltimore program using three years of earnings and AFDC data estimated that government budgets lost $203 per experimental sample member over five years (Friedlander, 1987, p. 30). This estimate assumed no decay in earnings gains, suggesting that recalculation with the additional earnings data would yield a similar result. The general absence of welfare effects makes additional AFDC data unlikely to affect the result.

percentage points for experimentals compared to controls, a reduction almost as large as Arkansas's. The annualized dollar impact in that year, which was the peak year, was $565, a 13.8 percent saving relative to the $4,088 paid, on average, to controls. With the new data, we now see five straight years of statistically significant AFDC effects. Effects do, as expected, eventually decrease with time. The experimental-control differential began narrowing in year three, and impacts in year five (the last full year of data) were down to about one-quarter of the peak amount, although this was still 6.2 percent of payments to controls during the year. Years beyond year six would appear likely to contribute some additional savings to the total AFDC impact estimate for SWIM. It is not clear how long the remaining experimental-control differential will last before convergence becomes complete, but benefit-cost computations, recently updated to include the new data, indicate that observed five-year savings alone are enough to allow the program to pay for itself more than twice over.[19]

SUMMARY AND OPEN QUESTIONS

A number of analysts have pointed out the somewhat surprising finding that almost all the welfare-to-work programs with experimental impact evaluations—a set of thirteen in all, beginning with the National Supported Work Demonstration in the late 1970s—have shown positive impacts on earnings for AFDC enrollees.[20] The new, extended follow-up data analyzed for this chapter also paint a positive picture. All four of the programs we looked at used their limited resources in a cost-effective manner to achieve several, though not all, of the goals laid out in the first part of this chapter. Judging from net costs, funds amounting to between 2 and 10 percent of the normal five-year AFDC payments to the program samples were invested in the welfare-to-work programs. With that modest investment, the programs increased employment among AFDC recipients; reduced AFDC receipt; increased the share of sample members' income coming

---

[19] Using the additional follow-up data, Friedlander and Hamilton (1993) estimate a net five-year budgetary gain of $1,234 per experimental sample member. Benefits amounted to $2,153 and net costs to $920, for a ratio of about 2.3 to 1.

[20] For reviews of recent social experiments involving welfare-to-work programs, see Friedlander and Gueron (1992), Greenberg and Wiseman (1992), and Gueron and Pauly (1991).

from earnings; and, except in Baltimore, broke even or saved money for government budgets.

Earnings impacts were found in all four programs. For all four, measured earnings impacts were greater than program net costs. In fact, total earnings gains, at a minimum, appear to exceed twice net costs even for the more expensive of the four programs, and this holds without adding in possible impacts in years beyond the current five-year observation period. Most importantly, earnings impacts appear larger in the programs with higher net costs, suggesting the possibility that greater investments might produce still greater effects. For AFDC impacts, we see a mixture of results across the four programs. Savings were not achieved everywhere, and the relationship between earnings gains and AFDC reductions was not straightforward. Two programs with comparable earnings impacts produced quite different AFDC impacts. We found, in particular, that relatively large earnings impacts could occur without AFDC reductions (Baltimore). Even fairly modest welfare reductions proved sufficient, however, to compensate government budgets for the modest costs incurred. In the cases of San Diego SWIM and Arkansas, government budgets were actually reduced as a result of the program.

The new data reveal some real limitations in low- to moderate-cost programs. In particular, the five-year follow-up shows that average earnings and average AFDC payments of controls eventually begin to overtake those of experimentals, narrowing the differential initially achieved by the program treatments. For AFDC impacts, this narrowing of the gap through convergence of experimental and control levels over time is a foregone conclusion and does not necessarily suggest a program failure, since the accumulated savings are "bankable" and don't disappear. Any experimental-control differential remaining at the end of five years, however, would signify a program impact on long-term AFDC receipt. In achieving the goal of reducing long-term AFDC receipt, these programs were not notably successful. Of the three programs with AFDC impacts, Virginia evidenced a decline of the experimental-control differential almost to zero, and Arkansas and San Diego SWIM showed declining absolute dollar effects, although they did show some possible longer-term persistence in those effects as a percent of annual outlays to controls. We return to the issue of effects on long-term AFDC receipt in Chapter 6.

The programs could, in theory, have created a permanent differential in earnings between experimentals and controls, a differential as large (or larger) at the end of five years as it was in any of the earlier years. As it turned out, three of the four programs appear to show a peak in earnings impacts, with a subsequent decline over time, rather than a continuing or increasing experimental-control difference. The peak is not particularly well defined, however, and for each program falls at a different time between years two and four of the follow-up period. Nor is the decline after the peak abrupt. In Baltimore, there also appears to be a peak, but there may be a continuing, perhaps permanent, long-term effect that is large relative to the peak effect. Such a continuing differential would constitute a major program achievement, greatly multiplying the observed impact on earnings. Analysis of the difference in earnings impacts over time between applicant and recipient subgroups in Baltimore suggests that the effect may persist indefinitely or even grow, but without still longer follow-up we cannot be certain. Even in Arkansas, where the services consisted almost entirely of low-cost job search assistance, the differential in employment rates was still nearly 5 percentage points (and statistically significant) at year six, although the experimental-control earnings differential had faded considerably. Elsewhere, however, there was generally little impact on employment remaining by year five, implying that those other programs did not achieve a sustained reduction in joblessness for a typical group of program enrollees.

In comparing the low-cost and moderate-cost programs, the longer-term follow-up is critical. Differences between programs ranked by cost are not readily apparent in the early years. Dollar impacts around the peak year do seem larger for Baltimore and San Diego SWIM than for Virginia and Arkansas, but the cost-effectiveness of the latter two in producing those earnings impacts—the dollar of earnings impact per dollar of net cost—may well be larger. It is only at the end of the added follow-up years that a possible advantage for Baltimore may be emerging from a lower rate of decline of earnings impacts over time. Even more follow-up for that sample would be helpful in deciding the point.

5

Patterns of Employment and Earnings

In this chapter we examine the nature of program effects on employment and earnings with some care. We are interested in establishing why the program impact occurred at each site and what might explain the distinctive patterns of earnings impacts across the four sites. The findings in the previous chapter clearly indicate that earnings impacts occurred in all four sites, but they do not show whether the kinds of jobs obtained by members of the experimental group differed from those obtained by members of the control group. In particular, it is not clear whether the programs speeded up job finding, or reduced employment turnover, or increased earnings on the job. These issues are examined here.

The conclusions from our analysis can be grouped into two categories. The first category covers initial program effects, and the second involves longer-term program effects. The main conclusions about initial program effects can be summarized briefly: in all four sites, the main initial impact of the programs occurred as a result of accelerated job finding. Experimentals found jobs that were similar to those found by controls, but they found them sooner.

The evidence for this conclusion is straightforward. During the first two to three years after random assignment, virtually all of the impact on earnings among members of the experimental groups was attributable to an increase in the average number of quarters of employment. Very little of it occurred because employed experimentals earned more during quarters in which they were employed than controls. Of the gain in quarters of employment, nearly all occurred because the initial spells of joblessness of experimentals were shorter than those of controls;

little occurred because experimentals held onto jobs longer. Initial spells of joblessness were reduced, in large part, because the programs speeded up job finding by enrollees who would have worked within a few years anyway. But from one-third (Baltimore) to three-quarters (Virginia) of the decrease in initial joblessness came from job finding by enrollees who would not have worked at all during the five-year follow-up period.

The reduced time that experimentals took to find their first jobs was translated into additional time in employment during the first two or three years after random assignment. In one of the sites—Arkansas—there is evidence that experimental-group members who found jobs were a bit more likely to remain employed than control-group workers. But in the other three sites, experimental-group workers were about as successful in remaining employed after finding their initial jobs as were control-group workers. The big difference between the two research groups was in the timing of initial jobs. Experimentals found employment first.

Our second set of conclusions, those regarding longer-term program effects, suggests that different mechanisms of longer-term program impact were dominant in each of the sites. The pattern in Virginia is easiest to understand. That program produced an initial acceleration of job finding. The program effect on employment and earnings grew until the third year. As more and more controls found jobs, however, the program effect gradually faded. Thus, the narrowing of the experimental-control differential over time resulted either from the normal job-finding behavior of controls or from their participation in employment services after the embargo imposed by the research design was lifted.

The earnings effect in Arkansas also reached a peak and then shrank. The employment effect persisted, however. In part, the program experience led some intermittently employed, part-time, or poorly paid workers to stay in the labor market when they might otherwise have left it. Employment at lower earnings levels remained more common in the experimental group than in the control group. We hypothesize that the experience of some enrollees, either in the program or on the job later, may have shifted their attitudes in favor of work and against welfare, which kept them from giving up on employment and going back to AFDC.

The Baltimore program was the only program that achieved sizable earnings gains persisting into the fifth follow-up year.

The program had little if any long-term effect on employment, but it slightly raised the percentage of workers with above-average earnings. The initial program effect in Baltimore, as in the other sites, came primarily from earlier job finding. But the longer-term effect of the program was achieved by boosting the earnings capacity of at least a few of the people enrolled in the program and thereby increasing their earnings on the job. This result is consistent with the program's greater emphasis on human-capital building activities.

San Diego SWIM produced the largest short-term employment and earnings impacts. Unlike Baltimore, however, San Diego SWIM showed no evidence of higher earnings on the job. As in the lower-cost programs, shorter initial joblessness (i.e., acceleration of initial job finding) accounted for the initial impact on earnings. As elsewhere, control group catch-up contributed to a narrowing of the experimental-control differential in earnings over time. But job loss also made a major contribution to the decline in longer-term earnings impacts.

The remainder of this chapter is organized as follows. In the next section, we attempt to decompose overall program impact on earnings into several component parts. To do so, we introduce some novel employment measures to capture the influence of accelerated job finding. We also examine the behavior of experimentals and controls during the part of the follow-up period after they first find jobs. The second section of the chapter analyzes the quality of initial employment of sample members who started to work early in the follow-up period. Because experimentals typically became employed earlier than controls, we try to examine whether they paid a penalty in the form of lower job quality, particularly lower earnings or shorter average duration of employment. The final section contains a comparison of the employment and earnings response in two different periods: the second follow-up year and the last follow-up year. This comparison is intended to shed light on the relationship between initial program response and the longer-term response that occurs well after an enrollee's initial involvement in the program has ended.

EMPLOYMENT RESPONSE AND THE CHANGE IN EARNINGS

We begin our analysis by examining the relationship between earnings impacts and the size and timing of changes in employment. As in the previous chapter, it is convenient to examine the pattern of employment and earnings changes first in Virginia and then in the other three sites.

Control-Group Behavior. Before we can fully understand the ways in which a program changes behavior, we must understand the patterns of employment that are typical for the program population when there is no special program. For this purpose, we examine the patterns of *control-group* employment over time, using quarterly data for Virginia. Figure 5-1 shows the trend in initial job entry and employment rates over the entire Virginia follow-up period, which is twenty quarters including the quarter of random assignment. The solid line towards the top of the figure represents the rate of "initial job finding" among members of the control group. We refer to this percentage as the *cumulative employment rate*, because it represents the cumulative percentage of sample members who have earned wages in at least one quarter by the end of the specified quarter. For example, by quarter nine, 57 percent of Virginia controls had found an initial job (that is, had earned wages in at least one of the quarters between enrollment and quarter nine). By the end of quarter twenty, the final quarter of follow-up, 72 percent had found at least one job covered by the Unemployment Insurance system.

Not all of these control sample members held onto their jobs, of course. Many left employment after initially finding a job. Thus, some who started work in an early quarter were not employed in a subsequent quarter. The *current employment rate* among controls, which is displayed in Figure 5-1 as the lower solid line, is therefore always less than the cumulative percentage of controls who found an initial job. For example, even though 57 percent of controls had held at least one job by the ninth quarter, only 34 percent were currently still employed in that quarter. That is, in less than two years, fully 40 percent ($100 - 100 \times [34/57]$) of job finders not only had lost their initial job but also had not yet regained employment.

Notice that the gap between the cumulative employment rate and the current employment rate for controls grew over time. Women who first became employed in an early quarter had more time to leave their initial jobs as time went on. This pattern highlights an important characteristic of the population becoming eligible for welfare-to-work programs. Members of this population find jobs with some difficulty, as indicated by the slow pace of initial job finding, and many of the jobs they find don't last long. To some degree, this behavior is typical of the low-wage labor market in general, where low skill levels are associated with high job turnover (i.e., short job tenure).

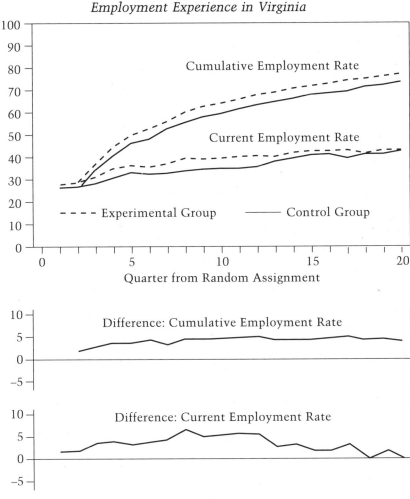

FIGURE 5-1
Employment Experience in Virginia

The dashed lines in the upper panel of Figure 5-1 show the rates of initial job finding and current employment for members of the Virginia experimental group. The experimental-control *differences* in cumulative and current employment rates are shown in the lower panel of Figure 5-1. These differences represent the effects or impacts of the program. We first observe that the current employment rate during quarters three through twelve was noticeably higher among experimentals than among controls. Thereafter, the differential decreased, approaching zero by the end of the observed follow-up. This pattern of impact growth and decline was suggested in Table 4-2 in Chapter 4.

We next see that the cumulative employment rate (or initial job finding rate) among experimentals was also higher in the program group than among controls (compare the dashed and solid lines in the upper panel of the figure). The gap between experimentals and controls peaked at 4.6 percentage points around quarter twelve and then began to narrow slightly. With the steady progress of the control group in finding jobs, they eventually began to "catch up" to the experimental group in the cumulative employment rate measure. By the end of the observation period at quarter twenty, the experimental-control difference was down to 3.5, although this is still a statistically significant difference. This remaining difference indicates that some experimentals who would not have been employed at all over the five-year interval did find work with the program's assistance.

Our discussion suggests that a program may have two kinds of job-finding effects independent of possible effects on rates of pay. First, the program may cause some people *who would eventually have worked anyway* to begin employment sooner. Second, the program may induce employment among some people *who would never have worked*. We will speak of both of these effects as *employment acceleration* or *employment speed-up*. In doing so, we mean to emphasize that the jobs found were either similar to jobs that would have been found eventually anyway or were otherwise typical of this population in the absence of special services. Our coinage specifically *excludes* placement in higher-wage or more stable jobs.

Virginia.   To separate the influences of job finding, employment, and pay changes on earnings, it is helpful to examine a variety of indicators of employment and earnings effects. In the top panel of Table 5-1 we show these measures for Virginia. The top two rows show the program impact on total earnings in quarter two through quarter nine and in quarter two through quarter twenty. Since we do not include the earnings obtained in the quarter of random assignment—that is, quarter one—readers should note that these follow-up periods comprise only eight quarters and nineteen quarters, respectively, of follow-up information. Quarter one is excluded from summary employment and earnings measures because it contains pre-program earnings for some persons randomly assigned in the second or third month of the quarter. In this table and all others in the chapter, we

TABLE 5-1
Impacts on Patterns of Employment Over the Full Follow-Up Period

ɔgram and Outcome	Experimentals	Controls	Difference	Difference/ Controls × 100
rginia				
Average earnings, annualized ($)				
Quarters 2–9	2,024	1,801	222**	12.3%
Quarters 2–20	2,758	2,509	248*	9.9%
Ever employed (%)				
Quarters 2–9	61.7	57.4	4.3**	(x)
Quarters 2–20	75.7	72.2	3.5**	(x)
Number of quarters employed				
Quarters 2–9	2.80	2.50	0.29***	11.8%
Quarters 2–20	7.28	6.74	0.55**	8.1%
If ever employed through quarter 20:				
Average earnings per quarter employed ($)[a]	1,798	1,769	29 (z)	1.6%
First quarter employed[b]	5.66	5.92	−0.26 (z)	(x)
Number of quarters of initial joblessness[c]	7.39	8.11	−0.72***	(x)
Fraction of quarters employed from first quarter employed through quarter 20 (%)	62.7	61.8	0.9 (z)	(x)
rkansas				
Average earnings, annualized ($)				
Quarters 2–9	1,049	815	234**	28.7%
Quarters 2–22	1,490	1,285	205	16.0%
Ever employed (%)				
Quarters 2–9	37.6	32.7	4.9**	(x)
Quarters 2–22	50.4	47.6	2.8	(x)
Number of quarters employed				
Quarters 2–9	1.70	1.31	0.39***	29.7%
Quarters 2–22	5.25	4.28	0.97***	22.8%
If ever employed through quarter 22:				
Average earnings per quarter employed ($)[a]	1,489	1,576	−87 (z)	−5.5%
First quarter employed[b]	6.41	7.28	−0.86 (z)	(x)
Number of quarters of initial joblessness[c]	12.64	13.52	−0.87**	(x)
Fraction of quarters employed from first quarter employed through quarter 22 (%)	62.8	57.2	5.7 (z)	(x)
altimore				
Average earnings, annualized ($)				
Quarters 2–9	2,454	2,137	317**	14.8%
Quarters 2–12, 19–21	3,317	2,923	394***	13.5%
Ever employed (%)				
Quarters 2–9	64.2	58.3	5.9***	(x)
Quarters 2–12, 19–21	77.9	75.7	2.1	(x)

TABLE 5-1 *(continued)*

Program and Outcome	Experimentals	Controls	Difference	Difference Controls × 100
Number of quarters employed				
Quarters 2–9	2.86	2.57	0.30***	11.6%
Quarters 2–12, 19–21	5.56	5.14	0.41***	8.1%
If ever employed through quarter 21:				
Average earnings per quarter employed ($)[a]	*2,088*	*1,988*	*100 (z)*	*5.0%*
First quarter employed[b]	*5.86*	*6.70*	*−0.84 (z)*	*(x)*
Number of quarters of initial joblessness[c]	7.43	8.41	−0.98***	(x)
Fraction of quarters employed from first quarter employed through quarter 21 (%)	*65.6*	*66.5*	*−0.9 (z)*	*(x)*
San Diego SWIM				
Average earnings, annualized ($)				
Quarters 2–9	2,461	1,963	498***	25.3%
Quarters 2–21	3,222	2,807	415**	14.8%
Ever employed (%)				
Quarters 2–9	62.5	50.8	11.8***	(x)
Quarters 2–21	74.6	67.5	7.1***	(x)
Number of quarters employed				
Quarters 2–9	2.73	2.15	0.58***	27.1%
Quarters 2–21	6.77	5.81	0.97***	16.7%
If ever employed through quarter 21:				
Average earnings per quarter employed ($)[a]	*2,378*	*2,417*	*−39 (z)*	*−1.6%*
First quarter employed[b]	*5.31*	*6.36*	*−1.04 (z)*	*(x)*
Number of quarters of initial joblessness[c]	7.54	9.43	−1.89***	(x)
Fraction of quarters employed from first quarter employed through quarter 21 (%)	*54.4*	*55.0*	*−0.6 (z)*	*(x)*

NOTES: "First quarter of employment" is defined as follows: for sample members with earnings, it is the first quarter with earnings, beginning with quarter two; for sample members without earnings, it is the last quarter of follow-up plus one. "Number of quarters of initial joblessness" is defined as the number of quarters following the quarter of random assignment (quarter one) and preceding "first quarter of employment," and is equal to "quarter of first employment" minus two.

Details may not sum to totals owing to rounding.

Italics indicate nonexperimental estimates.

A two-tailed t-test was applied to experimental differences. Statistical significance levels are indicated as: * = 10 percent; ** = 5 percent; *** = 1 percent. (z) indicates that the comparison is nonexperimental: no test of statistical significance was performed. (x) indicates that the percentage difference is not relevant.

[a]Calculated only for quarters with employment.

[b]Calculated only for sample members ever employed.

[c]Sample members never employed are assigned the value "last quarter of follow-up minus one."

follow certain conventions: Differences between experimentals and controls are shown both in absolute form (e.g., as dollars or quarters) and, where relevant and where space permits, as a percentage of the control-group mean. Estimates that are nonexperimental are displayed in italics. All experimental estimates are regression-adjusted, and all nonexperimental estimates are derived from regression-adjusted experimental estimates.

We present information on earnings and employment for two different periods in order to highlight the patterns across time that were found in Chapter 4. As we saw there, in all four sites the programs produced measurable effects on employment and earnings during the first two years following random assignment. In three of the sites, however, this effect shrank towards the end of the follow-up period. For each site, it is interesting to contrast the response during the period containing the strong initial effect with the response for the full follow-up period.

To facilitate comparisons, earnings are converted to annual terms by dividing by the number of quarters covered and then multiplying by four. As shown in the first row, the Virginia program boosted average annualized earnings by $222 during the first eight post-random assignment quarters. This dollar amount represented a 12.3 percent increase relative to the control mean earnings over the same period. The program raised annualized earnings $248 or 9.9 percent over the full nineteen quarters following random assignment. Note that, as usual, average earnings for experimentals and controls include zeroes for sample members who had no employment.

The third and fourth rows in the table show the cumulative percentage of women who obtained at least one UI-covered job by quarter nine and by the end of the full follow-up period, respectively. The numbers in these rows correspond to the cumulative employment rates shown in quarter nine and quarter twenty in Figure 5-1. As we noted when discussing that figure, the advantage of experimentals over controls erodes somewhat over time as a growing number of women in the control group find an initial job.

The next two rows of Table 5-1 show the average number of quarters members of the experimental and control groups were employed, from quarter two through quarter nine in row five and from quarter two through quarter twenty in row six. Once again, these estimates exclude the employment of sample members during the quarter of random assignment. During both follow-up periods experimentals were employed for more quarters than controls. In the early follow-up period, women could potentially have been employed for up to eight quarters. On average, Virginia controls were employed in a little less than a third of these quarters (2.50/8), and experimentals were employed in an additional 0.29 quarters, an 11.8 percent increase over the control-group mean. Over the full follow-up period, there are 19 potential quarters of employment. Of these, controls were employed in a little more than a third (6.74/19), and experimentals were employed an additional 0.55 quarters or 8.1 percent more quarters than controls.

With these statistics we can divide up the total impact on earnings into the contributions of additional quarters of employment and greater earnings per quarter employed. To make this decomposition, we rely on the following approximation: the percent change in a variable that is the product of two or more other variables is approximately equal to the sum of the percent changes in the component variables.[1] The contribution of the change in any one of the component variables to the change in the product may therefore be gauged by comparing the percent change in the component variable with the percent change in the product. For example, if the impact (i.e., the change) on one variable is 10 percent relative to its control-group mean and the impact on one of its components is 9 percent of its control-group mean, then the component variable in question may be said to account for about 9/10, or 90 percent, of the impact on the first variable. We make use of this decomposition at many places in this study.

[1] Formally, the case with two factors is represented as follows: if $Y = V \times W$, then $dY = W \times dV + V \times dW$ and $dY/Y = dV/V + dW/W$. If the differences are not infinitesimal—and program impacts are not—then the equality is approximate unless interaction terms are figured in. When applied to impacts, the formula for exact equality becomes, $(Y_e - Y_c)/Y_c = [(V_e - V_c)/V_c] + [(W_e - W_c)/W_c] + [(V_e - V_c)/V_c] \times [(W_e - W_c)/W_c]$, where the subscripts "$e$" and "$c$" indicate means for experimentals and controls. That is, the percent impact on the product equals the sum of the percent differences for the factors plus the product of the percent differences for the factors. When the last term is ignored, the formula becomes approximate. The approximation is closest where differences are fairly small, since the interaction term will then be close to zero. Given the magnitude of most effects examined in this study, the approximation yields an appropriate decomposition. The approximation holds even where some or all of the differences are negative. As an illustration of the potential discrepancy for a large difference and the influence of negative differences, consider the five-year earnings impact in Arkansas shown in Table 5-1. This 16.0 percent impact is the largest percent impact on five-year earnings in the table and is composed of a 22.8 percent difference in number of quarters employed and a -5.5 percent difference on average earnings per quarter employed. The sum of the two component effects is 17.3, with the product of the two component effects accounting for the small discrepancy of -1.3.

In the present case, we make use of the fact that total earnings equals the product of the number of quarters employed and average earnings per quarter employed. We can compare the overall percent increase in earnings with the percent impact on quarters employed. Up through quarter twenty, the percent increase in earnings for Virginia is only slightly greater than the percent increase in the number of quarters employed (9.9 percent versus 8.1 percent, respectively). This comparison implies that almost all (that is, 8.1/9.9, or more than four-fifths) of the program impact on earnings occurred because experimentals were employed in more quarters, not because they earned more in each quarter they worked.

This conclusion is reinforced by comparing the average quarterly earnings of experimentals and controls during quarters in which they were employed, shown in row seven of the panel.[2] Because these estimates are based only on quarters with earnings, we call them *conditional* earnings estimates, that is, earnings conditional on employment. During the full nineteen-quarter follow-up, experimental-group members in Virginia earned an average of $1,798 per quarter when they were employed. This is just $29—or 1.6 percent—more than the comparable mean for employed controls. Thus, the mean quarterly earnings on jobs held by Virginia experimentals was almost indistinguishable from the mean quarterly earnings on jobs obtained by Virginia controls. In later analysis, we show that not only the mean but also the distribution of earnings among employed experimentals was very similar to that of controls.

Some caution should be exercised when interpreting the preceding breakdown of earnings impacts into effects on quarters and effects on quarterly amounts. The decomposition is not exact. The percentage increases for the two components will not generally add up precisely to the percentage increase in total earnings. In addition, whenever we examine conditional estimates, we are going beyond the basic experimental-control comparison, and we may induce some nonexperimental biases. The possibility of such biases will reduce the certainty with which we can answer some research questions using conditional estimates.

In interpreting conditional earnings estimates, some uncer-

---

[2] "Average earnings per quarter employed" in the experimental and control groups was calculated by dividing the regression-adjusted mean of total earnings for a group by the regression-adjusted mean of total quarters employed for the same group.

tainty arises because there are two underlying behavioral patterns that could produce similar average earnings per quarter of employment across research groups. It could be that almost all the increase in employment was in jobs with quarterly earnings similar to those in jobs typically obtained by controls. Alternatively, it could be that some experimentals worked for higher quarterly earnings but no additional quarters while others worked for additional quarters at below-average pay rates.[3] This latter group of job finders would probably be individuals who would not have worked at all in the absence of intervention. Even under this second alternative, however, the increase in employment would still be a major contributor to the overall earnings gain unless earnings in the additional quarters were very low.

We next must look for the source of the increase in number of quarters of employment. Is it increased speed of employment or increased stability of employment? We begin with two statistics describing the interval between random assignment and the first quarter of earnings. The first of these we calculated only for sample members who found jobs during the follow-up period. The second is calculated for all sample members. The first statistic, shown in row eight in the top panel of Table 5-1, is the "first quarter employed," taken as an average over the subsample of individuals who worked. For control-group members who found jobs sometime during the follow-up period this number was 5.92 for Virginia, indicating that controls who found employment began to work at their first job, on average, just before quarter six. For working experimentals, the average quarter of initial employment was 5.66. The negative difference of 0.26 quarters implies that experimentals who found jobs in Virginia during the follow-up period found them a little earlier—about 3-1/2 weeks earlier—than controls who found jobs.

Recall, however, that 3.5 percentage points more experimen-

---

[3] An example here might be useful. Consider a simple experiment in which there are three controls, with the abilities to earn $1,000, $2,000, and $3,000 per quarter, respectively. There are also three experimentals of the same type. We find that individuals will switch from welfare to work only when they can earn more than $2,250 per quarter. Thus, in the control group, only one person will work, and the average earnings per quarter of employment will be $3,000. For experimentals, however, the program succeeds in raising everyone's earning power by $500 per quarter. We will then see that two-thirds of experimentals will be employed. They will have average earnings per employed quarter of $3,000, the same as controls. The newly employed experimentals have lowered the conditional average at the same time the other experimentals have raised it.

tals than controls found jobs during the follow-up period (fourth row of the table). Thus, the difference between the first quarter employed in the two groups is not a difference between two identically selected groups. Nor does it fully measure the influence of earlier job finding on the total number of quarters of employment in the experimental group. In order to measure the full effect of earlier job finding among the experimentals, it is necessary to construct an estimate based on the full research sample, including some information about those sample members who failed to find employment during the follow-up.

We have therefore calculated a second measure, which we call "number of quarters of initial joblessness." This variable is defined as the minimum of the number of quarters of initial joblessness up until (a) the first quarter employed or (b) the end of the follow-up period. For sample members who found a job, this measure is simply the number of quarters from the end of the quarter of random assignment until the beginning of the quarter in which they first started working. Someone who began work in quarter six, for example, spent four quarters after the enrollment quarter—quarters two through five—in an initial spell of joblessness. For sample members who did not find jobs, the initial spell of joblessness in Virginia is always nineteen quarters, the number of quarters in the follow-up period after the quarter of random assignment. For sample members employed in quarter two, the variable takes the value of zero.[4]

This statistic might seem peculiar. However, it conveniently divides every sample member's employment experience during the follow-up period into two parts, that which occurred before any employment was obtained and that which occurred after the start of the first job. We use information about both these periods to draw some useful conclusions about the nature of response to the program.

A simple diagram illustrates how our measure is constructed. In Figure 5-2, we display the pattern of job finding and job loss for a hypothetical member of the Virginia control group. We want to study the employment history covering the period fol-

[4]For people who did not become employed by the end of the last follow-up quarter, our measure of the spell of initial joblessness is truncated: it does not give the completed spell length, which we cannot observe. We do not know what happened after the end of the follow-up period. It may be that never-employed controls found jobs much faster than never-employed experimentals after the end of follow-up. Thus, our conclusions about the importance of early job finding in the experimental group should be understood to apply solely to the period we actually observe.

FIGURE 5-2
Illustration of Spells of Employment

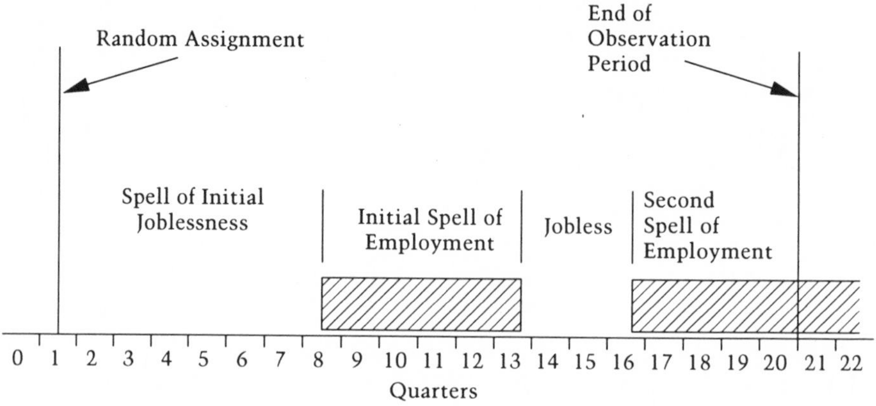

lowing the quarter of random assignment until the last day of the follow-up period, an interval of nineteen quarters. The person whose experience is depicted in the figure is jobless during the first six quarters after random assignment—quarters two through seven—but finds a job in quarter eight.

Note that the figure can tell us something about the stability of employment from the information it contains about the number of quarters of initial joblessness and the total number of quarters of employment. In particular, from Figure 5-2 we know that there are thirteen quarters remaining from the start of the first job through the end of the follow-up period (quarters eight through twenty). These are quarters in which the individual could, potentially, have remained employed. During this period, however, there were only eleven quarters of actual employment. Thus, the individual was employed 11/13 or 85 percent of the time after finding a job. Greater employment stability would make this percent as high as 100; less employment stability would make it lower, and it could go almost as low as zero. We make use of this kind of calculation later.

The number of quarters of initial joblessness is reported in row nine of Table 5-1. The average of this variable for the entire control sample in Virginia is 8.11 quarters.[5] Among experimen-

---

[5] The estimate of 8.11 quarters is simply the weighted average of 3.92 quarters for the 72.2 percent of controls who found jobs during the follow-up period and 19.0 quarters for the 27.8 percent of controls who did not find jobs. The 3.92 figure equals 5.92 for the conditional average first quarter employed minus 2.

tals the average is 0.72 quarters less—7.39 versus 8.11 quarters. This difference indicates that, *within the observation period*, experimentals spent about two fewer months than controls in finding their initial jobs.[6]

This difference can be usefully compared with the total effect of the program on quarters of employment, shown in row six. Within the observed follow-up period, experimentals worked 0.55 quarters more than controls. Within that same period, experimentals spent 0.72 fewer quarters before their initial jobs began or before the end of follow-up, whichever occurred sooner. The first point to make about this comparison is that the gains in overall employment and in earlier job finding are roughly comparable: 0.55 quarters versus 0.72 quarters. This suggests that experimentals worked more quarters during the follow-up period primarily because they spent less time than controls finding their initial jobs.

The decrease in number of quarters of initial joblessness can be apportioned between speedier job finding for individuals who would have found work within the follow-up period even without program assistance and employment by individuals who, without the program, would not have worked at all during the five years. As shown in Table 5-1, those who would have worked anyway were 72.2 percent of the sample, as indicated by the control group. In addition, the difference in "first quarter employed" between employed experimentals and controls was −0.26. Multiplying these two estimates together (and dividing by 100 to convert the percent to a fraction) gives −0.19 as the contribution to the impact on "number of quarters of initial joblessness" by experimentals who would have worked anyway. This contribution is about a quarter of the total −0.72 change in initial joblessness. The remainder, about three-quarters, can be attributed to job finding among experimentals who would not have worked at all. This calculation assumes that both groups started work, on average, at the same time. If the newly employed found jobs a bit faster than the average, then their share would be greater than three-quarters.

A second point is also important, however. The decrease in initial joblessness among experimentals was somewhat *greater* than the increase in total quarters employed. The time line in Figure 5-2 can help us to understand why. After finding her first job, the person represented in the figure soon lost it, suffering

[6]The fraction 0.72 of a calendar quarter is 2.16 months.

another spell of joblessness before finding another job. This experience is common in low-wage labor markets in general and in our research samples, too, and it has important implications for program impacts. If the individual in Figure 5-2 were an experimental instead of a control, then she might find her first job one quarter sooner (i.e., in quarter seven rather than eight, after five quarters of joblessness rather than six). But it does not necessarily follow that she will spend one additional quarter at work during the follow-up period. Because her employment experience is punctuated with intermittent spells of joblessness, part of the extra time after her initial job will be spent without a job. If the duration of the first job does not change, then the only effect of the program might be to move some joblessness from before the first employment spell to after it; the total quarters of employment might not change.

It is therefore important, in comparing the experiences of experimental and control groups, to determine whether the pattern of employment after the start of the first job differs in some systematic way between experimentals and controls. In the next section, we specifically examine the characteristics of workers' initial employment spells, including their average duration. But the numbers in Table 5-1 can tell us much about the overall frequency and duration of jobholding when all observable employment spells are counted.

Of the total of nineteen quarters we observe in Virginia, controls spent an average of 8.11 quarters before their initial jobs began. It follows, then, that there were, on average, 10.89 quarters of observation (19.00 − 8.11) remaining after those initial jobs began. The sixth row in Table 5-1 informs us that controls spent an average of 6.74 quarters employed. This is 61.8 percent of the quarters that occurred after controls found their first jobs (6.74/10.89).[7] Likewise, experimentals had 7.39 quarters before their initial jobs and 11.61 quarters (19.00 − 7.39) afterward. Experimentals spent more time employed: 7.28 quarters rather than 6.74. But the 62.7 percent of the quarters that experimentals worked after they initially found jobs (7.28/11.61) is virtually the same percentage of remaining time that controls spent in employment. In light of our earlier results, a reasonable interpretation of these percentage estimates is that the Virginia program

---

[7] Percentages, differences, and sums shown in tables are performed on unrounded estimates and may differ slightly from those obtained with a hand calculator on the rounded estimates.

accelerated initial job finding without noticeably affecting experimentals' success in holding their jobs or in finding jobs after the first one. The program speeded up initial employment but did not affect subsequent employment stability.

Before turning to results for the other three sites, it is useful to recapitulate briefly the main findings for Virginia. Over the entire follow-up period, members of the experimental group earned about 10 percent more than members of the control group. On average they were employed in about 8 percent more quarters, suggesting that the increase in their earnings was primarily the result of the increased likelihood that they would be employed in a given quarter. We found little difference between experimentals and controls in the average quarterly earnings of workers who were employed in a given quarter. In addition, all of the increase in quarters of employment occurred because the program reduced the amount of time that participants took to find their initial jobs, not because it led them to hold onto jobs longer. In fact, experimentals were about as likely to be employed in any quarter after starting their initial job as were controls.

Arkansas. We now discuss somewhat more briefly the findings from the other three experiments. As noted previously, Arkansas offered the least expensive package of program services and enrolled the most economically disadvantaged population. Arkansas residents who successfully applied for AFDC were poor even by the standards of the other three sites. Arkansas AFDC grant levels were very low, and the income threshold to qualify for public assistance in the state was correspondingly low. People who found welfare tolerable under those conditions probably faced quite bleak alternatives.

The poor earnings prospects of AFDC applicants and recipients in Arkansas are reflected in Table 5-1 by the extremely low levels of average earnings in both the experimental and the control groups. Through quarter nine, earnings among the controls averaged just $815 in annual terms. Through quarter twenty-two, control earnings averaged only $1,285 per year. Even though earnings in the experimental group were also very low, they were sharply higher in percentage terms than earnings in the control group. The annual gain in earnings during the early period was $234 per year, or 28.7 percent of the control mean; the average gain over the full follow-up period was $205 per year, or 16.0 percent of the control mean.

The average earnings of Arkansas women were necessarily

low because only a small percentage of them ever found jobs. By quarter nine, only about a third of controls had obtained a job. By the end of quarter twenty-two, less than half had found any UI-covered employment. Experimentals were more successful in finding employment, especially at the beginning of the follow-up period when they presumably were most affected by the program. The gap between the cumulative employment rates of experimentals and controls was 4.9 percentage points by the end of quarter nine but just 2.8 points by the end of the full follow-up period. As in Virginia, the cumulative employment rates in the two groups eventually tended to converge.

Because experimentals became employed earlier, it is not surprising that they were employed more quarters than controls. By the end of quarter nine, Arkansas experimentals held UI-covered jobs in 0.39 more quarters than controls. The percentage gain in quarters employed through quarter nine almost exactly matches the percentage gain in earnings. Quarters of employment rose 29.7 percent and total earnings rose 28.7 percent. In addition, during the first part of the follow-up period, experimentals and controls who worked earned almost the same, on average, in any quarter they were employed.

This picture changes strikingly over the full follow-up period. The percentage gain in experimental-group earnings was smaller than the percentage gain in quarters worked, indicating that the quarterly earnings of employed experimentals fell below those of employed controls in the later part of follow-up. Row seven of the Arkansas panel shows the size of the earnings drop. The quarterly earnings of employed experimentals were 5.5 percent lower than those of employed controls over the full follow-up period. Members of the Arkansas experimental group on average kept working at somewhat lower-paying jobs than did controls. Arkansas is unique among the four programs in exhibiting this kind of result. We consider explanations for it later in this chapter.

Even in Arkansas, however, most of total impact on earnings can be explained by increased employment. To see how much of the increase in number of quarters of employment is related to earlier job finding, we must examine our two statistics on the length of initial joblessness. Row eight in Table 5-1 shows the conditional speed of first employment. Among sample members who worked, experimentals found jobs nearly one full quarter earlier in the follow-up period than controls (in quarter 6.41 rather than quarter 7.28). The exact difference of 0.86 quarters is more than three times the effect in Virginia and suggests a correspondingly greater speed-up of initial employment.

In row nine, we include in the calculation the initial jobless spells of women who did *not* find employment. The difference between all experimentals and all controls in duration of initial joblessness is a negative 0.87 quarters. This differential is almost the same as the experimental-control difference in total quarters employed (0.87 quarters versus 0.97 quarters). A reasonable inference is that most of the gain in employment in Arkansas occurred as a result of earlier job finding. This is the same inference we drew regarding the program effect in Virginia. Applying the same formula as in Virginia indicates that about half the reduction in initial joblessness came from faster job finding for experimentals who would have worked anyway during the follow-up period (0.476 × −0.86/−0.87) and half for experimentals who would not have worked without the program.

Unlike the program in Virginia, however, Arkansas's program increased the average number of quarters employed by slightly *more* than it shortened the initial spell of joblessness. This implies that members of the Arkansas experimental group were somewhat more successful than controls in remaining employed once they initially obtained jobs. In Virginia, program-group members were just about as likely to remain employed as controls.

To see how much more successful experimentals were than controls in remaining employed, we performed the calculations whose results are displayed in the last row. To begin, the average control-group member in Arkansas was initially jobless for 13.52 quarters. The follow-up interval after the quarter of random assignment was twenty-one quarters, and it follows that there were 7.48 quarters remaining after the representative control initially found a job. Since controls had UI-covered earnings in 4.28 quarters, we can infer that they worked in 57.2 percent of the quarters after they first found employment (4.28/7.48). The same set of calculations for experimental-group members implies that experimentals worked in 62.8 percent (5.25/8.36) of the quarters after they first found jobs. Not only did experimental-group members find jobs 0.87 quarters earlier than controls, they were also more likely to hold a job in quarters after they first became employed.

In summary, the Arkansas program boosted employment in two ways. It accelerated initial job finding, and it raised the probability of employment in each of the quarters after experimental-group members initially found jobs. At the same time, however, employed experimentals earned less in each quarter they worked than did employed controls. The difference in these conditional quarterly earnings was most pronounced in the later half of the follow-up period.

One plausible explanation for this overall pattern is that the Arkansas program, in addition to speeding job entry, made work seem more attractive or the alternatives to work seem less attractive. Once they began to work, some program enrollees may have found they wanted to work more than they earlier thought they would. For others, overcoming initial barriers to employment (e.g., child care problems, fears about working, lack of knowledge about how to find a job) may have made continuing to work relatively easy. At the same time, by raising the perceived cost—the psychic cost, stigma, or "hassle"—associated with applying for and receiving AFDC, the program may have deterred members of the experimental group from leaving low-paying jobs to reapply for AFDC. The common aspect of these several explanations is a change in the relative attractiveness of work versus welfare, or a change in the "work ethic," without any change in actual enrollee earning power. As we see later in this chapter, a "relative attractiveness" hypothesis is consistent with other aspects of employment patterns among Arkansas experimentals.[8] In addition, the next chapter shows such a hypothesis to be consistent with the evidence on AFDC recidivism in Arkansas, too.

Baltimore. The full follow-up period in Baltimore runs through quarter twenty-one, but it contains two subperiods. The first of these covers the eleven quarters from quarter two through quarter twelve. The second covers the three quarters from quarter nineteen through quarter twenty-one. As already noted, earnings data for quarters thirteen through eighteen are lacking. In any discussion of the "full" employment and earnings follow-up in Baltimore, we utilize only the fourteen available quarters from quarter two through quarter twenty-one. The six-quarter gap does not seriously degrade the measures examined in this chap-

---

[8]The evidence appears to rule out the principal alternative hypotheses that the Arkansas program (a) placed some experimentals in low-paying jobs they otherwise would not have accepted or (b) increased employment among individuals with below-average earning power. As shown later, initial jobs of experimentals did not, on average, pay less than those of controls, a result which is at odds with both alternative hypotheses.

ter, although we restrict some measures to cover only the first three years of follow-up (i.e., the pre-gap period).[9] Even without any help from the program, Baltimore controls had better employment experiences than control-group members in other sites. Both their employment rates and their earnings exceeded those of the Virginia and San Diego control groups, at least moderately, and greatly exceeded those of the Arkansas control group. Members of the Baltimore experimental group did even better. The gain in annual earnings through quarter nine was $317, or 14.8 percent of the control mean. The gain over the full fourteen quarters of earnings data was $394 per year, or 13.5 percent of the control mean.

Earnings gains in the first part of follow-up were at least partly attributable to quicker job finding in the experimental group. By the end of quarter nine, 5.9 percentage points more experimentals than controls had found jobs in the UI-covered sector. As in Virginia and Arkansas, the cumulative employment rate for the control group tended eventually to rise towards the rate for the experimental group. At the end of the full follow-up period, the experimental-control difference had narrowed to just 2.1 percentage points.

Average earnings were higher in the experimental group than in the control group for two reasons. Experimentals were more likely to be employed, and when employed they earned somewhat higher quarterly wages. During the full follow-up period, experimentals were employed in 0.41 (or 8.1 percent) more quarters. Over this same period, the quarterly earnings of employed experimentals were $2,088, or 5.0 percent more than the quarterly earnings of employed controls. Thus, more than the other three programs, Baltimore apparently succeeded in raising the quarterly earnings of participants who found jobs.

We interpret this result as the natural consequence of the Baltimore program's somewhat greater emphasis on human capital development relative to low-cost job search assistance. The quarterly earnings gains were especially strong during the later part of the follow-up period. This apparent delay may indicate that human capital effects develop gradually from a lengthy investment period and lag behind any initial employment acceleration effects.

[9] The measures defined for Baltimore in Table 5-1 treat quarters thirteen through eighteen as nonexistent and count the last quarter as quarter twenty-one, following the same convention as in the other sites.

Although part of the Baltimore program's effect on *total* earnings came from increased quarterly earnings, much of the *initial* earnings gains came from increased employment. Most of this gain occurred because experimentals found their first jobs earlier than controls. Among the experimentals who found jobs, initial employment began 0.84 quarters earlier (quarter 5.86 for experimentals versus quarter 6.70 for controls), about the size of the same effect in Arkansas. Among all experimentals, including those who did not find jobs, the initial spell of joblessness averaged 7.43 quarters. This was almost one quarter—0.98 quarters to be exact—less than the average spell of initial joblessness among controls. In fact, the decline in the average length of the initial spell of joblessness was larger than the 0.41 increase in the average number of quarters of employment, indicating some loss of employment later on.[10] Multiplying the control-group fraction "ever employed" by the difference in "first quarter employed," as we did for the other programs, indicates that about two-thirds of the reduction in initial joblessness was associated with faster job finding by experimentals who would have worked during the follow-up period even without the program and one-third with job finding by experimentals who would not have worked.

On average, controls were initially jobless for 8.41 quarters through quarter twenty-one. They were employed for 5.14 out of the observed fourteen quarters. If we account for the six-quarter gap in earnings data,[11] we calculate that controls were employed in 66.5 percent of quarters after first becoming em-

---

[10] The six-quarter gap in Baltimore earnings data slightly affects the comparison in the sentence in the text. The −0.98 impact on number of quarters of initial joblessness applies to the interval between quarters two and twenty-one but is probably not affected much by the missing quarters, since employment starting in the missing interval would be counted as starting in quarter nineteen. On the other hand, the +0.41 impact on number of quarters employed may have been slightly reduced by the missing quarters. To assess the extent of any possible bias, we obtained a corrected estimate of the impact on number of quarters of employment by assuming that the employment rate for experimentals and controls for the missing six quarters is a simple average of the average quarterly employment rates of year three and year five (quarters nine through twelve and nineteen through twenty-one, respectively), as given in Chapter 4. This assumption gives +0.54 as the Baltimore program's estimated impact on number of quarters of employment over the full follow-up period, quarters two through twenty-one. This alternative estimate is not very different from +0.41 and is also smaller than −0.98. Thus, the comparison in the text appears not to be significantly biased or misleading.

[11] We interpolate the missing six quarters using the year before and the year after the gap, as described in the previous note. We obtain similar results if we interpolate using only year-five employment or using the full observed follow-up.

ployed. Experimentals were initially jobless for 7.43 quarters, on average, and were employed in 65.6 percent of the remaining quarters. Thus, like experimentals in Virginia, experimentals in Baltimore were about as successful as controls in remaining employed after finding their first job.

San Diego SWIM. Virtually the entire earnings impact in SWIM, both for the early period and the full follow-up, is associated with the increase in the average number of quarters employed. From quarters two through nine, the number of quarters employed rose by 27.1 percent in the program group, slightly exceeding the 25.3 percent increase in total earnings over the same period. From quarters two through twenty-one, the increases for employment and earnings were 16.7 percent and 14.8 percent, respectively. Average earnings per quarter employed in the experimental group were roughly the same as in the control group.

The gain in quarters of employment appears to have come mainly from accelerated job finding in the experimental group rather than from more stable, longer-lasting jobs. This acceleration can be seen in the "ever employed" and "first quarter employed" statistics. The increase in "ever employed through quarter nine" was quite large compared with the other programs. Some 50.8 percent of controls worked during the two years. This figure rose to 62.5 percent for experimentals, an increase of 11.8 percentage points. As elsewhere, the cumulative employment effect declined over time. Nevertheless, for the full five-year follow-up period, SWIM still had a 7.1 percentage point impact on this measure, two to three times the full follow-up effect in the other programs. This large five-year "ever employed" effect suggests that many experimentals who would never have worked—or would have worked only after a number of years— were induced to take jobs. At the same time, among sample members who worked, the first quarter of employment was earlier for experimentals than for controls: 5.31 versus 6.36, for a −1.04 difference, the largest among the four programs for this measure. These results are consistent with accelerated job finding. We calculate that about a third of the reduction in quarters of initial joblessness came from faster job finding by experimentals who would have worked during the follow-up period even without the program; about two-thirds came from job finding by experimentals who would not have worked in the absence of SWIM.

Members of the control group experienced 9.43 quarters of

initial joblessness, whereas members of the experimental group had only 7.54 quarters of initial joblessness. The negative difference of 1.89 quarters exceeds the 0.97 increase in number of quarters of employment, the result of some instability of employment after the start of the first job. This employment instability appears to be no greater for experimentals than for controls, however. The two groups were about equally successful in remaining employed at any point after they began their first jobs. In the control group, sample members were employed, on average, 5.81 quarters out of the 10.57 quarters that followed the end of the initial spell of joblessness (20.00 − 9.43 quarters), which translates into an employment ratio of 55.0 percent. In the experimental group, the corresponding figure was 54.4 percent, indicating that working experimentals were no more nor less successful in remaining employed after initially starting a job.

We conclude that the earnings impact of the San Diego SWIM program came from its impact on job finding. Members of the experimental group found more jobs during the observation period—especially during the first two years of follow-up—than did controls. Job finders in both groups were equally likely to remain employed after their first jobs commenced. Experimentals therefore worked more quarters in total. Jobs provided approximately the same quarterly earnings for employed members of both groups, but the larger number of quarters worked made total earnings larger in the experimental group.

QUALITY OF INITIAL EMPLOYMENT

In this section, we examine two aspects of job quality: quarterly earnings when employed and job turnover. Because the programs under study produced important effects on initial job finding, we now focus specifically on the quality of workers' initial employment. We hope to determine (a) whether the programs increased or decreased initial job quality and (b) whether there was a link between initial job quality and a program's longer-term earnings impact.

Program graduates may obtain higher-quality initial jobs if job search assistance improves their information about the labor market. It may help them find jobs they previously would not have encountered, possibly because they were not aware of such jobs or did not know where to look for them. At the same time, through better knowledge about labor market opportunities and the value of the skills they possess, enrollees may accept better jobs than they would have before. Efforts by program staff in developing higher-quality job placements may also contribute to this effect. Finally, better skills acquired through education or training, where these activities are offered, should increase the quality of jobs that enrollees obtain.

On the other hand, welfare-to-work programs could promote employment in inferior jobs for two reasons. In order to achieve high placement rates, job counselors might try to influence enrollees to accept lower-quality employment than they would in the absence of the program. Alternatively, AFDC applicants or recipients might regard the work program as an unwanted additional burden involved in receiving public assistance. In that case, the work program would raise the perceived cost—and, hence, reduce the attractiveness—of receiving AFDC. Even without aiding enrollees in their search for work, the program would produce an increase in employment because more enrollees would accept jobs they otherwise would have refused. We might expect these additional jobs to be of inferior quality.

In any case, the link between first job quality and longer-term program impacts on earnings may or may not be a strong one. Inferior initial jobs may well be followed by inferior future jobs and weak attachment to employment. But it may be that a rather wide range of jobs, even low-wage jobs, can provide valuable experience that will improve subsequent earning power. In addition, many labor economists believe that career paths leading to high-wage jobs often start at low wages.[12] When it comes to higher-quality initial jobs, later effects are also uncertain. Higher-quality first jobs may continue as high-quality jobs for a long time, adding to longer-term program earnings impacts. Conversely, enrollees placed in high-wage jobs may be unable to sustain those jobs or to move up to even better positions if they have not been given the requisite skills. As may be seen in the estimates reported earlier, average earnings among employed control sample members increase over time. What looked like a better quality placement early on may eventually begin to look like an inferior job if the program graduate is not equipped to advance.

---

[12] Human capital theory predicts that jobs with relatively high rates of wage growth will begin at relatively low wages. The lower initial wage level accepted by an individual is seen as an investment whose return comes in the form of higher wages later.

The information available does not enable us to identify specific "jobs" in the usual sense of work with a single employer. Instead we examine sample members' *first spell of employment* after the quarter of random assignment. We define the first spell of employment as the first continuous series of quarters with earnings, ended either by a quarter of zero earnings or by the end of the follow-up period, whichever comes first. This spell may begin in quarter two, or it may begin later if there are no earnings in quarter two.[13] For many sample members, there will be no initial spell of employment. In some cases the first spell will consist of only a single quarter, followed immediately by a quarter of joblessness. In other cases it will consist of a long string of quarters with earnings, continuing through the end of the follow-up period. This string might contain information from several different jobs, but we treat it as part of a single employment episode.

Analysis Issues.   Several analytical issues must be addressed before we examine the initial employment spell. One set of issues concerns the average duration of the first employment spell. Because sample members obtained their jobs in different quarters and because the follow-up period has a fixed duration, it would be misleading to calculate only the simple average of *observed* spell lengths. The average observed duration of initial employment spells could be longer in one group than in another, not because initial employment lasted longer, but merely because it began earlier. To eliminate this potential bias and create a level playing field, we restrict our attention to employment spells that began by the end of quarter five (i.e., by the end of the fourth quarter after the quarter of random assignment), and we track each initial employment spell for no longer than eight quarters. Under these conventions, all employment spells, whether they begin as early as quarter two or as late as quarter five, can contain

---

[13] If there are earnings in quarter two and quarter one, then the first employment spell is still deemed to start in quarter two. To make all aspects of our definition clear, consider a sequence of quarters with earnings beginning before random assignment and continuing through quarter one and thereafter. For some sample members, such an unbroken sequence will occur even when there is job loss and reemployment in quarter one or between quarters one and two. For those individuals, quarter two will contain earnings at the start of a new job (or at least near the start of a new job that began in quarter one). For others, a continuous stream of pre-/post-random assignment earnings quarters will represent one job held continuously. The start of the "first spell of employment" in quarter two will therefore represent the first post-enrollment spell but will not represent the start of a new job. For the purpose of studying program effects, this particular way of classifying such a sequence is the appropriate one.

only the same maximum number of quarters. In addition, only data through quarter twelve are used for the computations. We can therefore sidestep problems created by the gap in earnings data following quarter twelve in Baltimore. It should be understood, however, that our average duration statistics report the average "truncated" spell duration. They will serve to show us whether experimentals have more short (i.e., less than two years) initial employment spells, but they would seriously underestimate total spell duration if we were to use them for that purpose. We do, however, supplement our average duration statistic with graphs illustrating duration of the initial employment spell through the end of follow-up for Virginia and Arkansas.

To be sure, in every one of the four program samples, more members of the experimental group than the control group obtained employment by the end of quarter five. A comparison between the two groups is therefore not a true experimental comparison and must be interpreted cautiously when we attempt to infer the effect of each program on job quality. One example will show why. Suppose the comparison shows that experimental-group members who worked obtained, on average, inferior initial employment. The naive interpretation would be that the program reduced initial job quality. This interpretation might well be wrong. It might be that among those experimentals who would have obtained jobs in the absence of the program, initial job quality did not suffer. The apparent reduction in quality instead occurred as a result of employment by experimental-group members who would not otherwise have worked. The jobs such individuals found may well have been of below-average quality compared with those of other job finders simply because the new job finders do not have the experience or skills to find the better quality jobs. Their earnings capacity, although not yet on a par with the average, may even have improved as a result of the program. A naive interpretation of the empirical comparison would in this case completely misrepresent the real accomplishment of the program.

Comparisons between working experimentals and controls can provide information under certain conditions, however, provided the results are interpreted with caution. If initial job quality among employed experimentals is found to be lower than among employed controls, we cannot tell whether the program led to a real deterioration of job quality or increased employment among enrollees of lesser skill and earning power. On the other hand, if it turns out that initial job quality is just as high among employed experimentals as among employed controls, then it would be most unlikely that the program caused job quality to fall. Lastly, if job quality among employed experimentals were higher, then a plausible, though not certain, inference would be that the program improved job quality, at least for a few.[14]

One additional analytical issue must be dealt with, this time in connection with measuring initial earnings. In calculating initial earnings, we want to measure earnings as close to the start of the initial employment spell as possible. At the same time, however, we would like to measure earnings in a quarter when the worker is fully employed. But the first quarter of employment in a spell is unlikely to be one in which an individual is employed for a full thirteen weeks, if only because a new job hardly ever begins on the very first day of a quarter. On the other hand, if we were to ignore wage information from the first quarter of a spell, we would often exclude information about a nontrivial share of employment, since many initial employment spells last only a month. We therefore define initial earnings as the higher quarterly earnings amounts of (a) the first quarter of initial employment and (b) the quarter immediately thereafter. If the employment spell lasts only one quarter, or if the worker is paid less in the second quarter than the first, the first quarter's earnings are used. Otherwise earnings in the next quarter are used. To simplify interpretation, we annualize the quarterly earnings amounts by multiplying by four.

Virginia. The top panel of Table 5-2 contains information about durations of initial employment spells and the distribution of initial earnings in the Virginia sample. The first row of the panel shows the percentage of experimentals and controls who found employment by the end of quarter five. As noted earlier, experimentals enjoyed an advantage over controls in early job finding. Some 45.9 percent of controls found jobs, compared with 49.4 percent of experimentals, an increase of 3.5 percentage points.

All the rows after the first display statistics pertaining to the subsample of persons employed by quarter five. The third row shows that the advantage in job finding for experimentals did not lead to a measurable decline in average duration of initial

---

[14] Two other sources of potential error should be mentioned. First, since we examine only initial employment spells, we cannot be sure what happened in subsequent spells. Second, we do not examine all initial employment spells. In particular, women who first became employed after the fifth quarter are excluded from the results shown in Table 5-2.

employment spells. The average duration of initial employment spells, when spell length is truncated at eight quarters, is slightly higher for experimentals than for controls: 4.53 quarters versus 4.40 quarters, respectively.

The full distributions of spell durations through sixteen quarters, for both experimentals and controls, are displayed for Virginia in Figure 5-3(a). The downward sloping curved lines in the figure show the percentage of initial job finders who remained employed in successive quarters after first finding their jobs. Notice that, in Virginia, the experimental and control distributions are similar. The solid line beneath the main panel shows the experimental-control difference. For Virginia, this difference at first widened slightly over time and then narrowed, indicating that experimentals early on tended to remain employed a bit longer but later converged with controls. This evidence suggests that employment turnover was not increased by the program. It may well have fallen slightly, at least initially.

The fourth row of Table 5-2 shows average annualized earnings at the start of the initial employment spell. Average initial earnings were approximately the same for employed experimentals and controls. The distribution of initial earnings for the two groups is shown immediately below. Members of the experimental group were more likely to have low earnings (below $6,000 a year), but they were also slightly more likely to earn relatively high amounts (above $12,000 a year). These estimates therefore do not provide conclusive evidence that the Virginia program consistently either raised or lowered initial earnings.

Arkansas. Data on initial employment spells in Arkansas are presented in the second panel of Table 5-2 and in Figure

TABLE 5-2
Comparison of Initial Job Quality

Program and Outcome	Experimentals	Controls	Difference
Virginia			
Ever employed in quarters 2–5 (%)	49.4	45.9	3.5 **
If ever employed in quarters 2–5:[a]			
Length of first employment spell in quarters			
Truncated at four quarters	2.93	2.90	0.03 (z)
Truncated at eight quarters	4.53	4.40	0.14 (z)
Initial earnings, annualized[b]			
Average ($)	5,209	5,245	−36 (z)
Distribution (%)			
$1–$5,999	64.2	59.9	4.3 (z)
$6,000–$11,999	29.2	34.7	−5.5 (z)
$12,000 or more	6.6	5.4	1.2 (z)

TABLE 5-2 *(continued)*

Program and Outcome	Experimentals	Controls	Difference
Arkansas			
Ever employed in quarters 2–5 (%)	29.8	24.5	5.4**
If ever employed in quarters 2–5:[a]			
Length of first employment spell in quarters			
Truncated at four quarters	*2.94*	*2.83*	*0.11 (z)*
Truncated at eight quarters	*4.60*	*4.25*	*0.34 (z)*
Initial earnings, annualized[b]			
Average ($)	*4,744*	*4,516*	*228 (z)*
Distribution (%)			
$1–$5,999	*65.4*	*67.4*	*−2.0 (z)*
$6,000–$11,999	*30.8*	*29.9*	*0.9 (z)*
$12,000 or more	*3.7*	*2.7*	*1.0 (z)*
Baltimore			
Ever employed in quarters 2–5 (%)	51.0	43.9	7.2***
If ever employed in quarters 2–5:[a]			
Length of first employment spell in quarters			
Truncated at four quarters	*2.88*	*2.95*	*−0.06 (z)*
Truncated at eight quarters	*4.57*	*4.60*	*−0.03 (z)*
Initial earnings, annualized[b]			
Average ($)	*6,031*	*6,023*	*7 (z)*
Distribution (%)			
$1–$5,999	*58.0*	*58.8*	*−0.7 (z)*
$6,000–$11,999	*31.7*	*31.5*	*0.2 (z)*
$12,000 or more	*10.3*	*9.8*	*0.5 (z)*
San Diego SWIM			
Ever employed in quarters 2–5 (%)	51.7	40.4	11.3***
If ever employed in quarters 2–5:[a]			
Length of first employment spell in quarters			
Truncated at four quarters	*2.83*	*2.80*	*0.03 (z)*
Truncated at eight quarters	*4.25*	*4.20*	*0.05 (z)*
Initial earnings, annualized[b]			
Average ($)	*6,396*	*6,669*	*−273 (z)*
Distribution (%)			
$1–$5,999	*57.3*	*55.6*	*1.6 (z)*
$6,000–$11,999	*30.4*	*28.6*	*1.8 (z)*
$12,000 or more	*12.6*	*15.8*	*−3.2 (z)*

NOTES: Details may not sum to totals owing to rounding.

Italics indicate nonexperimental estimates.

A two-tailed t-test was applied to experimental differences. Statistical significance levels are indicated as: * = 10 percent; ** = 5 percent; *** = 1 percent. (z) indicates that the comparison is nonexperimental: no test of statistical significance was performed.

[a] Calculations in rows below are only for the subsample members ever employed in quarters two through five.

[b] "Initial earnings" are defined as the maximum of earnings in the first quarter of employment and the quarter following, multiplied by four.

FIGURE 5-3

Probability of Remaining Employed During First Employment Spell: (a) Virginia; (b) Arkansas

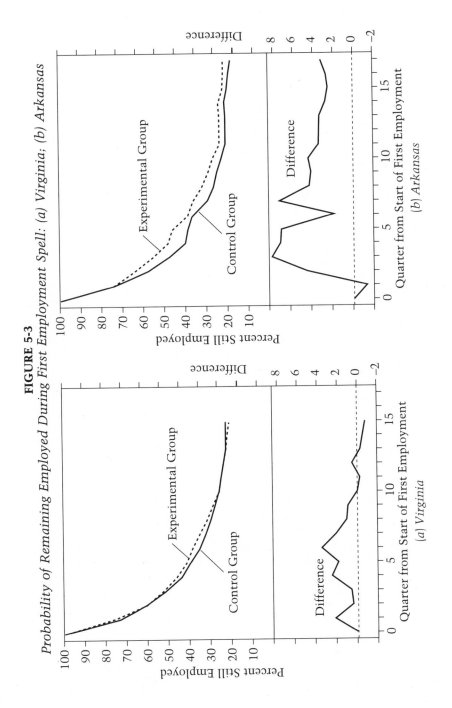

5-3(b). Both the table and the figure show that experimentals were somewhat more successful than controls in attaining long, unbroken spells of employment. As shown in the table, employment between quarters two and five was 5.4 percentage points greater for experimentals than controls. Initial employment spells (truncated at eight quarters) averaged 0.34 quarters longer for employed experimentals than for employed controls. The figure indicates that approximately 8 percentage points more experimentals than controls had initial employment spells lasting at least four quarters, and 7 percentage points more had spells lasting at least eight quarters. Experimental-group members not only found employment faster, they held onto initial employment longer.

The table provides little indication that experimentals who became employed in the first five quarters initially earned less than controls who became employed in the same period. Rather, the distribution of earnings among experimentals was slightly shifted towards the upper earnings brackets. Initial annualized earnings for employed experimentals were $228 (or 5 percent) higher than for employed controls. We have already shown, however, that average quarterly earnings among employed experimentals eventually fell below average quarterly earnings received by employed controls. This occurred later on in the follow-up, apparently because experimentals in intermittent, part-time, or low-wage employment were less likely than controls to leave the labor market. It is notable that initial job quality did not predict later employment and earnings patterns.

Baltimore. In Baltimore, the increase in employment from quarters two through five amounted to 7.2 percentage points, greater than in Virginia and Arkansas. Yet the evidence indicates that experimentals obtained jobs similar to those of controls. Employed experimentals and controls had almost identical initial spell durations. Initial earnings averaged about the same, and distributions of initial earnings were also quite similar. This absence of differences in initial employment quality is of some interest, given that Baltimore was the only one of the four programs to show larger earnings per quarter of employment over the full follow-up period and a statistically significant earnings impact in the final follow-up year. In light of these later differences, we might have expected some differences in the initial employment spell. The pattern we observe, however, does not suggest a strong association between initial employment quality and longer-term earnings impact.

San Diego SWIM. The increase in employment from quarters two through five for San Diego SWIM was the largest of the four programs, 11.3 percentage points. As in Baltimore, the duration of initial employment was almost the same for employed experimentals and controls. Earnings at the start of the first employment spell were lower for employed experimentals, however. Annualized initial earnings were $273 lower, or 4.1 percent of the control mean. The distribution statistics indicate that fewer experimentals began in the top earning bracket and more began in the bottom and middle brackets. This is the only evidence that any of the four programs led experimentals to take jobs of poorer quality than was typical for controls. It is not clear, however, that these initial earnings levels were associated with any lasting effect. For one thing, they were not accompanied by shorter initial employment duration. In addition, as we indicated earlier, average earnings per employed quarter over the full follow-up period and over year two and the final year were about the same for experimentals and controls.

Summary Assessment of Initial Job Quality. We find no evidence that any of the four programs produced shorter initial employment spells. We find some differences in initial earnings but no apparent connection between initial earnings and subsequent impacts on earnings. Arkansas, which showed a positive initial earnings difference, did not have large long-term earnings effects. Baltimore showed no difference in initial earnings, yet had relatively large earnings impacts later on, impacts which held up through the end of the observation period. San Diego SWIM showed a negative difference for initial earnings, but this did not appear to carry over into later quarters. In fact, it is noted in the next section that earnings per employed quarter for the full follow-up period and for year two and the final year in San Diego SWIM were similar for experimentals and controls.

This evidence does not support the view that *only* placement into "good" jobs (i.e., stable, high-paying jobs) can lead to impacts on earnings and AFDC receipt. At the same time, these results do not mean that higher initial earnings do not pay off for particular individuals. Nor do they rule out the possibility that other programs which placed many more enrollees in higher-paying jobs would have even greater long-term impact on earnings. Arkansas, the single instance we found of higher initial earnings, did not produce relatively large long-term earnings gains, but this instance may not generalize well to different kinds of programs. The Arkansas program featured only job search assistance and unpaid work experience. Programs which upgrade skills through education or training may produce graduates who are better able to sustain increased pay rates (and growth in pay) over the long term.

These results should be interpreted cautiously. We have only examined quarterly earnings data. Information on hourly wage rates, weekly hours, and start and end dates of particular jobs would clearly help our assessment. In addition, we looked only at jobs beginning in quarters two through five, a period in which these programs produced significant increases in employment. For long activity sequences, which might occur with extended training, it might be appropriate to look also at jobs beginning after that period. Our understanding would also be improved if we had information on more programs and other kinds of programs, especially those placing more emphasis on education or training. Finally, it should be remembered that the comparisons we have made between *employed* experimentals and controls are nonexperimental comparisons, which reduces our ability to describe with certainty the connection between group differences and causal effects.

EARLY AND LATER PROGRAM EFFECTS
ON PATTERNS OF EMPLOYMENT

In this section, we compare work patterns early on in the follow-up period with patterns at the end.

Virginia. Table 5-3 compares employment and earnings responses during the second follow-up year (quarters five through eight) with responses during the final follow-up year. The quarters that make up the "final year" may differ across programs. For Virginia, the final follow-up year includes quarters seventeen through twenty. Since random assignment occurred in quarter one, the final follow-up year in Virginia came well after program enrollees would have terminated their assigned activities and initial involvement with the program.

Program effects in the final follow-up year were clearly smaller than in the second follow-up year. A number of measures are shown in the table; for none was the experimental-control difference statistically significant during the final year. The impact on earnings declined from $282 to $201. The decline was actually somewhat greater than indicated by these numbers, since the dollar estimates in the table were not deflated.

Applying an inflation adjustment to earnings would make the average earnings gain in the final year less than two-thirds the gain during the second year.

The decline of employment effects was even more pronounced than the decline in earnings effects. In year two there was more than a 5 percentage point increase in the number of experimentals "ever employed" in the year, but this fell to 1.6 percentage points in the final year. The increase in number of quarters with employment was only one-fourth as large in the final year as in year two. The increase in the "percent employed all four quarters in year" fell from a statistically significant amount in year two almost to zero.

Differences in the earnings distributions, shown in the last four rows of this panel of the table, also shrank over time. During the second follow-up year, members of the experimental group were less likely to have no earnings for the year. They were more likely to earn in the bottom bracket (less than $6,000) and somewhat more likely to earn in the top bracket (more than $12,000). Each of these differences is statistically significant. By the final follow-up year, however, the earnings distribution of controls had shifted upward. Fewer controls remained jobless throughout the year, and more had entered the middle and upper earnings brackets. With this movement upward, controls began to catch up with experimentals. As a consequence, experimental-control differences in all brackets were far smaller in the final year than in the second. By that time, controls had attained almost the same employment rate as experimentals, and their earnings pattern was similar.

The only measure to show an increased differential over time was earnings per employed quarter. For this conditional measure of job quality, the difference between experimentals and controls more than doubled from the second to the final year. In year two, very little of the earnings gain was associated with greater earnings per quarter employed (1.6 percentage points of the 14.2 percent increase in earnings); in the final year, the share was about half. Larger earnings per quarter employed in the later part of follow-up suggests some impact on earnings capacity, either through skill development, additional experience in the labor market, or enhanced ability to find jobs with long-term earnings growth. Nevertheless, the difference in this measure amounted to only 3 percent of the control mean.

Taken together, the estimates shown in Table 5-3 are consistent with the conclusion that the main program effect in Virginia

TABLE 5-3

Short- and Longer-Term Impacts on Patterns of Employment

Program and Outcome	Year Two				Final Year[a]			
	Experimentals	Controls	Difference	Diff/Ctrls × 100	Experimentals	Controls	Difference	Diff/Ctrls × 100
Virginia								
Average earnings in year ($)	2,269	1,987	282**	14.2%	3,674	3,473	201	5.8%
Ever employed in year (%)	52.3	47.1	5.2***	(x)	53.4	51.9	1.6	(x)
Number of quarters employed in year	1.47	1.31	0.16***	12.4%	1.67	1.63	0.04	2.7%
Average earnings per quarter employed in year ($)[b]	1,546	1,521	25 (z)	1.6%	2,199	2,135	64 (z)	3.0%
Employed all four quarters in year (%)	22.6	19.4	3.1**	(x)	29.9	29.4	0.4	(x)
Earnings in year (%)								
None	47.7	52.9	-5.2***	(x)	46.6	48.1	-1.6	(x)
$1-$5,999	38.2	33.8	4.5**	(x)	28.3	26.4	1.9	(x)
$6,000-$11,999	10.5	11.1	-0.6	(x)	16.1	17.1	-1.0	(x)
$12,000 or more	3.6	2.2	1.4**	(x)	9.0	8.3	0.7	(x)
Arkansas								
Average earnings in year ($)	1,181	956	224	23.5%	2,019	1,935	84	4.3%
Ever employed in year (%)	31.7	26.7	4.9**	(x)	36.7	31.8	4.9*	(x)
Number of quarters employed in year	0.89	0.71	0.19**	26.1%	1.15	1.00	0.15*	15.1%
Average earnings per quarter employed in year ($)[b]	1,320	1,348	-28 (z)	-2.1%	1,762	1,944	-182 (z)	-9.4%
Employed all four quarters in year (%)	14.3	9.7	4.7**	(x)	19.8	18.2	1.6	(x)
Earnings in year (%)								
None	68.3	73.3	-4.9**	(x)	63.3	68.2	-4.9*	(x)
$1-$5,999	24.5	20.6	3.9*	(x)	21.4	19.5	1.9	(x)
$6,000-$11,999	6.5	5.3	1.2	(x)	12.0	7.5	4.5***	(x)
$12,000 or more	0.7	0.9	-0.2	(x)	3.3	4.9	-1.6	(x)

Baltimore

Average earnings in year ($)	2,784	2,389	395***	16.5%	5,307	4,832	475*
Ever employed in year (%)	53.6	49.0	4.6***	(x)	58.5	58.1	0.4
Number of quarters employed in year	1.53	1.37	0.16***	11.7%	1.95	1.89	0.06
Average earnings per quarter employed in year ($)[b]	1,819	1,743	76 (z)	4.3%	2,727	2,559	167 (z)
Employed all four quarters in year (%)	24.5	20.1	4.4***	(x)	38.4	36.3	2.2
Earnings in year (%)							
None	46.4	51.0	-4.6***	(x)	41.5	41.9	-0.4
$1–$5,999	34.4	33.2	1.2	(x)	24.4	26.3	-1.8
$6,000–$11,999	13.9	11.7	2.2*	(x)	16.3	15.7	0.6
$12,000 or more	5.3	4.2	1.1	(x)	17.7	16.1	1.6

(final column, Baltimore): Average earnings 9.8%; Ever employed (x); Number of quarters 3.1%; Average earnings per quarter 6.5%; Employed all four quarters (x); None (x); $1–$5,999 (x); $6,000–$11,999 (x); $12,000 or more (x)

San Diego SWIM

Average earnings in year ($)	2,735	2,109	626***	29.7%	4,126	3,978	148
Ever employed in year (%)	50.6	40.1	10.4***	(x)	43.3	41.7	1.6
Number of quarters employed in year	1.40	1.09	0.31***	28.4%	1.33	1.28	0.05
Average earnings per quarter employed in year ($)[b]	1,947	1,928	19 (z)	1.0%	3,100	3,108	-9 (z)
Employed all four quarters in year (%)	21.0	15.9	5.1***	(x)	23.6	22.2	1.4
Earnings in year (%)							
None	49.4	59.9	-10.4***	(x)	56.7	58.3	-1.6
$1–$5,999	32.6	26.8	5.7***	(x)	19.2	19.1	0.1
$6,000–$11,999	12.6	8.5	4.1***	(x)	11.0	8.9	2.1**
$12,000 or more	5.4	4.8	0.6	(x)	13.2	13.7	-0.5

(final column, San Diego SWIM): Average earnings 3.7%; Ever employed (x); Number of quarters 4.0%; Average earnings per quarter -0.3%; Employed all four quarters (x); None (x); $1–$5,999 (x); $6,000–$11,999 (x); $12,000 or more (x)

NOTES: Details may not sum to totals owing to rounding.

Italics indicate nonexperimental estimates.

A two-tailed t-test was applied to experimental differences. Statistical significance levels are indicated as: * = 10 percent; ** = 5 percent; *** = 1 percent. (z) indicates that the comparison is nonexperimental: no test of statistical significance was performed. (x) indicates that the percentage difference is not relevant.

[a]"Final year" of follow-up is defined as follows: Virginia, quarters seventeen through twenty; Arkansas quarters nineteen through twenty-two; Baltimore, quarters nineteen through twenty-one times 4/3; San Diego SWIM, quarters eighteen through twenty-one.

[b]Calculated only for quarters with employment.

was to accelerate the employment of experimentals into jobs similar to those that would be found by this population without program assistance. In addition, the decline of employment effects over time appears not to result only from "wearing-off" of program effects on enrollees. Rather, the narrowing of experimental-control differential in employment seems also to be the natural result of a steady increase in employment among controls: the various employment measures for controls eventually "catch up" with the rates for experimentals. For example, only 47.1 percent of controls were employed at all in year two, but this number rose to 51.9 percent by the final year, nearly a 5 percentage point increase. The corresponding increase for experimentals was only about one percentage point (from 52.3 percent to 53.4 percent). The number of controls employed for all four quarters increased even more: from 19.4 percent in year two to 29.4 percent in the final year, overtaking the corresponding experimental-group rate. Part of this catch-up may stem from receipt of services by controls late in the follow-up period, after the experiment-imposed embargo on services ended.

Arkansas. The time pattern of response in Arkansas is similar in some ways to the pattern just described for Virginia. But in certain crucial respects it differs: even though the program effect on earnings declined sharply by the final follow-up year, the employment effect remained in evidence; at the same time, average earnings per quarter employed among members of the experimental group *fell* in relation to earnings received by working controls.

The final follow-up year in Arkansas covers quarters nineteen through twenty-two. The experimental-control differential in number of quarters employed was almost the same in the final year as it was in the second. The earnings impact, however, went from $224 to $84 in current dollars, which translates to a decline of approximately two-thirds after adjusting for inflation.

In the final year, 36.7 percent of experimentals were employed compared with 31.8 percent of controls. The employment impact was therefore still 4.9 percentage points, the same as in year two. In the second year, experimental-group members worked in 26.1 percent more quarters than controls and earned 23.5 percent more earnings. In the final year, experimentals worked in 15.1 percent more quarters but received only 4.3 percent more earnings than controls. In that year, their average earnings per quarter employed was 9.4 percent *lower* than the comparable quarterly earnings of employed controls. Lower quarterly earnings offset nearly all the gain from increased employment.

In Virginia, the decline of the average earnings impact was associated with control catch-up in employment, offset by somewhat higher average earnings per quarter of employment among working experimentals. By contrast, the results for Arkansas suggest that other influences, in addition to catch-up, were at work in that state. The overall pattern of response suggests that the Arkansas program did not simply help enrollees search for employment. The response pattern is instead consistent with a change in enrollees' subjective appraisals of the costs and benefits of work relative to remaining on AFDC. That is, the program raised the willingness of some experimentals to remain with intermittent or part-time employment or with low wage rates they would have rejected in the absence of the program. If this relative cost hypothesis is correct, then the program would also reduce participants' willingness to accept the major alternative to employment, namely, receipt of public assistance. The program would, in effect, have deterred them from returning to the AFDC rolls. We investigate this possibility further in the next chapter.

To some extent, this kind of deterrence may be part of the explanation of program effects in other sites. That the effect was more evident in Arkansas may stem from the low monthly grant levels in that state. Small changes in perceptions or attitudes towards work and welfare may be more likely to have an effect where the benefit from remaining on AFDC—that is, the size of the grant amount—is low. In weighing these inferences, the reader should bear in mind that the small sample size in Arkansas reduces our confidence that the statistical estimates accurately reflect an underlying reality.

Baltimore. The later follow-up data for Baltimore include information from only the three quarters starting in the middle of the fifth year after random assignment (quarters nineteen through twenty-one). To make the final "year" earnings data for Baltimore comparable with those for Virginia and Arkansas, we have multiplied the three-quarter total of earnings and the number of quarters employed by 4/3. Short- and longer-term impacts of the Baltimore program are shown in Table 5-3.

Unlike the response in the previous two sites, the average earnings effect in Baltimore during the final follow-up year was greater than the effect observed during the second year. It was only slightly below the effect during the third year, when the earnings impact peaked. Hence, the evidence indicates that earnings response not only was relatively large to begin with but also shrank only slightly over the follow-up period.

The importance of earnings per employed quarter increased over time. In year two, more than two-thirds of the earnings gain was associated with increased employment, and less than a third was attributable to higher quarterly earnings. By the final year, much less of the earnings effect was associated with a gain in employment; two-thirds was attributable to higher quarterly earnings. In fact, as shown in the table, during the final follow-up year, 58.1 percent of controls were employed, only slightly less than the 58.5 percent of experimentals. Evidently, over time the Baltimore program raised the share of enrollees in better-paying jobs. The earnings distribution statistics, shown in the bottom four lines of the panel, suggest that there was a slight (and not statistically significant) shift towards jobs with annual earnings above $12,000. Even though the number of people involved is small, approximately 10 percent more experimentals than controls found employment paying more than $12,000 in the final year (1.6/16.1). Other estimates, not reported in the table, indicate that average earnings in the top earnings bracket were greater for experimentals than controls.[15] The long-term earnings impact of the Baltimore program, to a greater degree than for the other programs, thus appears to have been caused by an improvement in the earnings capacity of some enrollees. Earnings gains for the Baltimore program seem to have been concentrated in a small fraction of the sample who ended up in the top bracket. Though the gains were concentrated, they were large relative to the cost of the program.

San Diego SWIM. For San Diego SWIM, the final year is defined as quarters seventeen through twenty-one. As shown in Table 5-3, the earnings difference between experimentals and controls shrank from $626 in year two to $148 in the final year, and the decline of earnings impacts would look even greater if the amounts were adjusted for inflation. Impacts showed corresponding declines in other measures: in "ever employed in year," "number of quarters employed," and "employed all four quarters in year." Unlike Baltimore, earnings per quarter employed were never much different for experimentals and controls, early or late. There were experimental-control differences in the distribution of earnings, but these occurred only in year two and were concentrated in the bottom and middle brackets. There was virtually no change in the percent of experimentals in the top

---

[15] Increased employment in the $12,000 or more bracket in Baltimore accounts for the great bulk of final-year earnings gains (i.e., $396 out of $475).

bracket. By the final year, the only remaining differential in the earnings distribution was a modest increase in the middle bracket.

Part of the decline in employment and earnings impacts over time appears to be the result of control catch-up. To see this, we must examine the outcome levels for controls. The percent of controls who worked at all during the year changed very little from year two to year five (rising from 40.1 percent to 41.7 percent), but average earnings, number of quarters employed, average earnings per quarter employed, and percent employed all four quarters in year all increased. In addition, the distribution of earnings for controls shifted upward, from the bottom bracket to the middle and top brackets. These changes in control behavior steadily eroded the experimental group's initial advantage.

Another part of the decline of earnings impacts seems to stem from the program effect wearing off. Evidence for this comes from the pattern of outcomes for experimentals over time. Interestingly, San Diego SWIM was the only one of the four programs for which the "ever employed in year" statistic for experimentals *fell* over time. From 50.6 percent in year two, the "ever employed" rate declined to 43.3 percent in the final year, suggesting that a number of SWIM graduates who found jobs early on left them and did not return to work quickly. This decline suggests some wearing-off of the treatment effect. The number of quarters experimentals were employed fell, too, from 1.40 in year two to 1.33 in the final year. Other outcomes moved in a different direction, however. The percent employed in all four quarters of the year rose, as did average earnings and average conditional earnings. The distribution of earnings for experimentals shifted upward, with some experimentals moving into the top earnings bracket.

This complex set of findings suggests that SWIM produced two different kinds of accelerated employment behavior. Some experimentals entered fairly stable employment, beginning work sooner than they would have without SWIM. Their counterparts in the control group eventually found similar jobs and caught up, closing the experimental-control gap. Other experimentals began employment that did not last a long time, but they, too, started to work sooner than they would have without SWIM. For these individuals, the initial employment effect of SWIM, early in the follow-up period, appears as a peak or crest of employment followed by a gradual decline to a lower level, after the initial effect of the program wore off. The combination of these two kinds of accelerated employment behavior would have produced the observed pattern of effects. At one and the same time, it would have produced the increase among experimentals in earnings and stable employment as well as the initial high rate of "ever employed in year" followed by a lower rate later. It thus produced a narrowing of the experimental-control differential partly by catch-up and partly by wearing-off.

CONCLUSIONS

The empirical results in this chapter lead us to two main sets of conclusions. The first set pertains to the initial program effects on enrollees. The second set pertains to longer-term effects. In all sites, the principal initial program effect, evident through the first two or three years of follow-up, was an acceleration of job finding. Some members of the experimental groups who would have worked anyway found jobs faster. Some experimentals who would not have worked within the five-year follow-up period did so as a result of these programs. By and large, the initial jobs of experimentals were neither consistently better nor consistently worse than those obtained by controls. Initial employment spells lasted about as long for experimentals as for controls. And although initial earnings on the job were occasionally different for experimentals and controls, the amount of initial earnings difference did not reliably predict later earnings gains. In large part, the initial program effect was to move forward in time those employment experiences that would eventually have occurred even in the absence of the programs.

The second set of conclusions, regarding longer-term effects, is more complicated. If a speedup in job finding were a program's only effect, then the earnings advantage of experimentals over controls must eventually fade substantially if not completely. Controls would sooner or later find jobs and their employment rate would start to "catch up" with that of experimentals. We found, however, that other factors were also at work in producing longer-term results. Of particular interest are the results for Baltimore. There we found some evidence that a stronger focus on more intensive human capital development through education and training may pay off in longer-term improvements in earning power. These improvements do not necessarily show up quickly in the form of higher-paying first jobs. After some time, though, they may lead to higher levels of earnings on the job. It is these effects on earning power, not the faster initial employment, that seem to produce long-lasting increases in earnings for the program-eligible population. In these samples, it was higher earnings per quarter employed, not any employment effects, that produced the only large longer-term earnings gains that were observed. However, the response pattern in Baltimore also suggests that long-lasting earnings gains were concentrated on a small number of program participants.

There was some variation in the details of the behavioral patterns across the four programs. The employment and earnings response in Virginia came close to matching the stereotypical pattern expected from a simple acceleration of initial job finding. The size of the earnings effect grew during early follow-up quarters, and then eventually declined after the initial period of program participation. Workers in the experimental group started out earning approximately the same per quarter as working controls. And experimentals and controls were about equally successful in remaining employed after first becoming employed. Climbing rates of employment in the control group ultimately reduced the lead held by experimentals. By the end of follow-up, experimentals showed a small advantage in earnings per quarter employed, which was the only effect slowing the decline of the earnings differential.

In Arkansas, there was an impact on employment lasting through the final follow-up year. But the catch-up in earnings by controls was reinforced by a tendency among some employed experimentals to continue working at lower earnings levels. We ascribed this to a program effect on the subjective assessment of the relative value of working versus remaining on or returning to AFDC. This change in attitude led some experimentals by the end of follow-up to decide to stay in the labor market, continuing with low-wage, intermittent, or part-time employment, instead of reapplying for AFDC. In the next chapter, we attempt to confirm this hypothesis using evidence about deterrence of initial AFDC receipt or later reapplication.

The Baltimore program, which operated at moderate cost, placed somewhat greater emphasis on education and training than the others. It produced the clearest evidence of longer-term earnings gains. Initial effects, as elsewhere, came from employment acceleration, but by the end of follow-up most of the experimental-control differential in earnings was associated with greater earnings per quarter of employment for employed experimentals compared with employed controls. This effect was enough to make the overall Baltimore earnings impact persistent as well as comparatively large.

San Diego SWIM was also a moderate-cost program. Its initial impact on employment was the largest of the four, and SWIM produced the largest initial earnings impact. Again, we attributed this effect to employment acceleration rather than increased earning power. Unlike Baltimore, San Diego SWIM did not achieve higher earnings per quarter of employment in the long run, which would have helped sustain a long-run experimental-control differential in earnings. The fading of the experimental-control differential in average earnings over time resulted in part from control group catch-up. But SWIM also presents the clearest case of wearing-off of the treatment effect; there was an actual *decline* in employment among experimentals from the peak levels reached in the period of their initial program participation.

We hypothesize that this wearing-off of the SWIM treatment effect may have been the natural result of the limited duration of the SWIM demonstration. After the close of the demonstration, SWIM's distinctive maximum participation goal was no longer applied to experimentals still on AFDC or those returning to AFDC. If SWIM had continued operating in San Diego, and the separate treatments for experimentals and controls had been maintained, experimentals might have experienced earnings gains in later years. For example, experimentals who lost jobs and returned to AFDC might have obtained another job-finding stimulus from SWIM at that time. The employment and earnings advantage of experimentals over controls might have persisted indefinitely. In other words, a permanent SWIM program could have produced a permanent impact, with less wearing-off. The data used in this study do not permit us to confirm or refute this hypothesis, however.

Our empirical analysis enables us to address one other issue of importance to program operators. It is often suggested that low- to moderate-cost welfare-to-work programs do nothing but put enrollees in dead-end jobs which they soon leave. According to this argument, the poor quality of initial job placements causes any program effect on employment to wear off quickly as the new jobs are abandoned. In fact, we did observe a substantial amount of low-paying and short-term or intermittent employment in these samples. When we look five years after the initial program enrollment, we generally find only half or fewer of all enrollees who ever found jobs were still employed and working continuously in the entire final follow-up year. On the other hand, the high rates of job turnover these figures imply were generally no worse for experimentals than for controls. Program impacts would clearly have been much larger if all enrollees who started to work continued to do so. But there were earnings impacts nonetheless, and many experimentals placed by the programs did continue working for a long time.

The limitations of these low- to moderate-cost programs are apparent: the great majority of program enrollees did not obtain stable employment at above-average earnings levels. In fact, in any given year, a majority or sizable minority was not employed at all. This fraction of the enrolled sample was apparently unaffected by their program experiences. Or if it was affected, the influence of the programs was not enough to produce a change in actual work behavior. A principal question for future evaluations will be whether still larger outlays, particularly for more intensive human-capital development services or for more disadvantaged groups in the caseload, can produce correspondingly larger long-term impacts on employment and earnings.

6

AFDC Case Closure and AFDC Recidivism

This chapter analyzes program impacts on AFDC receipt. We examine three aspects of AFDC receipt: AFDC grant levels, exit from AFDC, and reentry to the rolls (i.e., AFDC recidivism). The analysis is similar in style to the earlier examination of program impacts on employment and earnings. The discussion is somewhat simpler, however, because the programs had very minor effects on average grant levels. Hence, our main concern is in tracing out the effects of the programs on welfare exit and reentry. In discussing "AFDC exit," we use that term interchangeably with "case closure," "departure," and "termination." We include as exits the departure of AFDC applicants who did not gain approval for aid and did not receive any AFDC payments during the observation period.

We find that AFDC reductions, where they were achieved, were associated almost entirely with speedier termination of AFDC receipt. Shorter AFDC spells translated into reductions in months on AFDC. These reductions in months of receipt account for the overwhelming bulk of impacts on AFDC payments. In Arkansas and San Diego SWIM, the two programs with the largest AFDC effects, reduced months on AFDC accounted for more than 80 percent of the total effect on AFDC payments. Sanctioning appears to have had much less *direct* effect in producing AFDC reductions, even in the program that used sanctioning most frequently, the SWIM program in San Diego. The *indirect* effect of the threat of sanction in promoting cooperation by program enrollees could not be measured, however. Reductions in monthly grant amounts for working recipients played, at most, a minor role in achieving AFDC savings.

AFDC recidivism was common in these samples. If we define

an individual's first month with a zero AFDC payment as an "exit," then about 40 percent of sample members who exited AFDC returned within a year. If episodes of one to two months off AFDC are not counted as true exits, the figure drops to about 20 or 30 percent. On average, the programs neither increased nor decreased recidivism. Between experimentals and controls who exited AFDC, there was little difference in the fraction of months in the observation period spent back on the rolls after having left. For Virginia and San Diego SWIM, we find a slightly greater percentage of one- or two-month spells off AFDC among exiting experimentals. For SWIM, we find that experimentals who exited AFDC spent a slightly greater fraction of succeeding months back on AFDC than did controls. For Arkansas, we found the reverse, with departing experimentals staying off somewhat longer than controls.

Recidivism thus did not markedly offset the effect of increased case closures in producing AFDC reductions. Altogether, time back on AFDC after a first exit may have reduced total AFDC impacts over the follow-up period by about 20 to 25 percent in Virginia and San Diego SWIM. The narrowing of the experimental-control differential in AFDC payments in the later follow-up years, pointed out in Chapter 4, appears not to be primarily the result of recidivism or any "wearing-off" of the effect of program services. Rather it seems mostly to be the inevitable result of normal AFDC turnover: over time, more and more controls leave AFDC, and case closings for them eventually "catch up" with those for experimentals. The catch-up by controls may have been partially induced by the availability of program services for controls after the end of the research project in each locality.

Decreases or increases in recidivism may have been more important had the programs produced greater initial impact on potential long-term AFDC recipients. In that case, a decrease in the recidivism of long-termers would have contributed to a decrease in long-term AFDC receipt; an increase in recidivism among long-termers after an initial impact on them could have undercut long-term AFDC effects considerably. For the most part, however, the programs studied were not successful in making dramatic inroads into long-term AFDC receipt. In the final year of follow-up, there remained a core of long-termers receiving AFDC, either because they had never left the rolls or because they had left and then returned.

Even modest effects on potential long-term AFDC recipients can make a disproportionate contribution to total impact, however. Arkansas and San Diego SWIM, the two programs with the largest total AFDC impacts, were also the only programs to show even modest effects on enrollees who would have still been on AFDC five or six years after random assignment. In SWIM, impacts on those potential long-term AFDC recipients may account for as much as one-third of the total AFDC impact over the observed follow-up, although the exact share cannot be determined with certainty. In Arkansas, the contribution of impacts on potential long-termers may have been smaller but still significant. Thus, effects on five- and six-year AFDC receipt, even modest effects, appear to have been integral to achieving overall AFDC reductions. Increasing program AFDC impacts further may well depend in large part on the ability of programs to develop and demonstrate approaches that will increase their effectiveness with potential long-term AFDC recipients.

The remainder of this chapter is organized as follows. In the next section, we consider the average impact on months of AFDC receipt and on AFDC benefits over the entire period covered by our follow-up data. We attempt to decompose the overall impact into several different types of effect: changes in monthly grant amounts, earlier exit from the assistance rolls, and so on. We then analyze the initial experiences of sample members *after* they leave public assistance. We seek to answer the question: How long do sample members remain off AFDC after their initial exit? The final section compares AFDC effects in year two, near the peak of AFDC impact, with those in the final twelve months of follow-up, after much of the narrowing of the experimental-control differential had occurred.

EFFECTS ON AFDC RECEIPT AND AFDC PAYMENTS

The basic impact estimates presented in Chapter 4 indicate a confusing variety of AFDC results across the four study sites. Two programs had large (relative to costs) and statistically significant AFDC impacts, and the other two had much smaller impacts. The two moderate-cost programs, although they achieved short-term earnings gains of similar magnitude, produced dissimilar results for AFDC: large reductions in San Diego SWIM and virtually no reductions in Baltimore. At the same time, large and sustained AFDC impacts were achieved in Arkansas, which achieved more modest earnings gains. Virginia's program achieved earnings impacts somewhat larger than Arkansas's but achieved AFDC impacts that were smaller.

The diversity of AFDC results, with no apparent link to earnings impacts or program cost, at first seems perplexing. In this chapter, we point out certain fundamental similarities across programs in the effects they achieved on AFDC receipt. We begin our analysis by examining the nature of the AFDC response over the full follow-up period. As before, we start by analyzing outcomes in Virginia in some detail and then discuss the findings for Arkansas, Baltimore, and San Diego SWIM in turn.

Analysis Issues.   There are three components of potential AFDC reductions: (*a*) lower monthly grant amounts, (*b*) fewer months on AFDC until case closure, and (*c*) reduced time back on AFDC after initial case closure. First, the amount of monthly payments to individuals who receive AFDC may decline. This might happen if some program enrollees obtain jobs with earnings low enough so that they do not lose their AFDC eligibility. In particular, part-time employment may in some cases reduce the monthly entitlement amount without closing the case. Monthly payments would also be lower for those enrollees who incur a sanction because they failed to comply with some program requirement.

Second, program enrollees may be induced to leave AFDC sooner than they would have left otherwise. They may leave because they have found a job. Or they may leave to avoid having to participate in the program, a *deterrence effect*. It may also be that the closer contact between program staff and enrollees results in more rapid or more complete reporting of earnings to the AFDC office, a *discovery effect*. In this way, more cases might be closed even without an increase in employment. In each of these scenarios, the effect of the program will be to shorten the time until case closure.

Lastly, the program experience may cause some individuals who leave AFDC to stay off the rolls longer than they would have otherwise. They may stay off because they work or hold jobs longer, or they may have decided that AFDC was too much "hassle." Regardless, the longer they stay off and the less recidivism there is, the larger will be the program reduction in AFDC receipt.

All the program samples contain a large proportion—from 40 to 60 percent—of sample members who were referred to the program while they were still in the process of applying for AFDC. Any of the effects described above may occur for these

AFDC applicants. In addition, some applicants may leave AFDC before they complete the application process. They may return to file another application only after a lengthy period. Or they may not reapply at all. This latter effect would appear as a decrease in the number of sample members who ever received AFDC during the follow-up period. Such a program-induced change in the ever-received rate we will call the *application effect*.[1]

Of the three components, lower monthly grant amount probably has limited potential for producing significant AFDC reductions in the programs under study. In general, only a small proportion of the AFDC caseload report earnings while on AFDC. Also, under existing rules, sanctions were only temporary and could not have a direct, long-term impact. Increased case closure and reduced recidivism have greater potential, since payments fall to zero when a case is closed and can remain at zero for a long time. Both increased case termination and reduced recidivism should show up as reductions in the total number of months on AFDC. It should be pointed out, however, that offsetting effects may occur. In particular, if cases are closed faster but more enrollees return to AFDC within a few months of exiting, then there may be little net impact on total months of AFDC receipt.

One additional point should be made. Unlike earnings, which could have an experimental-control differential lasting indefinitely, AFDC payments cannot show a permanent impact. All AFDC cases eventually close because the children on them grow too old to qualify for AFDC benefits. Thus, AFDC payments for any control group must eventually go to zero. Since the experimentals cannot have AFDC payments below zero, the experimental-control difference must eventually become zero, too. Nevertheless, it may take many years for this to occur. To say that a welfare-to-work program "merely" speeds up case closure may obscure the fact that substantial reductions in AFDC receipt and expenditures can be achieved in this way.

Virginia. We begin by examining AFDC benefits over the full follow-up period. Table 6-1 presents impacts on total AFDC payments along with the component statistics on months of receipt, monthly amounts, AFDC "ever received," speed of case

---

[1] A reduction in the number of completed AFDC applications is often called the "deterrence effect." We reserve that term to describe any departure from AFDC, whether by an applicant or a current recipient, that leaves the individual with lower money income than would have been the case in the absence of the special program.

closure, and recidivism. In the tables in this chapter, we follow the conventions adopted in the preceding chapter: Differences between experimentals and controls are shown both in absolute form (e.g., as dollars or months) and, where relevant and where space permits, as a percentage of the control-group mean. Estimates based on nonexperimental comparisons are displayed in italics. All experimental estimates are regression-adjusted, and all nonexperimental estimates are derived from regression-adjusted experimental estimates.

In the top row of Table 6-1 we show again the estimate of impact on total AFDC payments in Virginia. The follow-up period in Virginia consists of sixty consecutive months, starting in the month of random assignment (month one). Over that five-year period, members of the control group received, on average, $6,641 in AFDC payments. Experimentals received $6,318, implying a reduction of $323, or 4.9 percent of the control-group amount. Even though the difference between the two groups on this measure is not statistically significant at conventional levels, the year-by-year results presented in Chapter 4 do show that savings were statistically significant at the peak.

The 4.9 percent reduction in total AFDC payments can be

TABLE 6-1

AFDC Impacts Over the Full Follow-Up Period

Program and Outcome	Experimentals	Controls	Difference	Difference Controls × 100
Virginia: Follow-Up Period, Months 1–60				
Average total AFDC payments, months 1–60	$6,318	$6,641	−$323	−4.9%
Average number of months received AFDC, months 1–60	24.07	24.85	−0.78	−3.1%
Average AFDC payment in months receiving welfare[a]	$263	$267	−$5 (z)	−1.8%
Months observed in initial spell (max = 60)	16.39	17.38	−0.98	(x)
Initial spell did not end before month 60 (%)	7.7	9.3	−1.6	(x)
Ever received any AFDC, months 1–60 (%)	88.6	88.3	0.3	(x)
Fraction of months on AFDC from first exit through month 60 (%)[b]	17.7	17.6	0.1 (z)	(x)
Arkansas: Follow-Up Period, Months 1–66				
Average total AFDC payments, months 1–66	$4,390	$5,125	−$735 ***	−14.3%
Average number of months received AFDC, months 1–66	24.78	28.47	−3.69 ***	−13.0%
Average AFDC payment in months receiving welfare[a]	$177	$180	−$3 (z)	−1.6%

TABLE 6-1 (continued)

ogram and Outcome	Experimentals	Controls	Difference	Difference/ Controls × 100
Months observed in initial spell (max = 66)	16.09	19.12	−3.03***	(x)
Initial spell did not end before month 66 (%)	11.7	11.9	−0.1	(x)
Ever received any AFDC, months 1–66 (%)	79.9	83.0	−3.1	(x)
Fraction of months on AFDC from first exit through month 66 (%)[b]	*17.5*	*20.1*	*−2.6 (z)*	*(x)*
altimore: Follow-Up Period, Months 1–36				
Average total AFDC payments, months 1–36	$6,361	$6,424	−$62	−1.0%
Average number of months received AFDC, months 1–36	22.21	22.62	−0.41	−1.8%
Average AFDC payment in months receiving welfare[a]	*$286*	*$284*	*$2 (z)*	*0.9%*
Months observed in initial spell (max = 36)	17.92	18.42	−0.50	(x)
Initial spell did not end before month 36 (%)	26.5	27.6	−1.2	(x)
Ever received any AFDC, months 1–36 (%)	95.3	95.4	−0.1	(x)
Fraction of months on AFDC from first exit through month 36 (%)[b]	*24.0*	*24.2*	*−0.2 (z)*	*(x)*
an Diego SWIM: Follow-Up Period, Months 1–63				
Average total AFDC payments, months 1–63	$16,758	$18,688	−$1,930***	−10.3%
Average number of months received AFDC, months 1–63	30.53	33.40	−2.87***	−8.6%
Average AFDC payment in months receiving welfare[a]	*$549*	*$559*	*−$11 (z)*	*−1.9%*
Months observed in initial spell (max = 63)	22.41	26.30	−3.89***	(x)
Initial spell did not end before month 63 (%)	14.2	16.8	−2.6**	(x)
Ever received any AFDC, months 1–63 (%)	96.0	95.9	0.2	(x)
Fraction of months on AFDC from first exit through month 63 (%)[b]	*20.1*	*19.4*	*0.7 (z)*	*(x)*

NOTES: The initial welfare spell is defined as beginning at the month of the first positive AFDC payment, counting from the month of random assignment (month one) onward. It is defined as ending at the month of first zero AFDC payment. For sample members who received no AFDC payments in months one through three, the initial spell is defined as ending at month one and having a duration of zero months.

Details may not sum to totals owing to rounding.

Italics indicate nonexperimental estimates.

A two-tailed t-test was applied to experimental differences. Statistical significance levels are indicated as: * = 10 percent; ** = 5 percent; *** = 1 percent. (z) indicates that the comparison is nonexperimental: no test of statistical significance was performed. (x) indicates that the percentage difference is not relevant.

[a] Means equal total payments divided by total months.

[b] Equals the quantity total months of receipt minus months in first spell divided by the quantity length of follow-up minus last follow-up month of first spell. This last variable is not shown in the table. It differs slightly from length of first spell because sample members who begin receipt in months two or three are not counted as "off AFDC" before then. Hence, these sample members have an initial spell length of two or one month, respectively, less than the number of the follow-up month of last welfare receipt of the first spell.

decomposed into the contributions of reduced months on AFDC and lower monthly payment amounts. To do this, we compare the percentage versions of the differences for those measures with the overall 4.9 percent difference. For example, if the percent reduction in months is two-thirds of 4.9, then we may conclude that reduced monthly payment amounts probably account for two-thirds of the overall impact. As in the previous chapter, this kind of decomposition is not exact. The percent estimates for the two components will not generally add up precisely to the percent estimate for the total. Also, as we have stated, going beyond the basic experimental-control comparison may induce some nonexperimental biases, and the possibility of such biases reduces the certainty of our inferences. Nevertheless, when interpreted with care, the results of the decomposition can provide credible explanations for some of the underlying mechanisms of program impact.

There was an experimental-control difference in the number of months of receipt in Virginia. As shown in the second row, controls, on average, received AFDC payments in nearly twenty-five of the sixty months during the follow-up period. Experimentals received payments for 0.78 fewer months, or 3.1 percent fewer months than the control-group average. Note that the percentage decrease in the number of months spent on AFDC is about two-thirds of the percentage decrease in AFDC payments.

The balance of the total AFDC impact is explained by a small difference in the average amounts of monthly AFDC checks paid to experimentals and controls. The average check amounts are reported in row three. These monthly amounts are conditional averages, calculated by dividing total payments by the corresponding number of months of benefits received. Differences between conditional averages are nonexperimental, as in the previous chapter, and the same cautions on interpretation apply. In the case of Virginia, monthly amounts for months on AFDC averaged $5 less for experimentals than for controls. This 1.8 percent difference accounts for about a third of the 4.9 percent overall AFDC impact.

The remaining rows of the table for Virginia indicate that the reduction in months occurred as a result of earlier case closure, offset partly by recidivism. In row four, we report the average length of initial spells on AFDC observed during the follow-up period. We define initial AFDC spell length as follows: For an AFDC applicant who did not receive benefits within three months of random assignment, we assume the application was denied or not completed and count the duration of the initial spell as zero. For sample members who received benefits within three months of random assignment, we set initial spell length equal to the number of consecutive months of AFDC receipt until the first zero payment month or until the end of the follow-up, whichever occurred sooner. This definition of initial spell length classifies some sample members as exiting AFDC even though they left the rolls for only one or two months, possibly because of a missed check or administrative error.[2]

We want to compare the observed reduction in total months with the observed reduction in initial spell length. We should note that the average *observed* spell length, although appropriate for our purpose, will understate the average duration of *completed* initial spells, since the observation period ends at sixty months. For the 9 percent of controls and 8 percent of experimentals who never left AFDC during the sixty-month follow-up period (row five in Table 6-1), initial spell length exceeded sixty months. Because slightly more controls than experimentals remained on AFDC past sixty months, it seems likely that the full program impact on completed first spell length in Virginia was somewhat larger than the estimated effect on observed initial spell length.

As shown in the table, experimental-group members in Virginia received AFDC benefits for an average of 0.78 fewer months than controls, and they received benefits for 0.98 fewer months in their *initial* AFDC spells. At the same time, row six in the table shows that the same proportions of experimentals and controls—about 88 percent—received at least one month's benefits at some time during the follow-up period. We infer that none of the reduction in total months or initial spell length was achieved by reducing the number of successful AFDC applications. Virtually the entire reduction in months occurred because experimentals who actually received AFDC left the welfare rolls sooner than their counterparts in the control group. That is, the principal AFDC effect of the Virginia program was to accelerate exits from the rolls. The fact that the shortening of the initial spell was *greater* than the reduction in total months on AFDC indi-

---

[2]Discounting very short spells off AFDC produced slightly smaller impacts on length of first AFDC spell than those shown in Table 6-1. For example, under one alternative, utilized later (in Table 6-3), we did not classify a person as exiting AFDC unless we observed two or three successive zero monthly payment amounts. Under this definition, changes in initial spell length were −0.77 for Virginia, −2.43 for Arkansas, −0.35 for Baltimore, and −3.14 for San Diego SWIM.

cates that some of the experimentals who were induced to leave AFDC returned to the rolls not long after their first exit. In the next two sections of this chapter we examine the patterns of reentry onto the AFDC rolls after an initial exit. At this point, however, it is useful to derive a summary measure of AFDC receipt covering any recidivism in the period after the first exit.

Our summary statistic (last row of the panel) is nonexperimental, since it pertains to only a portion of the research sample selected on the basis of post-random assignment outcomes. For sample members who exited AFDC, we calculate the percentage of observed months they received AFDC benefits after the completion of the initial AFDC spell.[3] This measure is more complete than the usual measure of recidivism, namely, the length of time until reentry, since any differences in the number of months of receipt following reentry are included. The calculations reveal that Virginia experimentals who left AFDC received AFDC benefits in 17.7 percent of the months following their initial exit from the rolls; controls who left received benefits in 17.6 percent of the succeeding months. That is, the proportion of months on AFDC associated with recidivism is similar for exiters in the two groups.

In this sense, recidivism was no worse for experimentals than for controls: the *likelihood* of receiving AFDC in any given month after initially leaving the rolls was about the same. The *actual number of months* associated with recidivism was, however, somewhat greater for experimentals because they left the

---

[3] An example of the calculation, utilizing Virginia controls, is as follows: As shown in Table 6-1, the estimate of initial spell length for controls is 17.38. Since the total number of months that controls spent on AFDC was 24.85 (row two), we infer that controls received AFDC for an average of 7.47 months after their initial spells on AFDC were over (24.85 − 17.38). From another variable, not shown in the table, we know that initial spells ended, on average, in month 17.59 of follow-up, where we code this variable as the last follow-up month for sample members whose initial spell did not end during the observation period. Since the entire follow-up period is sixty months long, 42.41 months occurred after controls initially exited from AFDC (60 − 17.59). It follows, then, that Virginia controls, on average, received AFDC for 17.6 percent of the months after their initial exits (7.47/42.41).

This statistic pertains only to controls who exited; sample members who did not exit during the observation period cancel out of the formula. We should also point out that our estimate of the month the initial spell ended differs slightly from initial spell length owing to the way our definition of initial spell handles zero AFDC payments in month one or two. We did not count those zeroes as an AFDC exit if the sample member began to receive payments by month three. Thus, for example, initial spell length would be three for a sample member who received AFDC in months three through five and not in one, two, or six, but the last month of the initial spell would be month five.

rolls sooner and, consequently, had more months in which to be back on AFDC during a fixed follow-up period. We conclude, therefore, that the process of recidivism was not much different between research groups but that this process made impacts on total months of AFDC receipt smaller than the reduction in initial spell length. In other words, earlier departures from AFDC by experimentals were partly offset by a "normal" propensity to return to the rolls.

An estimate of the size of this offset can be calculated in a straightforward way. If there had been no recidivism in either research group, then the reduction in total months on welfare would have equalled the 0.98 reduction in initial spell length. The actual 0.78 impact on months of receipt was, by this reckoning, 0.78/0.98 or 80 percent of the potential impact. Based on this calculation, recidivism can be said to have reduced AFDC impacts in Virginia by about a fifth.[4]

Figure 6-1 illustrates the cumulative effects of AFDC exit and reentry for the experimental and control groups in Virginia. The figure shows the movement of three measures over time. The top graph shows percentage levels for the three measures, with each of the three solid lines representing controls and each dashed line representing experimentals. The bottom graph shows experimental-control differences for each of the three measures. Topmost on the graph is the percent of the sample that have ever been off AFDC (i.e., had at least one zero payment month) between the month of random assignment and the current follow-up month. Below that is the percent currently off AFDC for the month in question. The lowest curve is the percent currently in their first spell off AFDC following random assignment. Note in particular that at any point in time the percent of controls who have left the rolls at least once is always greater than the percent of controls who are currently off, which in turn exceeds those who are in their first spell off. In fact, this last measure,

---

[4]The logic behind this 80 percent estimate can be developed mathematically as follows: The relationship between total months on AFDC, length of first spell, and recidivism may be written as $M_{tot} = M_1 + p \times (M_{max} - M_1)$, where M_{tot} is total months on AFDC, M_1 is months in first AFDC spell, M_{max} is total follow-up, and p is the probability of being back on AFDC after the first exit. Impact on total months is $dM_{tot} = dM_1 \times (1 - p) + dp \times (M_{max} - M_1)$. If p is unchanged, then $dp = 0$ and $dM_{tot} = dM_1 \times (1 - p)$. That is, total impact equals impact on first spell length times the probability of remaining off AFDC in any month after first exiting. In Virginia, dp is almost zero and $100 \times p$ is about 18 percent (Table 6-1), which is consistent with the 80 percent estimate just given in the text (i.e., 80 is approximately $100 - 18$).

FIGURE 6-1
Virginia: "Off AFDC" Measures Over Time

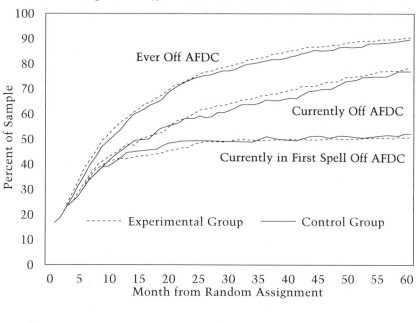

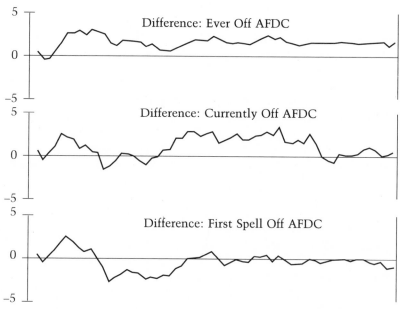

after its rapid rise in the first year, eventually becomes nearly flat.

These three curves depict the behavior we have just described using Table 6-1. First, the "ever off" curve on top rises continuously towards 100 percent (which it will eventually reach). Thus, no matter how large the effect on case closure for experimentals, controls must catch up in the long run, eliminating any differential between the two research groups on this measure. In the figure, we see, however, that a small differential in Virginia remains even at the fifth year. Second, we see recidivism coming into play in the measure "currently in first spell off": Experimentals at first exceed controls but soon fall below them as some of the first spells off AFDC end with a return to the rolls. Finally, we see changes in the experimental-control differential in current AFDC receipt tracking the experimental-control differences in "ever off AFDC" and "currently in first spell off AFDC" through the end of year four and then declining almost to zero.

On the whole, the AFDC effects just described for Virginia are modest—small enough relative to their standard errors so that we cannot altogether rule out chance as an explanation for the difference. The pattern is nevertheless consistent with a clear and reasonable story: The Virginia program reduced the level of AFDC outlays by reducing the AFDC rolls. It achieved this result by inducing women to exit AFDC about a month sooner than they would have in the absence of the program. The program's success on this score was partially offset by the fact that experimental-group members were just as likely to be back on AFDC in any month after their initial exits from the rolls as were controls.

Although program impacts on AFDC were small when averaged across all experimental sample members, one should not conclude that all effects on individuals were necessarily small. Individuals were almost certainly affected to quite different degrees. Most sample members probably experienced no change in their AFDC receipt. Among those whose cases were closed earlier than otherwise, some may have gotten off only a few months sooner, but some probably left at least a few years sooner. For them, the reductions in total AFDC payments would have been substantial, amounting to several thousands of dollars. Large effects on a small number of enrollees probably accounted for the bulk of the overall 5 percent AFDC reduction.

Arkansas.   The Arkansas program was much less costly than the one in Virginia but achieved considerably larger AFDC savings. The second panel in Table 6-1 shows the overall AFDC

impact in Arkansas and the breakdown for the various component effects. Over the full sixty-six-month follow-up period,
AFDC payments were reduced $735 per experimental-group
member, 14.3 percent of the control-group mean. As in Virginia,
virtually all of the decrease in benefits is explained by the decrease in average months on AFDC. Very little is explained by
differences in monthly grant amounts received by experimentals
and controls. Total months decreased by 3.69, or 13.0 percent
relative to months for controls. AFDC payments per month received were only 1.6 percent less for experimentals.

The decrease in months on AFDC was, in turn, explained
largely by a decrease in the length of the first welfare spell. Controls initially received benefits for an average of 19.12 months
during the follow-up period, while experimentals initially received benefits for an average of only 16.09 months. The difference of 3.03 is more than 80 percent of the 3.69 difference in
total months. It may be noted in passing that the estimate of
the experimental-control difference in observed first spell length
probably only slightly underestimates the difference in completed first spell length, since about the same number of experimentals and controls were observed to leave AFDC sometime
during follow-up (row five). The fact that the difference in first
spell length is *less than* the difference in total months on the
rolls suggests that recidivism among experimentals did not reduce AFDC impacts. Rather, experimentals who left AFDC may
have remained off welfare slightly longer, on average, than controls who left the rolls.

In Arkansas, unlike the other three sites, part of the decline
in initial spell length is explained by a reduction in the number
of successful aid applications among experimentals. As shown,
3.1 percentage points fewer experimentals than controls received
AFDC benefits sometime during the follow-up period (row six).
Some applicant experimentals may have taken jobs quickly
enough to make completing the AFDC application unnecessary.
Others may have been deterred from completing the application
by the extra burden of meeting program requirements. This "application effect" accounted for a portion—perhaps as much as a
quarter or a third[5]—of the total impact on months. Among those

---

[5] A rough estimate of the contribution of fewer completed applications can be
obtained by assuming that applicants who did not go on AFDC would have stayed
on about as many months as controls who went on. This conditional average number
of months for controls is 34.30 months (28.47/0.830). Multiplying this by the .031

experimentals who received AFDC payments, we calculate that the average initial spell lasted three months less than it did among controls who received payments (just twenty months rather than twenty-three). These earlier case closures for experimentals on AFDC account for about two-thirds of the effect on initial spell length.[6]

Interestingly, it appears that experimentals who left AFDC were more successful than controls in remaining off the rolls. Controls spent 20.1 percent of the months after their initial exit back on AFDC; experimentals were back on for only 17.5 percent of those months. Even if we restrict our attention to sample members who received AFDC benefits for at least one month during the follow-up period, the same conclusion holds: Experimentals spent less time after their initial AFDC exits back on AFDC.[7] Hence, recidivism clearly did not undercut AFDC impacts in Arkansas. Rather, a reduction in recidivism appears to have increased the size of the average AFDC impact.[8]

In summary, the Arkansas program achieved AFDC reductions primarily by speeding up case closure, shortening by about three months the initial AFDC spells of enrollees who received AFDC. Faster case closure was also the primary effect in Virginia; the effect in Arkansas was substantially larger, however. Indeed, as we will see, this was the primary effect wherever AFDC savings were obtained. Unlike the other programs, however, Arkansas's also reduced the fraction of women who ever received AFDC during the follow-up period. In addition, AFDC effects were not undercut by recidivism. In fact, only in Arkansas did the likelihood that experimentals would receive AFDC again

---

impact on "ever received" gives 1.06 months, which is 29 percent of the 3.69 reduction in total months. This may be an overestimate, since program enrollees who did not go on AFDC may otherwise have had fewer months of receipt than the average.

[6]Estimates of conditional spell length are obtained by dividing average spell length for a research group by the fraction receiving any AFDC. For experimentals, this is 16.09/.799 = 20.14; for controls, this is 19.12/.830 = 23.04. The difference multiplied by the percent of experimentals who "ever received" amounts to two-thirds of the difference in total months (20.14 − 23.04 = 2.90 × .799 = 2.3171/ 3.69 = 63 percent).

[7]The percent of months back on AFDC for sample members who received AFDC benefits for at least one month was 22.7 percent for experimentals and 24.9 percent for controls for a difference of −2.2 percentage points.

[8]As we have already indicated, nonexperimental differences are not unequivocal indicators of causality. The estimates revealing experimentals' lesser propensity to be back on AFDC after an exit may well result from a true program impact. But the same difference could also occur if the experimentals induced to leave AFDC by the program already had a lesser propensity to return. Conclusions about Arkansas's effects on recidivism must be interpreted with allowance for this uncertainty.

after they had left the rolls for the first time appear to be lower than for controls.

One final point must be made regarding the application effect in Arkansas. Even though such an effect was *observed* only in Arkansas, similar effects might be possible elsewhere. The research design in Arkansas was different from the other three in that randomization of AFDC applicants occurred earlier in the application/approval process. This meant that any application effect would more likely be captured by the Arkansas research design. On the other hand, low grant levels like those in Arkansas may be an important prerequisite for an application effect.

Baltimore. The Baltimore program achieved only small AFDC savings. Over the full thirty-six-month follow-up period, AFDC payments were 1.0 percent lower for experimentals than for controls (Table 6-1, third panel). Consistent with results for Virginia and Arkansas, all of this reduction occurred because experimentals received benefits in slightly fewer months than controls. Monthly grants received by experimentals were actually slightly higher than those received by controls.

The reduction in time spent on AFDC was similar to the reduction in initial spell length (0.41 months for the former versus 0.50 months for the latter). The slightly greater reduction in initial spell length implies that recidivism reduced AFDC impacts by about a fifth.[9] Our comparison of recidivism across research groups indicates that experimentals were about as successful as controls in remaining off the rolls after their initial AFDC exit. Experimentals spent 24.0 percent of the months after their initial AFDC exits back on AFDC, compared to 24.2 percent for controls. Thus, the effect of recidivism appears to stem from a normal rate at which exiters later received AFDC and not from any increase in that rate brought about by the program. There was no application effect.

We conclude, therefore, that the poor showing for Baltimore in AFDC impacts came from the lack of a basic effect on case closures rather than from an offsetting effect of recidivism. This suggests that raising the earnings of persons who are likely to find jobs anyway, which was the likely mechanism of the Baltimore program in producing earnings gains, may not be effective in achieving AFDC reductions. The reason is that individuals

---

[9] The 0.41 reduction in total months is about 80 percent of the 0.50 reduction in first spell length.

who are likely to find jobs anyway are also likely to leave AFDC fairly soon, and their short stays cannot be reduced by much.

San Diego SWIM. AFDC savings for San Diego SWIM were large, whether measured in absolute or percentage terms. Over the five-year follow-up, AFDC payments to experimentals were, on average, $1,930 lower than for controls, a 10.3 percent saving. About four-fifths of the San Diego savings can be explained by the 8.6 percent decrease in the number of months that experimentals received AFDC benefits. Only the remaining one-fifth is associated with lower monthly grant amounts for experimentals who received benefits in a given month.

The slightly lower monthly grant amounts may have resulted from a number of causes, including sanctions, increased part-time employment, and compositional effects on members of the experimental group who continued to receive AFDC benefits. The importance of any of these factors was at most minor, however. An overwhelming share of the cost savings in San Diego was clearly associated with the sharp fall in the average number of months that experimentals received benefits. The *direct* effect of sanctioning—that is, the partial reduction in monthly AFDC payments—could not have made a major contribution to AFDC impacts, even in a program with the relatively high sanctioning rate exhibited by San Diego SWIM. Indeed, by this reasoning, sanctioning could not have had a major direct effect on AFDC savings in any of the four programs. Whether the threat of a sanction had an *indirect* effect in promoting participation or in otherwise making programs more effective cannot be determined from this analysis.

The decline in months on public assistance is explained by earlier exits from the rolls. As shown in the table, experimentals were just as likely as controls to receive benefits for at least one month during the follow-up period (96.0 percent versus 95.9 percent). Thus, there was no application effect. But experimentals who received AFDC left the rolls nearly four months sooner within the observation period. In the entire sample, the total amount of time spent on AFDC fell by 2.87 months. The average duration of the initial spell on AFDC fell by 3.89 months. As in Virginia and Baltimore, the excess of initial spell reduction over total months reduction suggests that recidivism reduced overall impact in San Diego SWIM by roughly one-fourth.[10]

---

[10] As before, we divide the reduction in total months by the observed reduction in initial spell, which gives 74 percent (2.87/3.89), leaving 26 percent as the effect

Within the five-year follow-up period, experimentals who exited AFDC spent 20.1 percent of the months after their initial exit back on the rolls. Since the number of months occurring after the initial exit was greater for experimentals, their absolute number of months back on AFDC was also greater and somewhat offset their faster case closures. In addition, it appears that experimentals were slightly less successful than controls in remaining off AFDC after termination of their initial spells: controls spent 19.4 percent of the months after their initial exit back on AFDC, compared with 20.1 percent among experimentals. This difference slightly increased the offset to faster case closures of experimentals. SWIM was the only one of the four programs to show even a slight positive difference on this measure. Nevertheless, by far the dominant effect of San Diego SWIM, as for the other programs, was the reduction in the length of initial AFDC spells. And differences in overall AFDC impacts across programs appear to stem mainly from differences in program success in closing cases, not from differences in preventing recidivism.

RECIDIVISM AFTER INITIAL EXIT FROM AFDC

Our initial results suggest that experimentals and controls were usually about equally successful in remaining off welfare after an initial exit from the rolls. In one of the sites— Arkansas—we found evidence indicating that experimentals were more successful than controls in remaining off the rolls after initially exiting. In this section we undertake further analysis of recidivism among sample members who left AFDC during the first two years of the follow-up period.

Analysis Issues. In addressing recidivism, we have two concerns. First, it has been suggested, especially by program managers, that the impacts of welfare-to-work programs are short-lived. Enrollees, they argue, are sometimes helped to leave AFDC, but many who leave cannot maintain their independence and quickly return to the rolls. If so, then case closure will be less a once-and-for-all exit and more a revolving door.

---

of recidivism in reducing total AFDC impact. It should be added that the effect on the total length of the initial spell may be understated, since more experimentals than controls exited AFDC during the observation period. Conversely, additional follow-up may reveal a higher rate of recidivism in later years.

A second possibility is that the case closure effect of programs comes about merely from catching enrollees in paperwork mistakes that create technical AFDC ineligibility. For example, if an AFDC check were withheld in a particular month because a sample member failed to comply with some paperwork requirement arising from the program, then the individual might return to the rolls in the following month, perhaps with a check large enough to cover two months' payments. Such administrative case closings are known as "churning." They typically last only a month or two, just until the client has worked out the procedural problem. They do not constitute an important or sustained impact on behavior. Closings of this kind do not stem from increased earnings, nor are they likely to produce the large AFDC savings that permanent case closure will produce. They serve only to increase the effort required of enrollees to maintain continued AFDC eligibility.

If either of these possibilities, the revolving door effect or churning, is significant, we should observe an *increase* in returns to AFDC. As an illustration, if a program catches more individuals in paperwork errors, then we will see an experimental-control increase in case closures, but we will see an equally large increase in returns after one or two months. The analysis below is designed to uncover patterns of this sort.

Subsample Definition. In this section we focus on an important element of recidivism, namely, the length of the first spell off AFDC. Our analysis is based on the experiences of only a subsample of experimental- and control-group members. In order to estimate the duration of an initial spell off AFDC, it is obviously necessary to observe such a spell. Our calculations therefore exclude individuals who never leave AFDC during the follow-up period. In addition, we would like to observe a long enough interval after the initial AFDC exit to draw plausible inferences about the complete distribution of initial spells off AFDC. Since the observation period in one of the sites (Baltimore) is short, we are restricted to analyzing people who left the rolls relatively early in the follow-up period. We include as exiters those sample members who did not initially receive benefits at all.

The calculations that follow are based solely on the experiences of sample members who left AFDC within two years of random assignment. We identified the first exit from AFDC as follows. For individuals who did not receive AFDC at all in the first three months of follow-up, we assumed that case closure took place in month one (the month of random assignment). Thus, sample members who received no AFDC at all during the two-year period were classified as exiting the system in month one. For all other individuals, we identified case closure as the first zero AFDC payment month following at least one month in which a positive payment was received. Thus, for example, an applicant who was not approved for AFDC until month three and who therefore received zero benefits in months one and two, was not counted as exiting until after month three.

Virginia.   Figure 6-2 shows the percent of exiting experimentals and controls who remained off AFDC in each successive month after their initial departures.[11] In Figure 6-2(a), the curve for Virginia experimentals drops below that for controls during months one and two, indicating that there is initially a higher rate of return to AFDC among exiting experimentals than among controls, although the difference is not large enough to completely offset the speedier case closures for experimentals. After the eighth month off AFDC, the difference between the curves flattens out and then moves gradually towards zero over time, meaning that experimentals and controls who still remain off welfare have similar propensities for reentering the public assistance rolls, with controls tending to reenter just slightly more than experimentals.

Table 6-2 presents more detailed information about the initial spell off AFDC. We define the duration of the first spell off AFDC as the number of consecutive months of zero AFDC payments beginning with the month of case closure. If, for example, a woman returned to the rolls after only a single month off, the duration of her spell is coded as one month. In order to make comparable calculations for all of the sites, we top-coded spells lasting longer than twelve months, setting them equal to exactly twelve months. Top-coding implies that the tracking periods covered by Table 6-2 are truncated relative to the number of months covered by most of the curves in Figure 6-2 (i.e., in all sites except Baltimore).

Results for Virginia are given in the top panel of the table. The first row in the panel shows the percentage of experimentals and controls included in the calculations. Some 73.5 percent of controls and 74.5 percent of experimentals were off AFDC

---

[11] The figure tracks all initial exits. As explained above, these include departure from AFDC because an AFDC application was not approved as well as departure after some AFDC had been received.

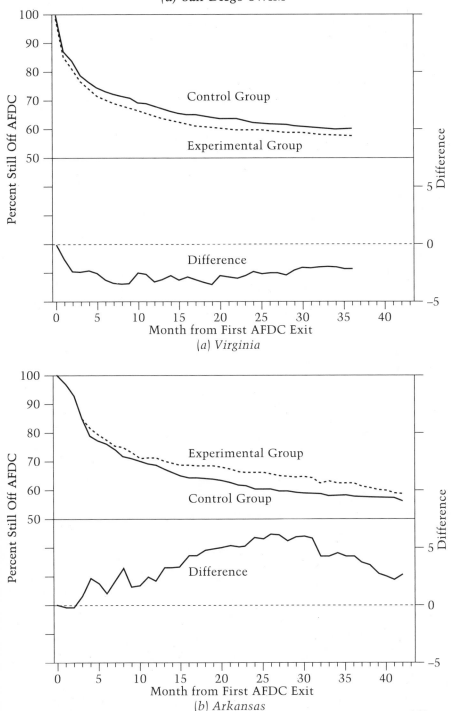

FIGURE 6-2
Probability of Remaining Off AFDC During First Spell Off:
(a) Virginia; (b) Arkansas; (c) Baltimore;
(d) San Diego SWIM

(a) Virginia

(b) Arkansas

169

FIGURE 6-2 *(continued)*

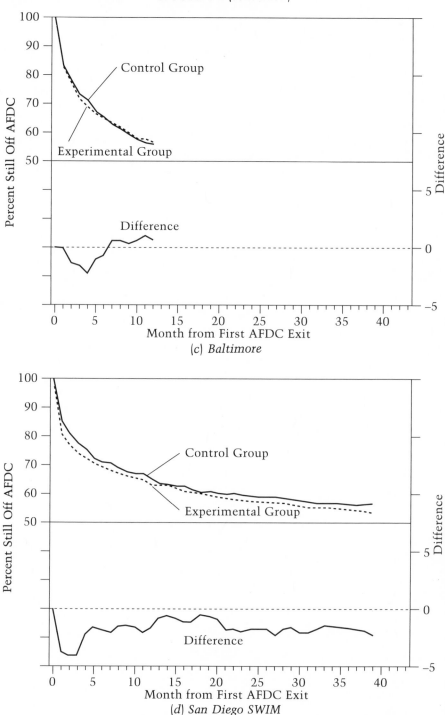

(c) *Baltimore*

(d) *San Diego SWIM*

within twenty-four months of random assignment, a difference of 1.0 percentage point. Since the percentages off AFDC differ—albeit only slightly—between the experimental and control groups, we cannot with complete certainty interpret any differences in reentry between the two subsamples as unbiased measures of program effect. Such differences may not be caused by the program. They may, instead, stem from differences in the composition of the two selected subsamples.

As stated above, exits include AFDC applicants who left the AFDC system because their applications were not approved. The second row of the table shows how many of these there were. The row selects sample members who exited and gives the conditional percent of exits that "never received" any AFDC payments within two years. In Virginia, as we already know from Table 6-1, group differences in this measure were minimal. As shown in Table 6-2, 16.6 percent of exiting controls never received AFDC; for exiting experimentals, that number was 16.3 percent.

We next select out this "never received" group, leaving only exiters who had at least one positive payment month before leaving. Row three shows the average length of the truncated first spell off AFDC for these experimental and control subsamples. Members of the experimental subsample remained off AFDC for 8.44 consecutive months of the maximum of twelve months we followed their first spell off. This is 0.33 months (or 3.8 percent) less than the average for controls.

The next several rows of the table show the distribution of length of first spell off AFDC for those who began to receive

TABLE 6-2
Distribution of Initial Spells Off AFDC

)gram and Outcome	Experimentals	Controls	Difference
ginia			
:ver off AFDC in months 1–24 (%)	74.5	73.5	1.0
f ever off AFDC in months 1–24:			
Never received in months 1–24 (%)	*16.3*	*16.6*	*−0.4 (z)*
If ever received in months 1–24:			
Observed average months off (max = 12)	*8.44*	*8.77*	*−0.33 (z)*
Distribution of length of first spell off (%)			
1 month off	*16.0*	*14.5*	*1.5 (z)*
2 months off	*4.9*	*3.6*	*1.3 (z)*
3–5 months off	*12.1*	*12.0*	*0.1 (z)*
6–11 months off	*7.8*	*7.6*	*0.2 (z)*
12 or more months off	*59.1*	*62.2*	*−3.1 (z)*
Total	*100.0*	*100.0*	*0.0*

TABLE 6-2 *(continued)*

Program and Outcome	Experimentals	Controls	Difference
Arkansas			
Ever off AFDC in months 1–24 (%)	75.3	70.8	4.5 *
If ever off AFDC in months 1–24:			
Never received in months 1–24 (%)	*32.0*	*28.4*	*3.6 (z)*
If ever received in months 1–24:			
Observed average months off (max = 12)	*8.66*	*8.60*	*0.06 (z)*
Distribution of length of first spell off (%)			
1 month off	*7.0*	*6.3*	*0.7 (z)*
2 months off	*5.9*	*5.6*	*0.2 (z)*
3–5 months off	*17.8*	*19.8*	*−2.1 (z)*
6–11 months off	*11.6*	*11.4*	*0.2 (z)*
12 or more months off	*57.8*	*56.9*	*0.9 (z)*
Total	*100.0*	*100.0*	*0.0*
Baltimore			
Ever off AFDC in months 1–24 (%)	62.4	60.1	2.3
If ever off AFDC in months 1–24:			
Never received in months 1–24 (%)	*7.9*	*7.9*	*0.0 (z)*
If ever received in months 1–24:			
Observed average months off (max = 12)	*8.09*	*8.12*	*−0.03 (z)*
Distribution of length of first spell off (%)			
1 month off	*18.1*	*17.8*	*0.3 (z)*
2 months off	*5.6*	*4.5*	*1.1 (z)*
3–5 months off	*11.8*	*12.0*	*−0.3 (z)*
6–11 months off	*9.8*	*12.2*	*−2.4 (z)*
12 or more months off	*54.7*	*53.4*	*1.3 (z)*
Total	*100.0*	*100.0*	*0.0*
San Diego SWIM			
Ever off AFDC in months 1–24 (%)	64.7	55.3	9.3 ***
If ever off AFDC in months 1–24:			
Never received in months 1–24 (%)	*7.0*	*8.0*	*−1.0 (z)*
If ever received in months 1–24:			
Observed average months off (max = 12)	*8.60*	*8.85*	*−0.25 (z)*
Distribution of length of first spell off (%)			
1 month off	*18.7*	*14.9*	*3.9 (z)*
2 months off	*5.0*	*4.6*	*0.4 (z)*
3–5 months off	*6.6*	*9.4*	*−2.8 (z)*
6–11 months off	*7.3*	*7.2*	*0.1 (z)*
12 or more months off	*62.3*	*63.8*	*−1.5 (z)*
Total	*100.0*	*100.0*	*0.0*

NOTES: The first spell off AFDC is defined as beginning with the first month of zero AFDC receipt after a positive amount has been received. If the sample members received no AFDC for the first three months, then the first spell off is defined as beginning with month one, the month of random assignment.

Details may not sum to totals owing to rounding.

Italics indicate nonexperimental estimates.

A two-tailed t-test was applied to experimental differences. Statistical significance levels are indicated as: * = 10 percent; ** = 5 percent; *** = 1 percent. (z) indicates that the comparison is nonexperimental: no test of statistical significance was performed.

and then stopped receiving AFDC benefits. A somewhat higher proportion of exiting experimentals than exiting controls had very short first spells off; correspondingly fewer experimentals had long first spells off. Some 2.8 percent more of exiting experimentals than exiting controls had spells lasting only one or two months. At the same time, 3.1 percent fewer experimentals had spells lasting twelve months or more.

This small increment in one- and two-month first spells off AFDC explains the small difference in curves in Figure 6-2(a)[12] and may be evidence of a small churning or revolving door effect. Overall, however, the effect exerted too little influence to be visible in our summary recidivism statistic of the previous section, "fraction of months on AFDC from first exit through end of follow-up," which yielded quite similar values for exiting experimentals and controls. The increment in one- and two-month first spells off AFDC was also too small to undercut program impacts on AFDC by much.[13]

This analysis of recidivism in Virginia confirms our previous conclusion: AFDC recidivism effects are not pronounced. The slightly higher recidivism rates in the first and second months after initial exit from AFDC may reflect some revolving door or churning effects, but these effects are too small to have had much significance for the total program impact. The dominant program effect remains the modest overall speedup in exit from AFDC, which resulted in a modest reduction in total AFDC payments.

Arkansas. Recidivism effects in Arkansas were also small, but were in the opposite direction of those in Virginia. As shown in Figure 6-2(b), the percent remaining off AFDC after the first exit, somewhat surprisingly, was actually *greater* for experimentals than for controls. This difference grew gradually during the tracking period and then declined. By the end of twenty-five

---

[12] In comparing the figure and the table it should be recalled that the former includes exiters who never received AFDC but the bell distribution in the latter does not.

[13] To further test this assertion, we altered our definition of an AFDC exit to exclude case closures lasting less than six months. We then used this new definition to reestimate the impact on length of the initial spell of AFDC receipt. In Virginia, the new estimate of impact on initial spell length was − 0.88 months. This is halfway between our original estimate of − 0.98 months for the impact on initial spell length and the − 0.78 estimated impact on total months on AFDC. We conclude that very short spells off AFDC accounted for about half the modest overall effect of recidivism in offsetting total AFDC impact in Virginia. That is, very short spells off AFDC reduced total AFDC impact by about one-tenth.

months, about 6 percentage points more exiting experimentals than controls remained off AFDC; by the end of forty-two months the gap was still about 2 percentage points. The Arkansas program not only accelerated exits but also made quick reentry less likely among those who left. It is clear that AFDC impact was facilitated rather than inhibited by effects on recidivism.

In Table 6-2, the first row in the Arkansas panel shows that 4.5 percentage points more experimentals than controls were off AFDC sometime within the first two follow-up years. Fewer experimentals than controls ever received AFDC benefits during this period, indicating that the program induced an application effect. The remainder of the effect occurred because a larger percentage of experimentals than of controls exited the rolls after receiving AFDC benefits for at least one month.

The rest of the information in Table 6-2 suggests that the difference in recidivism apparent in Figure 6-2(b) may be largely attributable to the application effect in Arkansas. As shown in the table, 3.6 percentage points more of experimental-group exiters never received any AFDC. Differences further down in the table are smaller than this. The average number of months off AFDC for sample members who went on then off fell only 0.06 months within the maximum twelve-month tracking period, which is virtually a zero effect. The distribution of months off does not show much difference in the frequency of short or long spells.

Baltimore. The Baltimore program had only a very small effect on early exit from AFDC. Differences in the length of first spell off AFDC were also small. As shown in Figure 6-2(c), the percent remaining off AFDC after the first exit was smaller for experimentals during the first four months of tracking, but this differential was wiped out over the next eight months. The third panel of Table 6-2 shows differences small enough so that the experimental- and control-group subsamples can be described as having essentially identical rates of AFDC recidivism. From these results we rule out recidivism as a factor in making AFDC impacts in Baltimore small.

San Diego SWIM. The distinguishing feature of AFDC effects for San Diego SWIM is the sharp increase in the rate of departure from AFDC during the first twenty-four months of follow-up. The final panel of Table 6-2 shows exits by 64.7 percent of experimentals and only 55.3 percent of controls, a difference of 9.3 percentage points. This is *twice* the difference in any of the other three sites. None of this effect in San Diego SWIM occurred as a result of an application effect. Similar percentages of experimental and control exiters left AFDC without any recorded AFDC payments during the observation period.

As shown in Figure 6-2(*d*), SWIM experimentals who exited the rolls were more likely to return to AFDC after one month. Some effect on short exits is also apparent in Table 6-2. The distribution of exit durations at the bottom of the table shows 3.9 percentage points more spells of one month off for experimentals, an effect larger than in Virginia, indicating a possible revolving door or churning effect. Other shifts offset the one-month effect, and the percent of spells twelve or more months long differed by only 1.5 percentage points between experimental and control exiters. The right of Figure 6-2(*d*), however, shows that somewhat more experimentals than controls had returned to AFDC after two or three years, producing a difference similar in magnitude to that in Virginia over the same interval. Thus, by the end of follow-up, AFDC recidivism was greater for experimentals than controls, but the difference is small and appears not to have had a pronounced effect on persistence of AFDC impacts over time. The truncated average duration of initial spells off AFDC (over the first twelve months) was only 0.25 months lower for exiting experimentals than for exiting controls (8.60 months versus 8.85 months, respectively).[14]

For San Diego SWIM, as for Virginia, Arkansas, and Baltimore, this analysis of recidivism supplements but does not fundamentally change our interpretation of the main program effect. For all these programs, most of the AFDC savings, whether small or large, occurred as a result of earlier exit from the rolls. Recidivism occurred among both experimentals and controls but did not substantially affect AFDC impacts. The largest AFDC effects were case closure effects in Arkansas and San Diego SWIM; none of the recidivism effects in any of the sites were as large as these effects. In two sites, Virginia and San Diego, the AFDC reduction from speedier AFDC exit was partly offset by short-term recidi-

---

[14] To further quantify the possible effect of very short spells off AFDC on overall AFDC impact, we redefined AFDC exit, as we did for Virginia, to include only spells of at least six successive months off. In San Diego SWIM, our reestimate of the program effect on initial AFDC spell length came to -3.53 months. This reestimate is about one-third the way down from our original estimate of -3.89 months for the impact on initial spell length towards the -2.87 estimated impact on total months on AFDC. We infer that very short spells off AFDC accounted for about one-third of the rather limited overall effect of recidivism in offsetting total AFDC impact in San Diego SWIM. Stated another way, very short spells off AFDC reduced total AFDC impact by about one-tenth, the same as in Virginia.

vism among some of the program enrollees, but the size of these offsets was modest. In Arkansas we found a reduction in recidivism among experimentals, whose initial spells off AFDC were somewhat longer than those of controls.

Recidivism is certainly an important phenomenon when considering the potential effect of a welfare-to-work program. Our analysis shows a significant rate of return to AFDC within a year of exit, among both experimentals and controls. Return within twelve months was about 40 percent for all people who left welfare; even among those who stayed off the rolls at least three months, 20 to 30 percent were again receiving AFDC within a year.[15] If interventions can be found which are effective in reducing reentry, they could clearly have an impact on AFDC receipt and expenditures. None of the programs examined here had a major effect of this kind, however.

AFDC RESPONSE DURING EARLY AND LATE PERIODS OF FOLLOW-UP

In this section, we examine AFDC case closure and AFDC recidivism with statistics from early and later follow-up periods. We will focus on Arkansas and San Diego SWIM, the two programs for which AFDC effects were largest. The data for Arkansas are displayed in the top half of Table 6-3. The left of the table displays estimates for the second follow-up year; the right shows estimates for the last twelve months of follow-up (months fifty-five to sixty-six). The same measures for San Diego SWIM are displayed at the bottom of the table. Corresponding results for the other programs may be found in Appendix Table A-1. The estimates for Virginia and Baltimore provide no new information beyond what has already been discussed.

The top portion of the Arkansas panel—rows one, two, and three—contains estimates of the AFDC impact measured in dollars, months of receipt, and amounts per month for early and

---

[15] These estimates are for experimentals. The total percent returning within a year is simply 100 minus the percent with a spell of twelve months or more. For example, in Virginia, this would be 100 − 59.1, or 40.9 percent. The estimates for experimentals who stayed off at least three months were obtained by dropping the one- and two-month leavers from the frequency distributions in Table 6-2. For Virginia, this would give (12.1 + 7.8)/(12.1 + 7.8 + 59.1) or 25.2 percent. Estimates for the other programs are as follows: Arkansas, 42.2 and 33.7 percent; Baltimore, 45.3 and 28.3 percent; and San Diego SWIM, 37.7 and 18.2 percent.

later years. These estimates reinforce our previous conclusions about the dominant role played by reductions in months of receipt. AFDC payments for year two in Arkansas were down by $192 or 19.2 percent; months of receipt were down by 0.96 or 16.4 percent, accounting for more than five-sixths the reduction in payments. Lower average payments per month of receipt during the year account for only a small part of total AFDC savings. By the final year, payment impacts were no longer statistically significant: the final-year saving was $63 per experimental, a third of the impact in the second year. The final-year dollar impact nonetheless still represents an 8.3 percent reduction relative to AFDC payments received by controls in that year. Months on AFDC were reduced by 0.27 or 7.1 percent in the final year, and the impact on months again accounts for about five-sixths of the year's AFDC reduction. Thus, although the total impact was much smaller by the final year, the mechanism of impact, namely, a reduction in months of receipt, was the same.

In the lower portion of the Arkansas panel, we display statistics on AFDC receipt among two classes of people in the sample. Sample members are divided into those who are "on AFDC" and "off AFDC" during the middle of the second and final years of the follow-up period. Sample members who were *on* AFDC are further subdivided into (a) those who were on welfare continuously after the month of random assignment, and (b) those who returned to the rolls after a spell off. In defining these statuses, we did not count brief spells of one or two months off the rolls as an exit. Sample members who had only one- or two-month strings of zero payments were assigned to the continuous receipt category rather than to the returnee category. In light of the findings reported in the previous section, it is useful to look at recidivism without reference to such short spells off the rolls. Sample members classified as off AFDC are subdivided into those who never received AFDC from the start of follow-up through the middle of the second or final years; those who initially received AFDC and then went off permanently (i.e., stayed off through the end of follow-up); and those who were off at midyear but would return before the end of follow-up.[16]

For the second follow-up year, the most notable result in Ar-

---

[16]There is a variety of ways to classify sample members by current, past, and future AFDC status. For the sake of simplicity, we elected to group together all those who had never received AFDC as of midyear, even if they subsequently reapplied and were approved later. Alternatively, those "future reapplicants" could have been assigned to the "will return" category.

TABLE 6-3
Short- and Longer-Term Impacts on Patterns of AFDC Receipt

Program and Outcome	Year Two			Final Year[a]		
	Experimentals	Controls	Difference	Experimentals	Controls	Difference
Arkansas						
Average AFDC payments during year	$812	$1,004	-$192***	$698	$761	-$63
Average number of months received AFDC during year	4.90	5.86	-0.96***	3.55	3.82	-0.27
Average AFDC payment in months receiving welfare	*$166*	*$171*	*-$6 (z)*	*$197*	*$199*	*-$2 (z)*
Midyear AFDC status (%)						
On AFDC at midyear						
Never off more than two months, month one through midyear	32.1	38.3	-6.2**	16.9	16.0	0.9
Off more than two months but returned by midyear	7.8	10.3	-2.6	12.5	15.5	-3.0
Off AFDC at midyear						
Never received AFDC from month one through midyear[b]	24.5	20.6	3.9*	20.1	17.2	2.9
Will not return to AFDC before end of follow-up	26.4	21.4	5.0**	47.6	48.6	-0.9
Will return to AFDC before end of follow-up[c]	9.3	9.4	-0.1	2.9	2.8	0.1
Total	100.0	100.0	0.0	100.0	100.0	0.0

San Diego SWIM					
Average AFDC payments during year	$3,523	$4,088	−$565***	$2,297	$2,461	−$164
Average number of months received AFDC during year	6.60	7.48	−0.88**	3.85	4.07	−0.23
Average AFDC payment in months receiving welfare	*$534*	*$546*	*−$12 (z)*	*$597*	*$604*	*−$7 (z)*
Midyear AFDC status (%)						
On AFDC at midyear						
Never off more than two months, month one through midyear	48.7	56.0	−7.3***	20.4	22.9	−2.5*
Off more than two months but returned by midyear	5.1	6.2	−1.1	11.4	10.2	1.2
Off AFDC at midyear						
Never received AFDC from month one through midyear[b]	4.7	4.4	0.3	4.0	4.2	−0.2
Will not return to AFDC before end of follow-up	29.7	25.5	4.3***	61.8	60.1	1.7
Will return to AFDC before end of follow-up[c]	11.7	7.9	3.9***	2.4	2.6	−0.2
Total	100.0	100.0	0.0	100.0	100.0	0.0

NOTES: Midyear AFDC statuses are mutually exclusive. Tests of statistical significance on those categories are not strictly independent. Year two is defined as months thirteen through twenty-four, and midyear is month nineteen. The final year is defined as the last twelve months of follow-up available, and the midyear month is the final month minus five.

Details may not sum to totals owing to rounding.

Italics indicate nonexperimental estimates.

A two-tailed t-test was applied to experimental differences. Statistical significance levels are indicated as: * = 10 percent; ** = 5 percent; *** = 1 percent. (z) indicates that the comparison is nonexperimental: no test of statistical significance was performed.

[a]The final year of AFDC follow-up is defined as follows: Arkansas, months fifty-five through sixty-six; San Diego SWIM, months fifty-two through sixty-three.

[b]Includes some sample members who will receive AFDC before the end of follow-up.

[c]Excludes sample members in the category "never received AFDC."

179

kansas is the large reduction among experimentals in the percentage who continuously received AFDC payments after random assignment. The drop in continuous benefit receipt was more than 6 percentage points by the middle of the second year. There was also a 2.6 percentage point drop in the fraction of people who received benefits in the middle of the second year after they had exited the rolls at some earlier point. At the same time, the proportion of people who never received AFDC benefits through the middle of the second year rose sharply in the experimental group, increasing 3.9 percentage points above the comparable rate in the control group. Even more striking is the rise among experimentals in the percentage of people who did not receive AFDC in the middle of the second follow-up year and who *never* received welfare during the remainder of the follow-up period (26.4 percent of the experimental group versus just 21.4 percent of the control group). Thus, in the short run, the Arkansas program deterred some applications for AFDC and speeded up exit from the rolls without increasing the rate of return to AFDC later on.

The differences between the treatment and control groups in Arkansas are narrower by the middle of the final follow-up year. Only two notable differences remain. A higher percentage of controls than of experimentals received benefits in the middle of the final year after having left the rolls at some earlier point (15.5 percent of controls versus 12.5 percent of experimentals). And a higher percentage of experimentals than of controls still had never received AFDC from the point of random assignment to the middle of the final follow-up year. The program had no noticeable effect in reducing the proportion of people who remained steadily dependent on AFDC for very long spells. About 17 percent of experimentals received benefits continuously through the middle of the final follow-up year versus 16 percent of controls. Thus, the main long-term effect of the Arkansas program was to deter completion of some applications for AFDC which otherwise would have been successful. Those who were deterred would not have received AFDC continuously for the full follow-up period. Rather, they were mostly individuals who would have left AFDC at some point and come back to the rolls later.

The Arkansas results clearly show that control-group catch-up was more important than wearing-off in explaining the decline in AFDC impacts over time. In Arkansas, we see a short-run reduction in continuous AFDC receipt. In the long run, the experimental-control difference has shrunk. The percent receiving continuously in the control group fell from nearly 40 percent in the second year of follow-up to only 16 percent in the final year. Case closures among continuously receiving controls caught up with those among experimentals. The narrowing of the experimental-control difference in continuous receipt can come only from catch-up. In fact, the difference between the effects in year two and the final year indicates the degree of control catch-up. Wearing-off implies an increase in the rate of return to AFDC among those who leave it. If wearing-off were the dominant mechanism, we would expect to see a large positive experimental-control difference in the percentage of people who left AFDC but returned by the final year. Instead, we see a negative effect.

We now turn to the results for San Diego SWIM. In some respects the patterns of AFDC effects of SWIM and Arkansas were similar. The $565 AFDC impacts for SWIM for year two amounted to a 13.8 percent reduction relative to the control mean. Months on AFDC were reduced by 0.88 (or 11.8 percent). As in Arkansas, the reduction in months accounts for about five-sixths the reduction in second-year payments. Lower average payments per month of receipt made up only a small portion of total AFDC savings for the year. The final-year AFDC impact was $164 (6.7 percent of the control-group mean), although it was not statistically significant. The corresponding impact on months was 0.23 (5.7 percent), which again accounted for about five-sixths of the total AFDC impact for the year. As in Arkansas, the dollar AFDC impacts in SWIM, both early and late, were largely determined by the reduction in months of welfare receipt.

We next examine the AFDC status outcomes for SWIM. By the middle of the second year, SWIM, like Arkansas, had produced a large reduction in the percent of experimentals receiving AFDC continuously from the point of random assignment. The decrease was more than 7 percentage points, even larger than the corresponding effect for Arkansas. SWIM achieved more than a 4 percentage point increase in the number of experimentals who left AFDC by the second year and did not return during the follow-up period. The size of this effect was similar to Arkansas's. Unlike Arkansas, SWIM produced no effect on the "never received AFDC" measure.[17] SWIM also produced nearly a 4 per-

---

[17] The percent of experimentals and controls who never received AFDC is much smaller in SWIM than in Arkansas, partly the result of differences in the locus of random assignment. Random assignment occurred earlier in the application/approval process in Arkansas than in San Diego SWIM. Consequently, in Arkansas, many more AFDC applicants entered the sample before their applications were acted upon than was the case in San Diego SWIM.

centage point increase in the percentage of experimentals who were off AFDC in the middle of the second year but would return before the end of the follow-up period. This effect did not show up at all in Arkansas. It indicates an increase in AFDC recidivism attributable to SWIM. Hence, in the short run, SWIM speeded case closure, although some of those induced to leave AFDC soon returned to welfare.

By the final year, all experimental-control differences in SWIM had declined substantially. Of particular interest is the decline in effect on continuous AFDC receipt. From 56 percent in year two, the percent of controls who were never off AFDC dropped by more than half to about 23 percent in the final year. The experimental-control difference fell from 7.3 percentage points in the second year to 2.5 percentage points in the final year. As in Arkansas, the decline in the difference could only have resulted from control catch-up. The wearing-off effect is comparatively small. By the middle of the final year, there was only a small difference (1.2 percentage points) between experimentals and controls in the number who left AFDC and then returned to the rolls. In the long run, SWIM differs from Arkansas in showing a small (but statistically significant) reduction in continuous AFDC receipt offset partially by a slight increase in returns to AFDC among those who had left.[18]

In sum, the analysis of early and later periods for Arkansas and San Diego SWIM reinforces our conclusion that impacts on AFDC payments came from reduced months on public assistance achieved by more rapid case closure. The main difference between Arkansas and San Diego SWIM is that Arkansas obtained an application effect whereas SWIM obtained its entire effect among enrollees who received AFDC but then left the rolls. The cases closed by the two programs were mostly among enrollees who would have received AFDC for three or four years but not for the full five and a half years we can observe. Control catch-up rather than AFDC recidivism was the principal mechanism of the decline in AFDC impacts over time.

---

[18] The two measures of recidivism show an apparent inconsistency for SWIM: The 3.9 percentage point increase in "will return to AFDC" in year two is larger than the 1.2 percentage point increase in "off but returned" in the final year. The greater magnitude of the two-year measure indicates that much of the increased recidivism it captured was a return to short-term AFDC receipt, followed by another departure from welfare before the final year. The off-on-off nature of recidivism in this case makes the offset to total AFDC impact less than we might have expected from looking only at the two-year recidivism measure.

EFFECTS ON POTENTIAL
LONG-TERM AFDC RECIPIENTS

The estimates in Table 6-3 offer us a convenient opportunity to consider program effects on long-term AFDC receipt. Long-term receipt can be approached from two quite different perspectives. Both are defined relative to the point of program enrollment, which is also the point of random assignment in these studies. First, we may be interested in *past* long-term AFDC receipt. That is, we may be interested in program impacts for enrollees who have been on AFDC for a long time before entering the program. The behavior of these long-term recipients may be studied even with short-term follow-up data. We may, for example, examine first- and second-year impacts of a program on enrollees who have been on AFDC for more than two years in the past. We can compare those impacts with impacts on enrollees who have been on AFDC for two years or less or enrollees who are just applying for AFDC for the first time.

We are interested in past long-term AFDC recipients, however, mostly because a long AFDC history is one of the best predictors of a long period of *future* AFDC receipt, especially in making predictions for adults. In fact, when we look at recipients with long past AFDC receipt, it is really the high proportion of "future" or "potential" long-term AFDC recipients among them that is of interest. The reason for this is that effects on long future AFDC spells will exert a disproportionately large effect on a program's total AFDC impact. As an illustration, closing an AFDC case that would have lasted ten more years will have the same impact on total months of AFDC receipt as closing ten cases that would have each lasted one more year; and impacts on AFDC payments will also be the same if payments for each year of receipt were the same for all cases. Against this, closing a case that is ten years old will have the same impact as closing a case that has just been opened (i.e., is zero years old) if both would have remained opened for the same amount of time in the future. It is only because a ten-year-old case is likely to stay open longer in the future than a new case that closing the former may produce a larger impact.

In practice, cases that are two years old or older at the time of program enrollment do tend to stay open much longer in the future. We can therefore make some important inferences about program effects on future long-term AFDC receipt by looking at short-term impacts for past long-term AFDC recipients. A study by Friedlander (1988c) using three of the four evaluations we study here, but with shorter follow-up, and two other similar evaluations, found that past long-term AFDC recipients and other disadvantaged groups contributed a major share of total program AFDC impacts. Impacts on earnings were not found consistently for this group, however, suggesting that low- to moderate-cost programs may not be effective in increasing the earnings of enrollees who are more disadvantaged than some threshold level (e.g., those with multiple barriers to employment). Job search and work experience, it was argued, will not be sufficient to repair the skills deficits common in this portion of the program population.

The correlation between past and future AFDC receipt is not perfect, however. Some individuals who have been on AFDC a long time will leave soon; others with short AFDC histories will stay on for many years. It would therefore be useful to study long future AFDC receipt directly. But we can only study long future AFDC receipt directly when we have several years of follow-up data, as we do in the present study. With long follow-up data, we now have some controls who are still on AFDC after five or six years, and we can see whether there are fewer experimentals still on AFDC at that time. Having data for five or more years of follow-up thus offers an important advantage over short-term follow-up if we want to study program effects on potential long-term AFDC receipt.

We can now turn to the data. In some sense, the definition of "long-term" is arbitrary. Some studies define a long-term spell as one lasting eight years or more. The data we have here, however, extend at most to five and a half years. We therefore define "future long-term AFDC recipient" as a sample member who is still on AFDC at the end of follow-up, five or six years after random assignment; we define "potential long-term AFDC recipient" as a sample member who is on or *would have been on* AFDC at that time in the absence of the program. We include individuals who remain on continuously and those who leave and then return. Looking back at Table 4-2 at year five of follow-up, we can see that between 24 percent (Virginia) and 36 percent (San Diego SWIM) of controls could be classified as potential long-term AFDC recipients under this definition. At the same time, fully 38 percent (San Diego SWIM) to 53 percent (Virginia) of controls were off aid by year two; many of these were off permanently, although some returned later on. The remainder of controls stayed on AFDC for an intermediate length of time between one and five years. Thus, we might think of three groups, roughly similar in size, of potential short-term, intermediate-term, and long-term AFDC recipients. This heterogeneity—this split between potential short-, intermediate-, and long-term AFDC recipients—is the reason long-term receipt is important. If there were no heterogeneity, if all control sample members were still on AFDC at the end of follow-up, then case closures for any one group would make the identical contribution to total program AFDC impacts as the same number of case closures for any other group. As it is, however, any case closures occurring among the minority of program enrollees who are potential long-term AFDC recipients must make a disproportionately large contribution to total AFDC impact, as discussed above.

Any sustained impacts on potential long-termers will show up as experimental-control differences in AFDC during the final follow-up year. If we look, again in Table 4-2, at year five in Virginia, we find that the experimental-control difference in AFDC payments is quite small. In addition, the average AFDC receipt rate in year five was 23.6 percent for experimentals and 24.1 percent for controls, a difference of only −0.4 percentage points. The small magnitude of these final-year impacts permits us to say with some confidence that program effects on potential long-term AFDC recipients at five years are small in Virginia and will be small beyond that point. In Baltimore, we think the effects on potential long-term recipients will be small because short-term AFDC effects, observed within three years of follow-up, are small.

The analysis for Arkansas and San Diego SWIM is more challenging. For those programs, the AFDC reductions in years five and six shown in Table 4-2 appear modest relative to the earlier years and are not statistically significant, except for year five in SWIM. In Table 6-3, we can see that dollar impacts and impacts on number of months are both much smaller in the final follow-up year than in year two. It is difficult to project these estimates out past the end of follow-up, and effects on AFDC receipt at eight years or more may be quite small. Nevertheless, even in the final follow-up year, the dollar impacts in Arkansas and SWIM represent reductions of 8.3 percent and 6.7 percent, respectively, in comparison with control mean AFDC payments during that year. Estimates of impacts on the number of months receiving AFDC in the final year are almost as large relative to control means: 7.1 percent and 5.7 percent reductions for Arkansas and San Diego SWIM, respectively.

Some speculative calculations suggest that effects on potential five- and six-year AFDC recipients may account for as much as one-third of total AFDC impacts over the observed follow-up period in San Diego SWIM—although the exact share cannot be determined with certainty—and a smaller but still significant share in Arkansas. To make these calculations, we first assume that the impacts on AFDC payments observed for the potential long-term AFDC recipients in the final year began around the end of year one and were then obtained by them in every succeeding year. Given that the peaks of AFDC impacts for both Arkansas and San Diego SWIM occur in year two, this assumption seems a plausible starting point. Using this assumption, we can multiply the final-year impacts by the number of follow-up years after year one (4.5 for Arkansas and 4.25 for San Diego SWIM) to obtain the total impacts on AFDC payments to potential long-termers. This amount we divide by the impact on total AFDC payments for the full sample, given in Table 6-1. The result is an estimate of the share of impacts on total AFDC payments accounted for by impacts on potential long-termers.

These calculations reveal that effects on potential five- and six-year AFDC recipients accounted for 39 percent of total program impact on AFDC payments in Arkansas and 36 percent in San Diego SWIM. As a check, we performed analogous calculations on months receiving AFDC. From these, we computed the contribution of potential five- and six-year AFDC recipients to total reductions in months as 33 percent for Arkansas and 34 percent for San Diego SWIM.[19]

For San Diego SWIM, these estimates of about one-third as the contribution of impacts on potential long-term AFDC recipients to total AFDC impacts appear justified. Table 6-3 has already shown that AFDC effects in the final year in SWIM came from a reduction in continuous five-year AFDC receipt, just the kind of effect assumed in our estimate. For Arkansas, our estimates appear too high. On the one hand, Table 6-3 indicates that the final-year AFDC impact in Arkansas was associated with a 2.9 percentage point increase in the rate of "never received AFDC," the application effect we have already examined. We

---

[19] The assumption we have made of a one-year delay in the onset of impacts is equivalent to an assumption of zero impact at the point of random assignment, followed by a steady, straight-line increase in impact through the end of year two, when the full impact on long-termers would then be reached. Replacing this assumption with the assumption of no impacts for the first two years would give a lower bound share of 26 percent (from the months estimate in Arkansas).

have already attributed about a third of the total AFDC impact to that application effect, which is in line with our estimate of the contribution of effects on long-term AFDC receipt. On the other hand, Table 6-3 reveals that the final-year AFDC impact in Arkansas came not from reducing continuous receipt but from reducing receipt among sample members who would have left AFDC and then returned. Savings for these sample members might therefore not have accrued over the full time period after year one. In particular, savings for them would not have accrued during periods when they would have been off AFDC anyway. Thus, the contribution to AFDC impacts from sample members who would have been on AFDC at the end of follow-up may have been less than one-third in Arkansas, although it was probably still significant.

From this discussion we draw two conclusions. First, as we have stated earlier, the major share of AFDC savings, even for Arkansas and San Diego SWIM, appears to come for short- or intermediate-term experimentals, who would have received AFDC for less than five years in the absence of the programs. Notwithstanding, even though the impacts on potential long-term AFDC recipients appear to be rather modest for these two programs, those effects do account for a significant share of the total AFDC impacts. Second, we note that Arkansas and San Diego SWIM had the largest AFDC impacts among the four programs and were also the only ones to show any effect at all on potential long-term recipients of welfare. It therefore appears that effects on potential five- and six-year AFDC recipients, even modest effects, were helpful in achieving large AFDC reductions. These findings are consistent with the AFDC impact findings of Friedlander (1988c).

CONCLUSIONS

In Chapter 4, we found that the experimental-control differential in AFDC in Virginia, Arkansas, and San Diego SWIM narrowed from the peak year to the final year of observation. The analysis in this chapter indicates that this decline in impact was not caused primarily by recidivism among experimentals. Instead, the narrowing of the experimental-control AFDC differential seems to stem mainly from "catch-up" by controls in welfare case closures. This catch-up in case closures may be mostly the result of normal welfare turnover, the month-to-month pattern of case closures observed even when no special assistance is offered to help people leave the rolls. To some extent, the process of catch-up may have been augmented by the availability of program services to control-group members after the research-imposed embargoes on serving controls were lifted.

Our overall assessment of the potential for welfare-to-work programs to achieve reductions in AFDC receipt and AFDC expenditures is, on balance, a positive one: If an initial impact on case closure can be obtained, then some reductions in receipt and payments are likely to persist over a period of several years. The savings for any one group of enrollees do not accumulate indefinitely, but this is a natural consequence of the fact that all AFDC recipients eventually leave welfare, even without special help in doing so. The decline in AFDC impacts is not so rapid that it eliminates the chance for low- to moderate-cost programs to make back in budgetary savings the initial cost of services.

At the same time, it is clear that the full potential for AFDC reductions was not achieved by any of these programs. Even in Arkansas and San Diego SWIM, about a third of the experimental group still received AFDC in the fifth year of follow-up. Working effectively with these long-term AFDC stayers may require more intensive education and training, special support components, or special ways of organizing activities and participation requirements.

For a program to succeed in reducing AFDC caseloads and spending, it must have two critical features. First, the share of the total AFDC caseload reached or covered by the program must be large. If a program actively serves a large share of the total caseload, then a 5 or 10 percent AFDC reduction for enrollees will translate into a visible aggregate impact. Programs or activities that can be implemented only on a small scale may have a large impact *per participant*, but the small number of participants places limits on the size of the aggregate impact.[20]

Second, the population receiving program attention must ac-

---

[20] For an elaboration of this point see Friedlander and Gueron (1992). An interesting comparison may be drawn between the San Diego SWIM demonstration and the National Supported Work Demonstration. SWIM, operating for two years in only two of the seven San Diego city offices, enrolled more than 10,000 AFDC recipients (only some of whom were selected for the research sample). In contrast, Supported Work, which was a much more intensive and expensive intervention, worked with only about 800 individuals, even though it was implemented in seven localities, including such large cities as New York, Chicago, Newark, Oakland, and Atlanta. The total impact of San Diego SWIM may therefore be many times larger, even if its impacts per enrollee are smaller.

tually include individuals who would otherwise have remained on AFDC for at least a few years. This may seem self-evident, almost a tautology. Yet the normal tendency of program staff will be to favor working with short-term AFDC recipients. Short-termers will seem comparatively easy to work with, and they leave AFDC with the least amount of staff time and attention. Program staff will tend to assign lower priority to working with program enrollees who would have remained on AFDC longer. Such individuals will appear to be poor prospects for rapid case closure, and staff will see them as "hard to serve." In order to offset this tendency, programs may adopt procedural rules and performance standards that discourage working with only short-term AFDC recipients.

At present, however, rules establishing service priorities must be crude, since the ability to predict who will leave AFDC only when provided with program assistance is currently quite limited.[21] Recall that San Diego SWIM, which achieved the largest AFDC reductions among the four programs studied here, operated under the simplest possible rule, namely, that *everyone* in the target population must participate.[22] In addition, SWIM, to a great extent, eliminated staff and client choice regarding the nature, sequence, and timing of activities. The inclusiveness of the SWIM participation protocols and their restrictions on discretion ensured that the longer-term AFDC stayers were not passed over for services. At the same time, however, it meant that a large share of program resources was spent on individuals whose future AFDC receipt remained completely unaffected by the services the program provided. Many of those unaffected were individuals who left AFDC and would have done so even without special attention; many were long-termers who stayed on AFDC but might have left with a more intensive (and expensive) effort. Research into better methods of matching the diversity of client types with the most effective low- or high-cost services for each type may be an important step for increasing program efficiency.

---

[21] Future AFDC receipt can be partially predicted from prior work and AFDC history and other demographics, or simply by adopting a wait-and-see approach. But even within groups having a long predicted length of stay on AFDC, there will be substantial turnover. Beyond that, identifying those in the long-term groups who will and will not respond to particular kinds of intervention is beyond present capabilities.

[22] In practice, not every SWIM enrollee was required to participate all the time. As permitted under program regulations, large numbers of "deferrals" from participation were granted for enrollees who faced family crises, sickness of a child, delays in course schedules, and other contingencies.

7

Interpreting the Empirical Findings

In this chapter, we provide some interpretation of the empirical results and discuss the implications for welfare employment policy. We do not believe our conclusions are definitive and final. We have examined only four evaluations, although we implicitly bring to our interpretation a wider knowledge of other program evaluation results. Data for newer programs and long-term follow-up data for more of the 1980s evaluations might reinforce or contradict the conclusions we draw here. Nevertheless, the empirical findings and our interpretation of them can contribute to the growing body of knowledge about the effects of welfare-to-work programs and can point out the critical tasks for policy and the important open questions for future field research.

OPERATIONAL OBJECTIVES

In interpreting our empirical findings, it is helpful to distinguish between the large number of individuals for whom joblessness and AFDC receipt are of short or intermediate duration and the smaller number who will be without work and on public assistance rolls for several years into the future. This distinction between short/intermediate-term and long-term AFDC recipients allows us to define three operational objectives for welfare-to-work programs. Each of these three operational objectives may require that program administrators develop different kinds of activities and support services. The three provide a framework for interpreting the empirical results of this study.

Two of the operational objectives apply to short- and intermediate-term AFDC recipients. As one possible objective, a program may attempt to shorten, perhaps substantially, the amount of time until an individual of this kind becomes employed. We find that all four programs achieved significant success in attaining this objective. They speeded up initial job finding and thereby increased the total amount of employment and the total sum of wages earned by program enrollees. Through faster job finding, the programs also shortened AFDC spells. Broadly speaking, the magnitude of employment effects was in line with the modest level of government resources committed to a program. In two of the four programs, budgetary savings from reduced AFDC payments substantially exceeded program net costs.

The second operational objective also pertains to individuals whose joblessness and AFDC receipt are short or intermediate in duration. A program may aim to increase the amount of earnings that these individuals obtain once they start to work. That is, it may try to increase hourly wage rates, weekly hours of work, and the duration of employment spells. Given the low levels of earnings observed among working members of the program population, these effects could improve the financial position of many families. In increasing on-the-job earnings, we find that only one of the four programs achieved significant gains, and that success was concentrated in a comparative handful of program enrollees. For the other programs, the mix of high-wage and low-wage, stable and unstable employment among program enrollees was similar to employment in the absence of the program (i.e., employment among controls).

The first two operational objectives we have discussed concern individuals who, within a few years, would find jobs or otherwise leave AFDC on their own, even in the absence of any intervention. The third operational objective for welfare-to-work programs concerns the important minority of program enrollees who face lengthy future spells of joblessness and AFDC receipt. Ideally, a welfare-to-work program would bring such individuals into the labor market and into stable employment at earnings levels that would maintain their families off AFDC at income levels higher than AFDC. Converting a spell of AFDC receipt that would last another ten years into ten years of employment represents an enormous program challenge but would be an enormous program achievement. None of the four evaluated programs was successful in attaining this objective. There was some increase in employment among program enrollees who would not have worked at all during the extended follow-up period. But the amount of employment gain remaining at the end of five years was small, indicating that the reduction in joblessness over the long term was not large. The programs made only modest inroads into long-term AFDC receipt, and a large fraction of program enrollees remained without work and on AFDC five years after their enrollment in a welfare-to-work program.

THE LONGER-TERM PERSPECTIVE

This study adds to existing knowledge by its analysis of the longer-term effects of mandatory welfare-to-work programs. Earlier studies with one-, two-, or even three-year follow-up did not capture the full picture of impacts changing over time. In their initial evaluations, the four programs in this study all showed short-term impacts on earnings if not on AFDC. None showed clear signs of how long those impacts might last for a group of enrollees. It was not known whether the impacts of low-cost job search activities and unpaid work assignments, which accounted for most of the activity in Arkansas and Virginia, would eventually decrease after the initial period of program participation. It was not known whether the more expensive education and training activities added by San Diego SWIM or Baltimore would cause impacts to persist or even grow. Thus, the full amount of impacts could not be determined with confidence, nor could the relative effectiveness of the more expensive versus the less expensive programs.[1] Longer-term program effects, it turns out, were important in determining the full worth and relative value of alternative program approaches. A large proportion of total earnings gains and total AFDC reductions came after two years from the date a group of enrollees first entered a program. And differences in the pattern of growth and convergence of earnings impacts over time emerged only in the extended follow-up data.

For AFDC impacts, the extended follow-up data did not change the rankings of the programs. Short-term data alone were apparently sufficient to distinguish programs that would ultimately have the largest effects from those that would have the smallest. But only the actual five-year earnings data were able to tell which programs had the largest total impacts on earnings. For example, the difference in earnings effects between Baltimore Options and San Diego SWIM did not become apparent

---

[1] Regarding the importance of longer-term follow-up in determining the relative effectiveness of programs, see also Friedlander and Gueron (1992).

until the end of the extended follow-up. Yet that final-year difference, to the extent that it predicts earnings impacts in year six and later years, indicates that Baltimore could gain a substantial lead over SWIM in total earnings impacts if additional follow-up were available.

The longer-term data were also important in determining the magnitude of financial gains for enrollees in programs that achieved government budget savings. Had Arkansas and San Diego SWIM shown more persistent earnings impacts, the total financial gains for enrollees would have looked much better than they did look. Thus, the long-term view of program effects, beyond the first job entry, appears particularly important in considering financial benefits for enrollees.

The longer-term data suggest that concerns about program effects wearing off were only partly realized in the programs studied. Rather it was catch-up by controls that was the major contributor to the eventual convergence in employment and AFDC receipt between experimentals and controls. This is an important finding for what it says about improving program effectiveness in the future. It implies that the programs produced effects for some kinds of enrollees but not for others. Future programs therefore do not have to start from scratch but, instead, can build upon the tested program approaches and add to them program components intended to reach a different part of the enrollee population. To reduce catch-up, programs will have to produce larger impacts on enrollees who would otherwise become the long-term jobless, long-term AFDC recipients.

The longer-term perspective helps explain a conundrum from past studies: How can there be earnings gains without comparable AFDC reductions? The new analysis makes clear that earnings impacts can accrue to many program enrollees who would not stay on AFDC long even without the program. Those earnings impacts therefore cannot produce much of a change in AFDC behavior. This insight illuminates the complex relationship between earnings gains and AFDC reductions observed in prior studies. One of the fundamental assumptions of policymakers in promoting welfare-to-work programs is that intervention that boosts employment will lead through work to reductions in AFDC receipt. But the data indicate that there is not a direct connection from earnings impacts to AFDC impacts. Rather, the connection is mediated by the characteristics of the group obtaining the earnings impacts. Efforts to achieve larger earnings impacts might be aimed either at individuals likely to become short-term AFDC recipients or at those likely to become long-term AFDC recipients. But focusing on the former has limited potential to increase AFDC impacts.

PROGRAM STRUCTURE AND THE PATTERNS OF IMPACTS

The kinds of activities a program offers, their sequence, procedures for assigning enrollees to them, rules for excusing enrollees from participation requirements, procedures for monitoring participation, enforcement practices—these elements of program structure interact with the mix of short- and long-term AFDC types to help determine the ratio of earnings gains to AFDC reductions. Different program structures may tend to elicit responses more from one or the other of these subgroups. The different responses of short- and long-termers can then produce two very different patterns of program results.

Among the four programs in this study, two produced substantial budgetary savings but much less financial benefit for enrollees. The other two produced financial gains for enrollees but no net benefits for budgets. That was particularly true for Baltimore Options, which had the largest income gains for enrollees but fell short of paying back program costs to government budgets. These results suggest the possible existence of a tradeoff between budgetary gains for government and financial gains for enrollees: the more for one, the less for the other. If this tradeoff is a general phenomenon, then policymakers will be forced to choose between competing goals. The particulars of the choice are best illustrated by the contrast between Baltimore Options and San Diego SWIM. To better understand the nature of the choice, it is helpful to speculate on how Options and SWIM affected underlying behavior.

The first goal of Baltimore program planners was economic security for enrollees. Options, as the name implies, offered a more customized program experience. This experience was based on an initial assessment of enrollee capabilities and needs in which the enrollee was asked to help choose the appropriate activity assignment. Education and training were frequently assigned as a first activity, although assignment to job search activities was also common. Program staff did not make much use of their sanctioning authority. Nevertheless, they treated the program as mandatory, told enrollees they had to participate, and pushed them to comply with their activity assignments.

Participation rates were as high as in most of the other program evaluations.

Baltimore Options produced persistent earnings impacts without long-term impacts on employment. Gains came to people who would have worked anyway, and there was not much in the way of AFDC impacts. The data suggest that a small proportion of enrollees gained a lot. In explaining this pattern of results, one plausible scenario is that the program structure elicited its main response from individuals who saw themselves leaving AFDC soon through employment and accepted guidance and services from the program to help get them working sooner and to improve their earnings prospects. This scenario is consistent with the very large earnings impacts estimated for recent applicants to AFDC, who, in the absence of special program intervention, tend to stay on the rolls for much less time than more established AFDC recipients. Under this scenario, individuals who expected AFDC to be their primary support for several years ahead would be less likely to see participation in Options as a benefit. They would be less likely to take up the program's offer of assistance and less likely to convert that assistance into a job.

San Diego SWIM provided a similar list of activities but was much less flexible. There was no initial assessment. The first steps in the participation sequence were usually fixed, with little staff and enrollee discretion. The prescribed sequence began with looking for a job; education and training came at the end. Participation was seen as an obligation for all, and that obligation was to be ongoing for as long as someone remained on AFDC. Achieving maximum monthly participation was a primary objective of the demonstration. Sanctioning rates were relatively high. It is possible that all these elements of program structure enabled SWIM to reach more deeply into its enrollee population, exerting its influence on many who did not necessarily see themselves as able to benefit from employment. This would be a different group from the one responding to the Baltimore program. This group in SWIM would have included more enrollees who expected their main income to come from welfare rather than work, at least for the next several years.

The difference in the kinds of people reached by SWIM combined with the up-front emphasis on job finding to produce a quite different pattern of results from Baltimore. Earnings impacts were large initially, but accrued primarily through more employment rather than increased pay on the job. The increased employment resulted in faster AFDC case closure because the group that responded contained more intermediate- and long-term AFDC recipients than did the group that experienced impacts in Baltimore. These case closures produced AFDC reductions in SWIM that were large relative to those of the other programs in this study and to those of other experimental evaluations of large-scale programs not examined here. These effects (and the effects on employment and earnings) might well have been even larger if SWIM had been a permanent program, since control-group catch-up would not have been facilitated by the ending of the embargo period and the superseding of SWIM by the GAIN program.

SWIM's impact on AFDC payments appears not to be the direct result of monthly grant reductions obtained through sanctioning. Rather, the evidence suggests that the dominant aspect of SWIM's "mandatoriness" was a tightening of constraints on enrollee behavior—quite different from the opening up of more "options" in Baltimore—achieved not only through sanctioning and threat of sanction but also through the program's fixed structure and possibly through expectations about work and welfare communicated by the staff to the enrollees. These are program influences independent of the content of program activities.

Although both were considered innovative welfare-to-work programs, Options and SWIM were very different programs, in themselves and in the effects they produced. They are, in fact, representative of opposing styles of program organization. Their results are consistent with existence of a tradeoff between savings for government budgets and income gains for enrollees. If that tradeoff is general, then federal and state policymakers will have an important choice between one or the other program style. That choice will depend on which program goal policymakers want to emphasize. For those who place top priority on increasing income, the assessment/choice model of Baltimore will appear the more desirable. Those who give greater weight to budgetary savings will favor models that are more like the fixed sequence, maximum participation approach of San Diego SWIM.

The existence of the tradeoff must be considered tentative. Baltimore is the only example of an assessment/choice model in the set of programs under study. Other adaptations of this model may be better able to produce AFDC impacts without sacrificing the long-term earnings impacts. It may also be possible to change the terms of the tradeoff on the SWIM side. Achieving larger earnings gains for the more disadvantaged, potential long-term AFDC recipients could increase the ratio of earnings gains to AFDC reductions for this group. A higher ratio would increase program impact on family income. Any program design capable of increasing earnings impacts for the more disadvantaged without sharply increasing program costs would still produce gains for government budgets and could reconcile some of the differing views of what welfare-to-work programs ought to be. We examine the possibilities for progress in this area in the next section.

THE MORE DISADVANTAGED

The results of the current study lead us to the view that welfare-to-work policy is at a critical juncture. On one hand, we have some indicators of favorable prospects for welfare-to-work programs in the future. We have a series of demonstrated successes from the 1980s, programs that have achieved results commensurate with a modest commitment of government funds. These programs not only increased employment and earnings but, for the most part, also produced enough in AFDC reductions and other savings to pay back government budgets all of program net cost. Even the least costly program produced impacts. Impacts on earnings were larger for the programs that spent more per enrollee, however, suggesting that increased effort can increase program effect. It would therefore seem to be worthwhile to continue and expand the use of 1980s approaches, even if it were not possible to increase program effectiveness by adding more activities and improving program structure and management.

Several provisions of JOBS do, in fact, greatly extend the reach of welfare-to-work programs. JOBS programs must be run statewide in all states, and there are additional federal matching funds to support those programs, up to a total federal share of $1.3 billion in 1995 and $1.0 billion per year thereafter.[2] The JOBS legislation also removed the participation exemption for many single AFDC parents with preschool children. The large group of AFDC case heads whose youngest child is three to five years old has been reclassified as mandatory under JOBS—the limit had previously been set at age six—and states have the option

---

[2] The federal matching rate begins at 90 percent, up to a state's fiscal 1987 WIN allocation. Above that amount, basic JOBS expenditures are matched at the larger of the state's Medicaid rate or 60 percent.

to lower the youngest child age exemption further to one year. States must guarantee child care if needed for an adult to participate, and the federal contribution to child care funding is not capped.[3] Finally, in a significant departure from past practice, the JOBS legislation imposes minimum participation levels for states that want to claim their full allotment of federal funds.[4] These provisions of JOBS are intended to bring program services and requirements to more people in more places. The evaluation results for programs for the 1980s have furnished a short list of proven activities and ways of organizing them that could provide a foundation for this effort.

On the other hand, it is not certain that what worked in the 1980s will prove effective for the new JOBS-mandatory groups or that it will achieve results across the full range of labor markets served by JOBS programs. In addition, the research has enabled us to identify important shortcomings with the approaches evaluated in the last decade. Those approaches helped enrollees find employment but did not give many of them a leg up to better-paying jobs. As a consequence, the programs did not directly alter the financial calculus by which AFDC parents must choose to support their families with income from welfare or from work. The programs also did not produce a sizable impact on the more disadvantaged, who make up a significant percentage of the program caseload. If these shortcomings cannot be effectively addressed, they will impose definite limits on the potential impact of welfare-to-work programs.

The more disadvantaged constitute a key subgroup in JOBS. As already discussed, greater earnings impacts for the more disadvantaged could ease the tradeoff between income gains and AFDC savings. In addition, because the more disadvantaged tend to become the long-term AFDC recipients, achieving greater impacts for them is the only way—by definition—that JOBS can fulfill its legislated mandate to reduce long-term dependency. It is also a path to increasing overall program impact. As we have seen in the current study, impacts on short-termers eventually fade over time as control sample members catch up. Potential long-termers in the control group will not catch up, or will catch up much more slowly. That means that impacts for any particu-

---

[3] The federal child care matching rate is the Medicaid rate for a state (varying from about 50 to 80 percent).

[4] The participation rate target was set initially at 7 percent of the nonexempt caseload (for fiscal 1990) but is scheduled to rise to 20 percent by 1995. States must attain these minimum participation rates in order to receive more than a 50 percent federal match rate for JOBS.

lar group of potential long-termers can be sustained for a much longer period, greatly multiplying the initial program effect. Total program impact will also increase simply because long-termers make up a large portion of the JOBS caseload. Obtaining better results for them will therefore naturally contribute to total JOBS impact in proportion to their numbers.

Certain features of JOBS were designed to increase program attention to the more disadvantaged and to better address their labor market problems. States are required to offer basic and remedial education, high school or equivalency, and English as a Second Language (ESL).[5] JOBS thus expands significantly the potential to address basic reading and math skills deficits, one of the key difficulties facing the more disadvantaged. States must also offer job skills training. JOBS further encourages the use of time-intensive education and training activities by specifying that only participation averaging at least twenty hours per week may be counted in the program participation rate. To ensure that the more disadvantaged receive attention, JOBS requires that states spend at least 55 percent of their funds on target groups containing relatively high proportions of potential long-term AFDC recipients.[6] Under JOBS, states have, in fact, been able to expand the geographic coverage of their welfare-to-work programs, have offered services to more people than before, and have increased the emphasis on education.[7] They are exceeding the 55 percent requirement for target-group spending.[8,9]

---

[5]For JOBS participants age twenty or over who lack a high school diploma or equivalent and cannot demonstrate basic literacy, states must include education unless the employability plan for that individual identifies a long-term employment goal that does not require a diploma or equivalent. States may require custodial parents under age twenty who do not have a high school diploma or equivalent to participate in education full-time, regardless of child age.

[6]Groups included in the target population include: (1) families in which the custodial parent is under age twenty-four and has not completed high school or has little or no work experience in the preceding year; (2) families in which the youngest child is within two years of being too old to be eligible for assistance; (3) families who have received assistance for thirty-six or more months during the preceding sixty months; and (4) applicants who have received AFDC for any thirty-six of the sixty months immediately prior to application.

[7]Hagen and Lurie (1992).

[8]U.S. General Accounting Office (1992).

[9]Problems as well as successes have marked the first years of JOBS. For one, JOBS has been experiencing serious problems with unspent funds. In fiscal 1992, for example, only two-thirds of the $1 billion in authorized federal funds were claimed by states (U.S. Congress, 1993, page 641). In addition, participation data gathered by the states under federal regulations have recently been judged inaccurate and not comparable across states, making them an unreliable basis for assessing this aspect of states' performance under JOBS (U.S. General Accounting Office, 1993).

Beefing up basic education and job training for the more disadvantaged addresses a critically important policy challenge posed by the results of the 1980s program evaluations. At the same time, however, the innovations of JOBS in this area entail considerable risk. JOBS goes several steps beyond what has been demonstrated to work in field studies. In theory, education and training increase earning power, which, in turn, increases the attractiveness of choosing work over welfare, leading to an increase in employment and a concomitant reduction in receipt of public assistance. A large number of empirical studies have documented the fact that groups with more education and training tend to have higher earnings. But it has been difficult to establish education and training conclusively as the *cause* of higher earnings. Moreover, the bulk of the evidence comes from studies of the general, nonwelfare population, using data in which people voluntarily choose the amount of education and training they acquire. The effect of *mandatory* participation in adult basic education and skills training for the AFDC population has only recently come under systematic scrutiny through field tests, and the final results of those studies are not in.

The large commitment of resources by JOBS would by itself make it important to test the theory in practice. Thorough testing is also recommended because there are a number of reasons why achieving success in this area may prove quite challenging. Teaching basic literacy and job skills and making up for weak prior labor-market experience is a major undertaking by itself. But programs also face the task of motivating enrollees who have done poorly in school in the past, and who have built up negative expectations about their own capabilities to learn and to benefit from education. Many enrollees will be daunted by the effort entailed, by meager self-esteem and self-confidence, and by what they believe to be poor earnings prospects for themselves. Programs may find that existing adult basic education and occupational training, which are designed for motivated, voluntary participants, may require special adaptations to work well with the AFDC population. Developing efficient education and training systems under JOBS may require several years of innovation, testing, and dissemination of proven "best practice" techniques.

Programs that work more intensively with the more disadvantaged will also have to be more concerned about job loss and AFDC recidivism than might be inferred from the findings in this study. These were limited in their role as offsets to long-term impacts in this study because the bulk of program impacts did not accrue to potential long-term AFDC recipients. Faster case closure is less likely to result in recidivism for short- and inter-mediate-term AFDC recipients simply because they would be off AFDC soon anyway. It is the program enrollees who would ordinarily stay on AFDC a long time who are more likely to return if an AFDC spell is interrupted. Efforts to work harder with this group may find employment instability accompanied by AFDC recidivism to be a much more serious problem. Achieving sustained impacts for potential long-termers may require an-cillary, post-job entry services and other measures to reduce job loss and recidivism and to support the initial investment in skill development.

In moving forward with human capital development services, JOBS programs face a number of unknowns. How much of an increase in reading and math skills can be produced by welfare-to-work programs using basic education? How many program enrollees can be assisted in obtaining their high school diploma or equivalent? How much do such educational impacts improve participants' earning power? How much can job skills training increase earning power? To what extent do greater investments in education and training lead to higher-wage, more stable jobs, with reduced likelihood of return to AFDC? Will the AFDC im-pacts produced by these investments compensate for the increase in program expenditure on more intensive services? Can such impacts be realized for the more disadvantaged? Can programs produce impacts for the new JOBS-mandatory group of single parents with preschool children, which were not part of the 1980s evaluations?[10]

The experimental evaluations of the 1980s, including those we examined here, did not have to address these questions. They were not meant to be tests of the human capital development approach. The first-generation programs we studied did not oper-ate with the encouragement provided later by JOBS for the use

---

[10] Examples can also be given of questions relating to the details of implementing education and training in JOBS programs: How closely should basic education and specific occupational training be linked? How much monitoring and counseling will be needed to get enrollees through these long and (for many) demanding activities? How much are child care and other support services needed to facilitate participation in education and training, especially among the new JOBS-mandatory group of single parents with preschool children?

There are also questions about how to best promote high quality in adult education and training. For example: How well can objective tests, such as academic achieve-ment tests or skill certification tests, predict future labor market success for educa-tion and training participants? Would impacts on earnings and AFDC increase if programs were rewarded based on the number of education and training participants who pass such tests?

of basic education and job training. Their evaluations were primarily designed to find out whether large numbers of AFDC recipients could be reached with any services and what the impact of such a broad program effort might be. To learn specifically about the impacts of education and training, we have to look to later field research.

Two important field experiments currently under way should provide information about the effectiveness of basic education and occupational training for adults in JOBS. The first of these is the experimental evaluation of California's Greater Avenues for Independence (GAIN) Program, which is the state's JOBS program. GAIN lays heavy emphasis on mandatory participation in basic education. Immediately upon entry into GAIN, enrollees are classified as in need or not in need of basic education,[11] and those deemed to need it are usually assigned to basic education as a first program activity. Only short-term results are available for GAIN.[12] Participation data reveal that there has been a substantial amount of activity in basic education. Impacts on achievement test scores and receipt of high school equivalency certificates have been found in some GAIN counties but not in others.[13] Whether or not these educational effects are associated with longer-term impacts on earnings and AFDC must await collection of additional follow-up data.

A broader set of empirical results should come from the National JOBS Evaluation, currently under way in seven cities. The scope of these studies goes beyond that of the GAIN evaluation in several ways. Unlike GAIN, the human capital focus of these programs includes occupational training as well as basic education.[14] These experiments should also yield a substantial amount

---

[11] Basic education in GAIN includes adult basic education, preparation for the General Educational Development (GED) examination for high school equivalency, and English as a Second Language (ESL). GAIN enrollees are deemed to need basic education if they lack a high school diploma or GED certificate or if they fail to score above 215 on both a reading test and a mathematics test (developed by the Comprehensive Adult Student Assessment System, or CASAS). Enrollees who are not proficient in English are also classed as in need of basic education, but non-English speakers were not included in the follow-up literacy test for the GAIN evaluation.

[12] For short-term impacts on earnings and AFDC, see Friedlander, Riccio, and Freedman (1993).

[13] For the complete analysis of educational outcomes in GAIN, see Martinson and Friedlander (1994).

[14] As part of the analysis of the effects of basic education, the National JOBS Evaluation will implement achievement tests, both before random assignment and during follow-up, to three thousand sample members in three sites. The study will also obtain participation and school attendance data and will interview enrollees,

of information about program effectiveness for the new JOBS mandatories, who were not part of GAIN at the time the evaluation was launched. This group of single parents with preschool children is in the JOBS evaluation sample at every site. In addition, at four sites, single-parent AFDCs with a child as young as one year have been classified mandatory. Finally, among its other innovations, the evaluation is using three sites to test human capital development head-to-head against a competing JOBS strategy aiming for rapid employment instead of a lengthy period of education or training. Sample members are being assigned randomly either to the rapid employment or human capital approach or to a no-JOBS control group. This adaptation of the experimental method will allow unbiased estimates of the impacts of the alternative approaches and of the *difference in effectiveness* between them.

The three-group experimental design is particularly suited to determining whether intensive education and training is the best way to maximize the effectiveness of JOBS. This methodology makes comparisons of alternative program approaches more accurate than can be achieved when those approaches are tested in separate, unrelated studies. The three-group design overcomes severe problems posed when the studies to be compared are carried out under differing local labor market and AFDC conditions, with samples having different characteristics, and with different research methodologies. In a fundamental way, this change in method enhances the nature of the information that may be obtained from the evaluation. With the two-group, experimentals-versus-controls designs of the 1980s, the research question was: Is Approach A effective? In head-to-head trials, the additional question may be asked: Is Approach A more effective than Approach B? It is just this kind of information on comparative effectiveness that is essential for identifying and validating the "best practice" (i.e., most effective) program approaches. And demonstrating what techniques work best is the first step in moving JOBS systematically towards widespread use of those techniques.

TASKS AHEAD

The four programs we looked at in this study predated JOBS and do not necessarily predict what the impact of JOBS will be. They do show that localities can build integrated systems of

---

teachers, and administrators for information about the content and quality of participants' education experiences in the programs.

job search assistance, unpaid work assignments, and, to a lesser extent, education and training. The evaluation results demonstrate that requiring AFDC recipients without preschool children to participate in those systems affects their work and welfare behavior. One important task for planners is to verify from the forthcoming evaluation research that JOBS can achieve impacts for AFDC recipients with younger children. Making them mandatory greatly increases the number of individuals who could go through JOBS. Even if the average impact per enrollee for this new group is no greater than it was for the old mandatory enrollees in the four programs we looked at, then JOBS' *aggregate* impact on the employment and earnings of AFDC recipients will still be substantially larger. How much those labor market effects might be accompanied by reductions in AFDC depends on the style of implementation adopted by the majority of localities. Our findings indicate that a range of results is possible: Net program costs could exceed reductions in AFDC and other transfers by a fairly modest amount. Or the returns to government budgets, over and above program costs, could be substantial.

The findings for these four programs also clearly indicate where progress needs to be made. If JOBS is to move beyond the first-generation welfare-to-work programs, it will have to achieve a larger and more sustained impact on the more disadvantaged program enrollees. JOBS will have to accomplish this to achieve its legislated mission to reduce long-term AFDC receipt. If it is successful, it would increase total program impact at the same time. Larger earnings impacts for this group could also ease the tradeoff between income gains for program enrollees and budgetary savings for government. The JOBS legislation has taken the first steps towards this goal by encouraging the use of basic education and occupational training on a large scale and by establishing targeting rules intended to promote attention to future long-termers.

Investment in basic education and skills training for the more disadvantaged is a strategy that carries some risk from the perspective of government budgets. It is not certain that more intensive effort really can produce larger impacts and do so cost-effectively. It is not certain which specific education or training strategies might work and which will not. For the more disadvantaged, it may not be possible, within the constraints of affordable services, to remedy skills deficits enough so that enrollees will believe they can afford to choose work over welfare. The ability of JOBS to achieve more for the more disadvantaged may be strengthened by changes in the social context that would increase the rewards of work for AFDC recipients, changes that would "make work pay," as it were. The recent extension of the Earned Income Tax Credit (EITC) increases the financial attractiveness of work over welfare by supplementing earnings directly with cash. Passage of a national health insurance plan with coverage mandated for all employed persons would eliminate another major incentive to remaining on AFDC. Currently, the jobs available to large numbers of AFDC recipients do not provide health insurance, whereas AFDC (through Medicaid) does. National health insurance that covered AFDC recipients when they left welfare to work at those jobs would shift the financial calculus more in favor of work. Lastly, measures to increase child support payments from absent parents, which were part of the Family Support Act and other federal legislation, also increase the value of work. When AFDC families receive child support, the monthly AFDC benefit is adjusted downward.[15] In essence, child support is "taxed" heavily by the AFDC grant formula. But the full amount of child support is kept by people who leave AFDC. Increased child support can therefore increase income more if a family leaves AFDC than if it remains on. As a consequence, increased child support acts as an inducement to leave AFDC. Moreover, child support added to earnings could raise family income above the level of AFDC in many cases where the custodial parent's earnings alone are not sufficient to accomplish that.

How we approach the future of JOBS is also contingent on other developments in welfare reform. The current national debate about converting AFDC to transitional assistance heightens the importance of achieving larger impacts for the more disadvantaged in JOBS. Clearly, if AFDC is to become a period of transition leading to work, then getting more potential long-term AFDC recipients into employment is consistent with that goal. Furthermore, under a system of time-limited welfare, recipients who reach the time limit would include most of the more disadvantaged, including people who cannot make much money working and do not have alternative secure sources of income. If time-limited welfare is not to require the creation of a dauntingly large supply of government "workfare" jobs, then it will be up to JOBS to increase the number of people who leave AFDC before

---

[15]The first $50 of current monthly child support received by a family is disregarded, but the remainder is counted in determining AFDC eligibility and benefit amounts.

reaching the time limit. And if a time limit without workfare is not to throw a very considerable number of AFDC families suddenly off aid completely and sharply reduce their income, then ways must be found to increase their income from other sources. Earnings are one alternative source, and increasing the ability to produce earnings is the role of JOBS. The extent to which JOBS can achieve its goals with the more disadvantaged will determine what kind and how much of a broader welfare reform is feasible.

The research tools developed over the last twenty years can help reduce the risk of pursuing ineffective strategies in JOBS and contribute to a step-by-step improvement in program practice over time. The greatest potential payoff for program development in the near future lies in research into the effectiveness of more intensive education and training coupled with more intensive monitoring and enforcement of program participation requirements and provision of supports and incentives that will foster compliance. The question for this research is: Can we convincingly demonstrate that particular program approaches can increase earning power enough to produce sustained increases in self-sufficiency and income among groups that otherwise would remain on welfare a long time? Some answers to this and other high-priority questions should be available soon from ongoing field experiments.

References

Bane, Mary Jo; and Ellwood, David T. 1983. *The Dynamics of Dependence: The Routes to Self-Sufficiency.* Cambridge, Mass.: Urban Systems Research and Engineering, Inc.

Ellwood, David T. 1986. *Targeting "Would-Be" Long-Term Recipients of AFDC.* Princeton, N.J.: Mathematica Policy Research, Inc.

Friedlander, Daniel. 1987. *Supplemental Report on the Baltimore Options Program.* New York: MDRC.

Friedlander, Daniel. 1988a. "An Analysis of Extended Follow-Up for the Virginia Employment Services Program." New York: MDRC.

Friedlander, Daniel. 1988b. *Employment and Welfare Impacts of the Arkansas WORK Program: A Three-Year Follow-Up Study in Two Counties.* New York: MDRC.

Friedlander, Daniel. 1988c. *Subgroup Impacts and Performance Indicators for Selected Welfare Employment Programs.* New York: MDRC.

Friedlander, Daniel; and Gueron, Judith M. 1992. "Are High-Cost Services More Effective Than Low-Cost Services? Evidence from Experimental Evaluations of Welfare-to-Work Programs." In Charles F. Manski and Irwin Garfinkel, eds., *Evaluating Welfare and Training Programs.* Cambridge, Mass.: Harvard University Press.

Friedlander, Daniel; and Hamilton, Gayle. 1993. *The Saturation Work Initiative Model in San Diego: A Five-Year Follow-up Study.* New York: MDRC.

Friedlander, Daniel; Hoerz, Gregory; Long, David; and Quint, Janet. 1985. *Maryland: Final Report on the Employment Initiatives Evaluation.* New York: MDRC.

Friedlander, Daniel; Hoerz, Gregory; Quint, Janet; and Riccio, James. 1985. *Final Report on the WORK Program in Two Counties.* New York: MDRC.

Friedlander, Daniel; Riccio, James; and Freedman, Stephen. 1993. *GAIN: Two-Year Impacts in Six Counties.* New York: MDRC.

Friedlander, Daniel; and Robins, Philip K. 1992. "Estimating the Effects of Employment and Training Programs: An Assessment of Some Nonexperimental Techniques." Presented at the Thirteenth Annual Research Conference of the Association for Public Policy Analysis and Management, Bethesda.

Greenberg, David; and Wiseman, Michael. 1992. "What Did the OBRA Demonstrations Do?" In Charles F. Manski and Irwin Garfinkel, eds., *Evaluating Welfare and Training Programs.* Cambridge, Mass.: Harvard University Press.

Gueron, Judith M.; and Pauly, Edward. 1991. *From Welfare to Work.* New York: Russell Sage Foundation.

Hagen, Jan L.; and Lurie, Irene. 1992. *Implementing JOBS: Initial State Choices, Summary Report.* Albany, N.Y.: The Nelson A. Rockefeller Institute of Government, State University of New York.

Hamilton, Gayle. 1988. *Interim Report on the Saturation Work Initiative Model in San Diego.* New York: MDRC.

Hamilton, Gayle; and Friedlander, Daniel. 1989. *Final Report on the Saturation Work Initiative Model in San Diego.* New York: MDRC.

Martinson, Karin; and Friedlander, Daniel. 1994. *GAIN: Basic Education in a Welfare-to-Work Program.* New York: MDRC.

Price, Marilyn. 1985. *Interim Findings from the Virginia Employment Services Program.* New York: MDRC.

Quint, Janet. 1984a. *Interim Findings from the Arkansas WIN Demonstration Program.* New York: MDRC.

Quint, Janet. 1984b. *Interim Findings from the Maryland Employment Initiatives Programs.* New York: MDRC.

Riccio, James; Cave, George; Freedman, Stephen; and Price, Marilyn. 1986. *Virginia: Final Report on the Employment Services Program.* New York: MDRC.

"A Symposium on the Family Support Act of 1988." Fall 1991. *Journal of Policy Analysis and Management* 10(4):588–666.

U.S. Congress, House of Representatives, Committee on Ways and Means. 103d Congress, 1st Session. 1993. *Overview of Entitlement Programs: 1993 Green Book.* Washington, D.C.: U.S. Government Printing Office.

U.S. General Accounting Office. 1992. "Welfare to Work: States Serve Least Job-Ready While Meeting JOBS Participation Rates." Washington, D.C.

U.S. General Accounting Office. 1993. "Welfare to Work: JOBS Participation Rate Data Unreliable for Assessing States' Performance." Washington, D.C.

Appendix

TABLE A-1
Short- and Longer-Term Impacts on Patterns of AFDC Receipt

Program and Outcome	Year Two			Final Year[a]		
	Experimentals	Controls	Difference	Experimentals	Controls	Difference
Virginia						
Average AFDC payments during year	$1,488	$1,528	-$40	$760	$769	-$9
Average number of months received AFDC during year	5.63	5.64	-0.01	2.84	2.89	-0.05
Average AFDC payment in months receiving welfare	*$264*	*$271*	*-$7 (z)*	*$268*	*$266*	*$2 (z)*
Midyear AFDC status (%)						
On AFDC at midyear						
Never off more than two months, month one through midyear	38.4	38.0	0.4	13.5	14.9	-1.4
Off more than two months but returned by midyear	8.2	7.7	0.5	9.7	9.4	0.3
Off AFDC at midyear						
Never received AFDC from month one through midyear[b]	12.4	12.5	-0.1	11.4	11.7	-0.3
Will not return to AFDC before end of follow-up	32.3	32.6	-0.3	62.8	62.1	0.7
Will return to AFDC before end of follow-up[c]	8.7	9.1	-0.5	2.6	2.1	0.6
Total	100.0	100.0	0.0	100.0	100.0	0.0
Arkansas						
Average AFDC payments during year	$812	$1,004	-$192***	$698	$761	-$63
Average number of months received AFDC during year	4.90	5.86	-0.96***	3.55	3.82	-0.27
Average AFDC payment in months receiving welfare	*$166*	*$171*	*-$6 (z)*	*$197*	*$199*	*-$2 (z)*
Midyear AFDC status (%)						
On AFDC at midyear						
Never off more than two months, month one through midyear	32.1	38.3	-6.2**	16.9	16.0	0.9
Off more than two months but returned by midyear	7.8	10.3	-2.6	12.5	15.5	-3.0
Off AFDC at midyear						
Never received AFDC from month one through midyear[b]	24.5	20.6	3.9*	20.1	17.2	2.9
Will not return to AFDC before end of follow-up	26.4	21.4	5.0**	47.6	48.6	-0.9
Will return to AFDC before end of follow-up[c]	9.3	9.4	-0.1	2.9	2.8	0.1
Total	100.0	100.0	0.0	100.0	100.0	0.0

Baltimore

Average AFDC payments during year	$2,057	$2,092	-$35	$1,783	$1,815	-$31
Average number of months received AFDC during year	7.15	7.34	-0.19	5.83	6.00	-0.17
Average AFDC payment in months receiving welfare	*$288*	*$285*	*$3 (z)*	*$306*	*$303*	*$3 (z)*
Midyear AFDC status (%)						
On AFDC at midyear						
Never off more than two months, month one through midyear	51.7	52.5	-0.7	38.2	39.6	-1.4
Off more than two months but returned by midyear	6.9	7.1	-0.2	9.4	9.9	-0.6
Off AFDC at midyear						
Never received AFDC from month one through midyear[b]	5.0	4.8	0.2	4.8	4.7	0.1
Will not return to AFDC before end of follow-up	27.6	27.1	0.6	43.2	42.2	1.0
Will return to AFDC before end of follow-up[c]	8.7	8.5	0.2	4.5	3.6	0.9
Total	100.0	100.0	0.0	100.0	100.0	0.0

San Diego SWIM

Average AFDC payments during year	$3,523	$4,088	-$565***	$2,297	$2,461	-$164
Average number of months received AFDC during year	6.60	7.48	-0.88***	3.85	4.07	-0.23
Average AFDC payment in months receiving welfare	*$534*	*$546*	*-$12 (z)*	*$597*	*$604*	*-$7 (z)*
Midyear AFDC status (%)						
On AFDC at midyear						
Never off more than two months, month one through midyear	48.7	56.0	-7.3***	20.4	22.9	-2.5*
Off more than two months but returned by midyear	5.1	6.2	-1.1	11.4	10.2	1.2
Off AFDC at midyear						
Never received AFDC from month one through midyear[b]	4.7	4.4	0.3***	4.0	4.2	-0.2
Will not return to AFDC before end of follow-up	29.7	25.5	4.3***	61.8	60.1	1.7
Will return to AFDC before end of follow-up[c]	11.7	7.9	3.9***	2.4	2.6	-0.2
Total	100.0	100.0	0.0	100.0	100.0	0.0

NOTES: Midyear AFDC statuses are mutually exclusive. Tests of statistical significance on those categories are not strictly independent. Year two is defined as months thirteen through twenty-four, and midyear is month nineteen. The final year is defined as the last twelve months of follow-up available, and the midyear month is the final month minus five.

Details may not sum to totals owing to rounding.

Italics indicate nonexperimental estimates.

A two-tailed t-test was applied to experimental differences. Statistical significance levels are indicated as: * = 10 percent; ** = 5 percent; *** = 1 percent. (z) indicates that the comparison is nonexperimental: no test of statistical significance was performed.

[a] The final year of AFDC follow-up is defined as follows: Virginia, months forty-nine through sixty; Arkansas, months fifty-five through sixty-six; Baltimore, months twenty-five through thirty-six; San Diego SWIM, months fifty-two through sixty-three.

[b] Includes some sample members who will receive AFDC before the end of follow-up.

[c] Excludes sample members in the category "never received AFDC."

215

Index

Entries in **boldface** refer to figures and tables.

W